SOCIAL ISSUES, JUSTICE AND STATUS

ASSAULTS

INTERVENTIONS, PREVENTIVE STRATEGIES AND SOCIETAL IMPLICATIONS

Social Issues, Justice and Status

Additional books in this series can be found on Nova's website
under the Series tab.

Additional e-books in this series can be found on Nova's website
under the e-book tab.

SOCIAL ISSUES, JUSTICE AND STATUS

ASSAULTS

INTERVENTIONS, PREVENTIVE STRATEGIES AND SOCIETAL IMPLICATIONS

KEITH V. BLETZER
EDITOR

nova publishers
New York

For permission to use material from this book please contact us:
Telephone 631-231-7269; Fax 631-231-8175
Web Site: http://www.novapublishers.com

Additional color graphics may be available in the e-book version of this book.

Library of Congress Cataloging-in-Publication Data

Assaults : Interventions, prevention strategies and societal implications / editor, Keith V. Bletzer.
pages cm
Includes index.
ISBN: 978-1-62808-051-3 (hardcover)
1. Assault and battery--Prevention. 2. Violent crimes--Prevention. 3. Sex crimes--Prevention. I. Bletzer, Keith V.
HV6618.A87 2013
364.4--dc23

Published by Nova Science Publishers, Inc. † New York

CONTENTS

PREFACE

When we speak of "assault," we move our discussion from that of violence in its varied injurious forms toward the needs of the victim, prevention of future acts of harm, societal education and policy development, and mobilization of community resources, which should include the support of both nation-states and responsible institutions. Violence as a manifestation of human aggression has long been with our species. Defining that aggression in its manifest forms as "assault" provides a foundation for intervention with both the perpetrator (offender in legal terms) and survivor victim (person attacked in legal terms).

Contributors to this volume on assault have varied professional responsibilities. Some hold faculty positions with colleges or universities; others are affiliated with university institutes and/or medical hospitals. A few are students in the final steps of completing graduate training. All of them in some way are at the forefront of making direct contributions to prevention and intervention, if they themselves are not the practitioner or clinician who in some way provides direct services to individuals harmed by violence.

Most chapters are based on professional experience at the front lines of delivery, where real people come or, owing to severe instances of violence, are brought, for services. Each contributor has repeatedly seen evidence for and/or heard about the outcomes of harmful acts of violence, perpetuated on those most vulnerable in society, owing to sex, age, socio-economic status, professional standing, and/or the momentary inability to take personal action that could prevent or protect one against perpetration of an act of violence.

As you read these chapters, consider the role of the researcher and practitioner in their chosen profession to make a contribution. View the language with a critical eye. You will find carefully reasoned proposals for change, calls for social justice, explanations of models for prevention strategies and development of public policy, and articulated reasons why violence falls short of the human right for societal protections that each member of our species deserves. What may be a potential solution or, conversely, negative consequence, what might be a dilemma or beneficial outcome, and what can happen when people work collaboratively: These chapters portray the nuanced reasoning that permits the professional to work toward development and confirmation of more effective models of prevention and intervention, which can reduce the need for prolonged care and services.

It should come as no surprise that violence takes place in many forms across a range of various communities and countries. It can affect anyone, although some individuals face greater susceptibilities, owing to their structural vulnerability. This volume, sad to say, however extensive and nuanced its offerings, covers but a few forms of human assault. The coverage nonetheless is focused and well-attuned to social-psychological-physical-economic realities of harmful impact and the short-term and long-term post-incident consequences of assault on another human being.

Chapter 1 – Theories of human aggression to account for developmental characteristics are mainly biological. There has been an increase in scientific work related to the importance of *amygdala* and other brain regions in recalcitrant aggressive reactions. This relationship has been proven to a certain degree, because "amygdalotomy" as it is performed by neurosurgeons is still considered a form of effective treatment for "aggressive reactions." From self-mutilation to hetero-aggression, the role of the frontal lobe has often been associated with concepts of impulse control or the lack of such. Schizoid psychopathology offers proof of the biological roots of the disorder. The role of neurotransmitters, hormones (mainly sexual) and drugs of abuse offer another enlightening perspective for the intricate issue of effective solutions for human aggression.

The phenomenology of human aggression as it is sketched for the early-starters (involved in school bullying to minor thefts) is another theme. A positive spiral through the period of early-starter development is more applicable, with aggressive acts that become more and more severe. Comparing the increasing severity of early-starter aggression will help to better explain the course of development for the recalcitrant aggressive reactions.

Chapter 2 – Bullying is a risk factor that can impede children's physical and psychological health. The act of bullying is often described as physically aggressive behaviors and/or verbal aggression toward someone who is portrayed as socially and emotionally weak and/or defenseless. The occurrence of bullying might seem to take place without specific reasons. Verbal bullying is expressed through insults and/or aggressive language to harm the victim, whereas physical bullying involves actual bodily harm through aggressive acts. Bullying happens within various settings including families, educational settings, work places, and over the Internet and other electronic media (i.e., cyber bullying). Specific types of bullying across various settings are discussed within the context of prevention efforts to reduce their occurrence as well as their negative psychological impacts. Overall, bullying is associated with both short-term and long-term negative effects that impact the development of children, adolescents and adults. These effects range from having low self-esteem to the possibility of suicide. However, the presence of programs in schools and involvement of the parents in the educational system can help to reduce bullying and its associated consequences.

Chapter 3 – Commonly called "IPV," interpersonal violence (i.e., physical and/or sexual assault) perpetrated on women is a major public health concern. A considerable number of studies have demonstrated the devastating effects it can have on both the psychological and physical health of women who have been harmed. This is especially true when we consider the harmful consequences that physical and sexual assault can have on women's reproductive health. Although the prevalence of such assault on women in the general population is unfortunately high, ethnic minority women living in low socio-economic, urban neighborhoods are at even greater risk of being victims of IPV, when compared to women who do not have these socio-demographic risk factors. Assault experiences confer a greater likelihood of obstetric and gynecological health problems, such as sexually transmitted infections, pelvic pain, sexual dysfunction, unintended pregnancy, infertility, miscarriage, cervical cancer, and maternal and fetal complications during pregnancy and birth. In addition, women who have been assaulted report greater fear and avoidance of obstetric and gynecological exams and are less likely to receive preventive health care services, which increases risk for medical complications that go undetected. The aim of this chapter is to review the known literature on the association between women's reproductive health and both physical and sexual assault, with specific attention to pregnancy outcomes for mother and baby. The authors present preliminary descriptive data from a prospective study of female patients who sought both obstetric/gynecologic and psychological care from a major, urban medical center. They discuss the implications of these associations on psychological treatment and obstetric care, and highlight the need for multi-disciplinary interventions for pregnant survivors of IPV.

Chapter 4 – Although assault victims can receive important support and assistance from others by disclosing their assault, victims report a range of barriers to disclosure (e.g., self-blame, perceived stigma). Further, those victims who do disclose might encounter a range of positive and negative reactions from others, of which the latter can have a deleterious impact on post-assault outcomes. These responses to disclosure vary for a number of reasons, including factors related to the victim (e.g., perceived coping ability), the assault (e.g., perpetrator type) and the disclosure recipient (e.g., informal versus formal recipient).

Unfortunately, little information is available regarding disclosure recipients, despite the critical role that they play in the disclosure experience. Further examining disclosure recipients and their experiences with sexual assault disclosure is important for better understanding this group, as well as how they can best help victims. To that end, this chapter reviews the literature on sexual assault disclosure, including the prevalence of disclosure and disclosure receipt, the people to whom assaults are disclosed (i.e., formal versus informal support sources) and the range of responses provided to victims, both positive and negative. Responses of disclosure recipients are examined within the relevant theoretical framework provided by Victimization Perspective Theory. Possible outcomes of, and barriers to, disclosure are discussed. Finally, implications are provided, including suggestions for ways to improve the disclosure process for both victims and recipients.

Chapter 5 – United States federal law mandates all colleges and universities that receive federal funding to implement some type of violence prevention program. Despite this initiative, women on college campuses continue to experience sexual victimization at alarmingly high rates. The high rates of sexual victimization and the range of psychological after-effects associated with sexual violence underscore the importance of developing effective programs to reduce women's risk for sexual violence. As such, this chapter reviews the rationale, content, structure, theoretical underpinnings, and efficacy of sexual assault risk reduction programs for women in college. Recommendations for developing and administrating risk reduction programs are also delineated.

Chapter 6 – Using theatre of the oppressed techniques as the basis for sexual assault prevention interventions is becoming increasingly popular. Interventions that use *theatre of the oppressed* aspire to change values and norms that perpetuate the acceptability of sexual assault and teach bystanders how to intervene in situations where sexual violence might occur. This chapter provides an overview of theatre of the oppressed theory and practice, review of scholarship investigating critical pedagogy prevention interventions, and personal stories from theatre of the oppressed practitioners about their experiences using theatre for social change techniques to prevent sexual violence. The goal of this chapter is to provide practitioners and researchers with a general understanding of theatre of the oppressed theory, practice, and research that target sexual violence prevention.

Chapter 7 – Corporal punishment remains a controversial issue in today's society. One of the ongoing concerns has been the relationship between use of corporal punishment and its impact on a child's overall well-being and development. A thin line exists between what is considered *corporal punishment* and what is considered *assault*, as the former often escalates into the latter. Research has provided insight as to what factors might lead a parent to engage in corporal punishment, which generally includes parental, child, and environmental factors. Researchers have conducted numerous studies to determine negative effects and outcomes that are associated with corporal punishment, but little is known as to what methods of intervention will reduce public opinion that currently seems to take a position of favorability toward its use. Some studies have focused on using education to demonstrate negative outcomes associated with corporal punishment to parents, school administrators and students, and community groups. Overall, the use of corporal punishment has been shown to be ineffective and correlated with negative outcomes. Corporal punishment in schools has declined markedly in recent years due to organizational efforts and new laws. Yet corporal punishment remains a lawful form of school punishment in many districts throughout the United States. Much still needs to be done to intervene against corporal punishment in the home. Providing solid information on the harmful effects and ineffectiveness of corporal punishment to the public has been shown to be an effective method in changing people's opinions on its use and everyday practice.

Chapter 8 – Nurses often take care of victims and perpetrators of violence from the communities in which they live. They are our friends, families, and neighbors. Violence occurs in areas of the hospital such as emergency rooms and trauma units that are the symbols of safety and care yet have become battlegrounds where people are maimed and killed rather than cured. The upsetting but basic fact is that violence occurs everywhere in the health care system, not just psychiatric units. In fact, the general hospital has less control over the facility environment than does a locked psychiatric ward.

Homicides make national headlines, but in hospital settings verbal threats, non-fatal physical assaults, and unwanted sexual advances are often under-reported or not reported at all. Part of the problem is nurses' perception that assaults come with the territory. Most nurses would not think of reporting a patient with Alzheimer's disease who strikes out, as he's being fed. Nor would they report the girlfriend of a young man who is pronounced dead on arrival, who lashes out because, she believes, you did nothing to save him. Increased rates for both physical and non-physical violence have been identified for working in a nursing home, long-term care facility, intensive care unit, emergency room, or psychiatric/behavioral department. Providing patient care and supervising patient care, as well as working with primarily geriatric patients, resulted in increased rates for physical violence. A national Veterans Administration (VA) survey was conducted in which 48% reported at least one verbal or physical assault within a 12-month period. Many published studies document assaults, but health care institutions have a long way to go toward implementing these findings, especially as they apply to staff working conditions. I hope this Multiple Pronged Approach helps you to decrease assault on nursing staff.

Chapter 9 – Many forms of torture exist. One of them is a burn that leaves marks on the skin in addition to physical impediments and mental trauma. The physical damage and outcome of an intentional burn is often worse than an accidental burn. When available, the hospital history is important for diagnosis and management of cases of injury by burns. Identifying the features of an intentional burn and correlating them with tools of harm that were used, motives and the victim's associated socio-economic status, makes it possible to discern injuries that are non-accidental, whether perpetrated by the injured individual or another person. Acids among which is sulfuric acid are the most used chemicals for attack. Motives vary for why a person or group might intentionally inflict burns on another individual. However severe the injuries might be, particularly for women and/or children, the burns usually are inflicted by persons known to the victim. Contact burns on servants might occur for punishment or to obtain a confession of an alleged theft. Some victims have psychological impairment before they are burned, while repeated assault leads to psychological disorder in others. Assault by burning leads to a risk of death and disability from physical/psychological scarring. For legal purposes injury certificates from the hospital can provide strong assistance to victims. As they are poor and often without resources, these victims fare poorly in seeking justice from perpetrators that have higher social ranking; for them, the process of justice is difficult and complicated. Legal and social support for victims and families are frequently inadequate to compensate for losses. A statement from a qualified doctor regarding the nature and causation of the burn wound would be a major assistance for them in seeking justice and compensation.

Chapter 10 – New means of communication have made it easier to communicate worldwide. They enable contact in real time, irrespective of distance and borders. However, these new means of communication have been diverted from their primary use to feed deviant fantasies or to satisfy a need of superiority. There are particular situations that can directly affect people: child pornography, grooming and cyber-bullying. The Internet is the main tool that is used in these three situations. However, the extensive use of cell phones should not be overlooked. In all three situations, the essential factors that explain the growth of offences are virtual aspects of communication and anonymity. Apart from child pornography, the main victims of cyber-grooming and cyber-bullying are adolescents, as, by definition, the victim must be able to establish virtual contact with an aggressor and thus have the capacity to master telecommunication tools. Likewise, the appeal of these tools for adolescents inevitably leads to their deviant use by other young people who are not always aware of the danger of virtual contacts and do not always recognize the impact of bullying. Criminal and victim profiles have been identified. De-materialized aspect of these offences makes it difficult to apprehend the perpetrators. States must take steps to deal with cyber-criminality. New methods need to be set up to apprehend the perpetrators and protect the victims.

Chapter 11 – Sexual assault is a current problem that reaches public awareness, owing to the presence of improved documentation of violence-related injuries. Specialists assist victims of sexual assault face several difficulties, where a comprehensive examination must evaluate physical and mental health of the victim, circumstances of the assault, and a possible relationship between the victim and the perpetrator. Managing victims of sexual assault means, first, provision of medical care for their health and, second, facilitation of forensic assessment. Nevertheless, the juridical necessities are significant and therefore they must not be disregarded. Actions that aim to restore the victim's health must be performed with effective procedures to acquire useful information of forensic significance. This management needs to be advantageous beyond healing the victim. Correct collection of evidence, even if it is not the immediate purpose, can become the all-important "cultural capital" that is used in a courtroom trial.

The elaboration and introduction of a standard procedure is crucial, whereby it standardizes collection of evidence and management of the victim in the immediate setting. It is essential that an accurate case history is combined with blood tests, including research of toxics, drugs and microbes, as well as different types of sampling for sperm detection. These analyses are necessary because in most cases the medical examination and genital inspection do not reveal specific evidence of violence. Moreover, the earlier that examinations and tests are performed, the more useful and reliable the information (e.g. sperm in the vagina can be retrieved up to 72 hours, whereas toxics and drugs remain for a limited time in blood and urine). Therefore, for these same reasons, it is important to prove genital and extra-genital injury that may heal in a short time and lose its evidential validity. The importance of a proper methodology to obtain objective information stems from psychological and emotional consequences to the victim, caused by the trauma or, possibly, to drugs that could make the victim's deposition unreliable. The professional consultant who faces a sexual assault victim for medical assistance should, first of all, provide immediate health care and psychological support and, secondly, provide for documentary evidence by preserving the victim's clothes, sampling the appropriate body fluids and photographing possible wounds. In conclusion, it is essential that specialists be highly trained and knowledgeable regarding the effective approach in working with a victim of sexual assault and as contributing member of the multi-disciplinary cooperation team.

Chapter 12 – *Objective*: To refine boundaries and characteristics of the late-night entertainment precinct in Cairns to facilitate refined measurement of alcohol-related assaults, assess stakeholder perceptions regarding interventions to reduce them and explore the contribution that this process can make to sustainable interventions.

Methods: 29 semi-structured interviews incorporating cognitive mapping techniques, 12 focus groups with key service providers, and community-action research methodology to elicit feedback on preliminary findings.

Results: The rate and severity of violence in the Cairns precinct has fallen over time; reducing alcohol availability would further reduce violence but have negative economic consequences. A generational culture of 'drinking to get drunk' exists. Community-level education programs addressing this are important. A majority of interventions identified by stakeholders were situational and environmental. Participants generally agreed on a defined precinct boundary, at the same time they highlighted unexpected violence 'hot-spots'. Coordination and communication between relevant stakeholders is essential.

Conclusion: The precinct is viewed as a safe place by stakeholders and they expect to continue working together to reduce violence. The emphasis on stakeholder communication endorses current government programs to address alcohol-related violence. Independent community-action research facilitates information transfer and is a key strategy to coordinate data collection, and in implementing and monitoring coordinated interventions.

Implications: This study supports the importance to stakeholders of defined precincts for enhanced data collection to measure alcohol-related assaults, and previous studies indicate the importance of research as an independent driver to reducing this sort of violence. The methodology is a foundational stage of establishing scientific veracity in studying this public health issue, and in guiding policy and research directions.

Chapter 13 – There is much interest in how state policies might reduce firearm deaths. For example, a recent study found that using local agencies to perform background checks prior to a firearm purchase was associated with reductions in firearm homicide and suicide-deaths. The authors re-visit this issue, using sophisticated empirical model specifications that help reduce bias from confounders. They also explore the effects of comprehensiveness of other state policies related to gun background checks. State-level data for 1996-2005 are used. Data on state policies are from from the Survey of State Procedures Related to Firearm Sales, and data for firearm deaths are from the National Center for Injury Prevention and Control. Multivariate negative binomial models are used to estimate the relationship between agency levels and state policies for background checks, and firearm homicides and suicide-deaths, by race (all races, whites and blacks) and age (youth and adults). Models control for contemporaneous state characteristics, past firearm violence, past state-policy on background checks, and other proxy variables for unmeasured state-level heterogeneity.

We found little evidence that using local or state agencies as opposed to federal agencies impact firearm deaths. In fact, the use of state agencies as opposed to federal agencies except in certain instances is associated with higher firearm deaths. Firearm homicide-deaths were 11% and 37% higher respectively among Whites and Blacks in states using state agencies for background checks (reference group: federal agency). Firearm suicide-deaths among Whites and all adults were about 13% and 9% higher respectively in the states using state agencies. The authors found evidence that more comprehensive background checks at the state level are effective in reducing firearm deaths. They also found significant variation in results between suicide deaths and homicide deaths, and between races and age-groups and states that have had background checks in place since before the Brady Act had fewer firearm deaths. The use of local or state agencies as opposed to FBI is not associated with lower firearm homicide-deaths or suicide deaths, whereas more comprehensive background checks regardless of agency before firearm purchase were associated with fewer firearm purchases.

In: Assaults
Editor: Keith V. Bletzer

ISBN: 978-1-62808-051-3

Chapter 1

AGGRESSION AS A DEVELOPMENTAL DISORDER: FROM BULLYING TO ADULT DELINQUENCY

***Gentian Vyshka*[1,*] *and Admir Sinamati*[2]**
[1]Human Physiology, Faculty of Medicine, University of Tirana, Albania
[2]Institute of Legal Medicine, Tirana, Albania

ABSTRACT

Theories of human aggression to account for developmental characteristics are mainly biological. There has been an increase in scientific work related to the importance of *amygdala* and other brain regions in recalcitrant aggressive reactions. This relationship has been proven to a certain degree, because "amygdalotomy" as it is performed by neurosurgeons is still considered a form of effective treatment for "aggressive reactions." From self-mutilation to hetero-aggression, the role of the frontal lobe has often been associated with concepts of impulse control or the lack of such. Schizoid psychopathology offers proof of the biological roots of the disorder. The role of neurotransmitters, hormones (mainly sexual) and drugs of abuse offer another enlightening perspective for the intricate issue of effective solutions for human aggression.

The phenomenology of human aggression as it is sketched for the early-starters (involved in school bullying to minor thefts) is another theme. A positive spiral through the period of early-starter development is more applicable, with aggressive acts that become more and more severe. Comparing the increasing severity of early-starter aggression will help to better explain the course of development for the recalcitrant aggressive reactions.

Keywords: Aggression, impulsivity, explosive behavior, anti-social personality, criminogenic environment, developmental theory

* Corresponding author: Email: gvyshka@yahoo.com.

INTRODUCTION

Law professionals, social workers, clinicians and psychologists have continuously attempted to define *anti-social behavior* in childhood, adolescence and adulthood, albeit without reaching a commonly accepted definition of the phenomenon. Even the basic definition of *aggression* per se is confusing. Should an action be accompanied by the *intention to harm*, for such an act to be considered an aggression? In that case, an important implication would derive itself from the intentionality of the wrongdoing. On the other hand, and much more incisively, should the models of anti-social behavior be treated or sketched universally, or should such conclusions be drawn within the context of the culture and the environmental setting? It is clearly stated, that ethnic composition and cultural background play important roles in bullying behavior and in victimization (Vervoort, 2010; Spriggs, 2007).

Actually, under a legal point of view, anti-social behavior among children and adolescents is noted as "micro-criminality," "delinquency" or merely "vandalism" (a rough term approximating the others), when anti-social behavior among adults is strictly defined as "criminal," Those definitions suffer from inconsistencies when it comes to psychological analysis of the latter. More attention is given to the fact that the wrongdoings are noted as such, following from a police intervention, rather than attempting to define the anti-social behavior as such. It is important to consider that micro-criminality is represented as a single, solitary act, rather than a complex of intermingled behaviors. Furthermore, early anti-social or aggressive behavior cannot be underemphasized or underestimated. Some authors have found associations between behavior at the age of three years, with future convictions and criminality as an adult (Stevenson, 2001). It is important to distinguish between the *officially reported* micro-criminality of an action deemed to be illegal and *self-reported* actions that characterize the life phase of an individual from children, parents, peers, school and similar entities.

Psychological research makes a clear distinction between the so-called *externalizing* behavioral models characterized by impulsive/anti-social actions and other aggressions, and *internalizing* behaviors such as anxiety, dysphoria, social isolation, somatization and anger (Cohn, 2012; Kim, 2011). We should of course concentrate on these externalizing issues, but clearly the two problems overlap, with internalizing behaviors playing their part as well.

Another important issue is the classificatory distinction between anti-social behavior and aggression at one side with a large spectrum of the symptomatology of attention deficit and hyperactivity disorder (ADHD), where the concomitance of ADHD and anti-social behavior is extremely high. Within this frame, aggression and anti-social behavior fit along a continuum of psychopathology, starting with basic defiance and opposition toward social rules and authority (known as *oppositional-defiant disorder*); progressing to the lifelong *conduct disorder*, and upgrading (or degrading for some) to the anti-social personality. Conceptually speaking, these disorders deserve their own description, because differences do exist (Jensen, 1997). Within the exaggerated attempt and tradition of modern psychiatry to coin categories, conduct disorder and oppositional defiant disorder are grouped within the "explosive" behavioral disorders. Both types refer to disorders starting before the eighteenth year of life. Typically the phenomenology is often visible at the age of ten. Inevitably, although not always, those categories will switch to an anti-social personality disorder as soon as the person reaches adulthood. Since the description of anti-social personality disorder recently was reviewed and thus determined by legal transgressions produced by these certain individuals, the severity of the disorder is interrelated to the frequency of such violations. Thus, it might be a product of the legality for the proposed dichotomy between childhood explosive disorders and the anti-social personality of adulthood. In fact, declining to register or legally prosecute these rule violations by individuals of minor age might be erroneously interpreted as a lower frequency of the phenomenon in that age. It is a fact, however, that some or most of the juvenile law violators abandon their specific behavioral model during adulthood, which once dominated their childhood (McCurley, 2006).

Returning to the developmental perspective of the anti-social personality and/or his-her behavior, early childhood law violations will not necessarily produce a recidivist. Authors have focused on researching the roots of deviant behaviors of psychopathology. The more callous traits of personality and externalizing psychopathologies have been largely discussed (Barry, 2000; Cohn, 2012).

Descriptive attempts to define a "delinquent" child or individual are difficult, because anti-social behavior is to a certain degree, a personally communicative way for a subject to respond to the social environment. The delinquent subject in contrast is positioned within a psychological context, often with a different familial and social background. Personality traits and the severity or character of a personality disorder are not proportionally related to the severity of the offences produced. Specific risk factors have been well identified, regarding the persistence of offences (the so-called *persisters*) and cessation of such a phenomenon (so-called *desisters* where former child delinquents have later stopped such an activity). Here again familial risk factors and the role of the peers are considered of primary importance (Remschmidt, 2010).

Early studies of juvenile delinquency have mainly been focused on frequent psychiatric co-morbidities. In fact, delinquent minors diagnosed with conduct disorder show a very high prevalence of internalizing pathologies (Ulzen, 1998). Co-existence of a psychiatric nosology with criminal behavior is derived from the fact that during some period of life, many wrongdoers have been under psychiatric treatment. Nevertheless, because many psychiatric patients do not commit crimes, and many criminals are considered mentally sane and thus competent to stand trial and accept prosecution, efforts are needed to identify the "protective factors" that separate the disorders from each other. That is, the psychiatric diagnosis must be separated from the criminal behavior. In the psychiatric literature conduct disorder and oppositional-defiant disorders are among the most frequent in child and adolescent samples. A high proportion of adolescent delinquents have been diagnosed with conduct disorder (Ollendick, 1999). Albeit diagnosing a conduct disorder or deviating behavior might seem a simple task, where over-diagnosis is the rule overtaken from laymen, we should consider that few adolescents face police and legal consequences even during a single criminal act, such as rape or murder. The act might be a severe law violation, but it might not suffice to diagnose a conduct disorder. The task of detecting behavioral deviations in an adolescent sample within detention facilities is even more difficult, because individuals under those conditions become extremely diffident and non-cooperative, regardless of assurances that they are given for a total respect of confidentiality.

METHODOLOGIES

Terminological Considerations

When prosecuting and eventually condemning someone for perpetration of a crime, law professionals request two pre-conditions before defining the presence of individual responsibility: *actus reus* (guilty act), and *mens rea* (the state of mind indicating culpability) which are necessary components for a statutory definition of a crime (Cornell University Law School, 2012). When speaking about "the deed" [*die Tat*], Johann Goethe in his famous *Faust* foreshadowed the latter very clearly with "the force" [*die Kraft*]. Yet even the force had to be preceded from "the sense" [*der Sinn*] (Goethe, 1808). Therefore, from a historical and humanistic point of view, a misdeed (deed) has to be preceded from the sense (intentionality), and meanwhile it has to be perpetrated with some consistence, or force, to deserve its name and notoriety.

If culpability and guilt are to be proven, there is a need to justify classifications, and to grant different subtypes and categories a theoretical and empirical basis, sufficient to substantiate their meaning. Under a terminological point of view, we might distinguish:

1. An inter-personal *verbal* aggression consists in menacing, teasing or mocking, and differs substantially from *physical* aggression such as beating and thus assaulting the victim. Such a difference is not only descriptive, it is developmental as well. In fact, physical aggression appears early, achieving its peak in the pre-school years of life (4th to 6th year of life), whereas acts of verbal aggression come in later years (Parke, 1983). This is not the only timing parameter of such an aggression, because such physical acts become gradually more and more serious through time, where the severity of crimes increases and the individual becomes a medical and societal concern.
2. The aggression might be direct or indirect (relational; i.e., revenging through a third person, discrediting publicly the hostile figure, excluding such a figure from social events etc.). Indirect aggression seems a particularity of female individuals. Inter-sexual differences in aggression and the ways of expressing hostility are a well-known biological phenomenon, involving almost all taxonomic species (Miczek, 2007).
3. Anti-social (aggressive) behavior might be defined as overt or disguised (clandestine); the latter includes behavioral categories such as lying, stealing, property destruction, substance abuse, cheating and arson. Problematic children generally manifest both these types, but distinction between the overt and the disguised type is an important one.
4. Aggressive behavior might be proactive (beating, menacing) or reactive (revenging). There is an abundant amount of data regarding both these subtypes that we will detail in the table below, and discuss thereafter.

Table 1. Some differences between proactive and reactive aggression

Proactive and Reactive Aggression		
	PROACTIVE	**REACTIVE**
Use of violence	Purposeful and clearly oriented	Toward an environmental event
Acting way	Calculated and manipulative	Spontaneous
The crime	Controlled	Uncontrolled
Period of criminal activity	Longer	Sudden and unexpected
Correlation with organic brain damages	Unknown	Prefrontal lobe cortex; amygdale
Implied neurotransmitter	Unknown	Serotonin

The distinction between a proactive and a reactive assault or aggressive behavior is an important one, not only regarding the environmental frame which elicits each kind of reactions, but also due to different neuroanatomical circuits that are triggered therein, implying the presence of different neurotransmission agents as well.

Authors have coined and used equivalent terms for proactive and reactive aggression. For example, predatory aggression and defensive aggression have been used almost synonymously (Peterson, 2004) with terms we used above. The same meaning should have *impulsive aggression*, which is a synonym of the reactive type of aggression, and *instrumental aggression*, namely the proactive one (Montoya, 2012).

Anthropological Approach

The anthropological research on aggression is long running and for centuries has been a favored domain of psychiatrists. Lombroso published at the end of XVIII century two major works, whose titles will clarify from the start the author's meaning. The first one, "The criminal - the inborn delinquent - the morally insane - the epileptic" details all possible crimes one might commit, and the ways that society was dealing with them during that historical epoch (Lombroso, 1887). The anthropological theories of Lombroso went far beyond with his published atlas and descriptions he made of the anthropological features and somatic parameters of criminals of certain nations (Lombroso, 1887). He studied 383 skulls of criminals of the time, making autopsies and describing pathological changes in the viscera of these individuals, including their stomachs and so on. His atlas on the "Criminal Individual" is very sophisticated for the time. It was concentrated on skulls, but very intuitively the author grasped the relation between tattoos and anti-social behavior (Lombroso, 1887). The relation between tattoos and aggression or anti-social behavior even today is at the center of debates and current research (Cardasis, 2009). Tattoos are not the only external body marking made visible and presumably related to criminality and anti-social behavior. Skinheads and the Skinhead Movement have been blamed for aggressive acts, among others, even micro-criminality (Menicocci, 2012).

What remains from anthropological theories of Lombroso and others are of course not the skull parameters, although the actual trend is reinforcing the anthropological point of view. Instead of speaking of "small" or "big" cranium, research has concentrated on more sophisticated - still anthropological - parameters, such as size of amygdala and other surrogates of brain structure or activity (Matthies, 2012). If some authors support the idea a small amygdala leads more easily to aggression, others might hold a contrary opinion; this is not the only contradiction found within specialist circles (Whittle, 2008). Researchers obviously might not converge in their conclusions, as one might logically suppose; size of pre-frontal regions and amygdala is frequently discussed, with cingulum and other limbic regions, regaining importance in the literature (Boes, 2008).

The amount of data collected and discussed in the above mentioned studies, and many others, were not dealing with samples of damaged or injured brains. That is, they focused on persons without any traumatic lesions. In fact, the study of post-traumatic personality change and aggression is another important field of research.

Developmental Theory

Developmental theories insist that age of onset for anti-social activity and the persistence of "micro-criminal" acts are important clues that determine the gravity and the persistence of the anti-social behavior, as well as the co-existence of inter-personal and social problems of the individual. A conceptual distinction has been made between lifelong anti-social behavior and anti-social behavior manifested only and exclusively during adolescence (Moffitt, 1993). Such a distinction is contrasted with other criminological views, which consider the trend for anti-social behavior as a constant independent of age.

Developmental theories suffer from the fact that studies generally are started at a late moment of someone's life, i.e. in individuals that, having manifested their aggression and anti-social behavior, already have reached a certain age. The actual focus and the consistent bulk of studies regarding the bullying phenomenon inside schools might be a compensation of the previous lack of interest or of sensible medical and/or psychological studies, aiming at detection of potential anti-social traits in the early childhood. Bullying was initially considered a moral issue that had to be dealt with, only by schools and teachers. That was obviously not true: bullying that resulted in schools was much more than that (Leblanc, 2001). When defining bullying as *direct* (open attacks) and *indirect* (social isolation, exclusion of the victim), it might become difficult to find any substantial difference between the concept of bullying and that of aggression generally. However, power imbalance is a characteristic in the process of bullying, especially noted inside schools (Leblanc, 2001). Aggressive behavior, on the other hand, will not necessarily be denoted through the presence of power imbalance.

According to Moffitt's findings, there should be a criminogenic environment, giving rise to a stable aggressive model of behavior, and such an environment will find its prey in an individual with "slight neuropsychological deficits." Adolescents that demonstrate life-course-persistent anti-social behavior, live in high-risk environments. Disadvantaged families, socio-economic hardship, inconsistent parental figures and attention deficit disorder, are all considered important risk factors (Ferguson, 1996). Moffitt goes further, through describing the life-course-persistent behavior as a kind of psychopathology per se. On the other hand, the anti-social behavior that lasts only during adolescence has as its main characteristic the lack of continuity over the life course.

Both models (life-course-persistent and adolescence-confined) are somehow related to imprudent parenthood. Adelaide Johnson coined the term "superego lacunae," which was embedded deeply in the psychiatric and psychological research of delinquency (Meloy, 2001). Thus, the psychodynamic hypotheses of conduct disorder and childhood delinquency suggest that children unconsciously act-out their parent's anti-social wishes (Sadock, Sadock & Kaplan, 2008, pp. 95-96). If parents are not culpable for everything, of course, according to the psychoanalytic sources, they should play an important role in the entire process.

The classification offered from Moffitt has been generally accepted, albeit other authors have modified it substantially. There exists in fact another category of delinquents, the so-called *repentant group*, composed of individuals that manifest anti-social behavior early during the developmental process (before adolescence) who withdraw from it thereafter (Loeber, 1998). Another drawback of Moffitt's model has to do with female delinquency, because girls that show a completely distinct developmental trajectory in the criminal career mainly defined as late-onset. This might not be a female characteristic in the entire issue, because adult-late-onset delinquency has been described from several sources even for male individuals (Zara, 2009; Wiecko, 2012).

Neurobiological Proof of Assaultiveness

Post-traumatic behavioral changes have been at the focus of several studies since 1848, when the first case of post-traumatic psychopathy in the modern time was registered. Phineas Gage survived a severe head trauma with no amnesia, no decline in his intelligence, without any speech disorder nor any motor deficit (Damasio, 1994). The irrespective, insolent and asocial behavior this famous patient showed after the head trauma surprised his contemporaries. Afterwards, the post-traumatic behavioral disorder depicted in the Gage case, became the neuropsychological model of social deviations of behavior and of the medical interventions that were justified on those bases (Macmillan, 1992, 1996). In this case the wide damage to the left and the right frontal cortex were documented, and the concept of acquired psychopathy was translated into a biological model of anti-social and/or asocial behavior. The amount of data raised the question whether violence and anti-social behavior might have a neurobiological basis. Be it so, the entire issue could be simplified in terms of neurotransmitters and imbalance of the latter. Another famous case of post-traumatic personality changes was that of the French poet Apollinaire, although in this case the temporal lobe seems to have been involved (Bogousslavsky, 2003). Apart from the poet's case whose personality changes were of another type far different from the theme were dealing with, in general, authors converge on the frontal lobe post-lesion changes (mainly post-traumatic). Thus, if amygdala is implied in anti-social or aggressive behavior, it should or must be inborn or at least a developmental issue, which differs from the post-traumatic equivalent, when the frontal lobe becomes a central concern.

Psychobiological and neurobiological influences have been implied in aggression generation and assaultive tendencies. Although internalizing disorders such as anxiety and depression might seem quite opposite to externalizing disorders such as conduct disorder and oppositional-defiant disorder, nevertheless, it has been suggested that both these types of disorders might accompany each other (Zoccolillo, 1992). Conduct disorder and depression have a high comorbidity. Important questions are raised (a) whether major depression might give rise to aggressive actions; (b) whether conduct disorder and the problems it creates might cause dysphoria and demoralization; (c) whether other overt or covert factors might influence the symptomatology.

A decreased serotoninergic activity seems to be related with impulsivity and aggression, as well as suicidal tendencies. It was Raleigh (1991) who studied initially the role of serotoninergic medication on aggressive behavior, through agonists of serotonin [*tryptophan*, *fluoxetine*] or antagonists of this neurotransmitter [*cyproheptadine*]. From the neurobiological point of view, auto-aggression and hetero-aggression (respectively translated into suicide and attempted homicide) are related to a low concentration of brain serotonin. Serotonin is a neurotransmitter whose main synthesis is embedded in the brainstem. Nevertheless, axonal structures originating therein reach the forebrain structures (i.e., frontal lobes and orbitofrontal cortex), among others.

Amygdala, an almond-shaped nucleus located bilaterally in the temporal lobes, as mentioned above, has as well been at the center of different studies. Its role in the emotional and vegetative life, as a substantial part of the limbic cortex, has been studied since Klüver-Bucy syndrome was first described in humans, after initial symptomatology was detected in monkeys (Lilly, 1983). This syndrome is an expression of hyper-orality and hyper-sexuality; yet lesions of temporal lobes were initially found to have a taming effect in animals. Goltz, a famous German physiologist of the 19th century, published several papers on localization values of different lesions inside the brain (Pauly, 2005).

Surgical removal of both amygdalae was experimented in high primates more than half a century before (Morgane, 1957; Schwartzbaum, 1960). The behavioral changes following bilateral destruction of these nuclei led to the idea that amygdalectomy might be a solution for refractory aggressive behavior. Although the procedure has serious ethical implications and its application in human patients is very restricted, some neurosurgeons still perform it, using the alternative form of amygdalotomy, through stereotaxic approaches (Fountas, 2007).

It is worth mentioning that neurobiological theories of aggressive behavior are not restricted to cortical or sub-cortical territories. Of course, hormonal changes registered when testosterone or cortisol are implicated, might quite well not be peripheral-originated, but rather a disturbance of the hypothalamic-hypophyseal axis, translated in the form of disequilibrium in the target endocrine gland, be it the testicle or adrenal gland. Thus, pharmacological or surgical castration has been found effective in decreasing aggressive behaviors in different mammals. Low cortisol levels have as well been related with persistent anti-social and disruptive behavior (McBurnett, 1999). Cortisol and testosterone, both playing a part in the complicated human aggression behavioral mechanisms, seem also to be interrelated, with the basal levels of the second hormone predicting the changes noted in the hypothalamic (Mehta, 2008).

Forensic Approach

Post-traumatic or not, the fact is that behavioral traits of criminals have been studied extensively during the last decades. Technology has improved through modern imaging methods. Authors have scanned convicted criminals, trying to deepen our knowledge of human aggression, particularly the anti-social behavior and misdeeds that have been perpetrated by criminals. The question has become more complex. Remote studies were focused originally on anatomical changes, being gradually being replaced by functional studies. New horizons have been explored toward explaining functional brain changes through mostly positron emission tomography (PET) and magnetic resonance imaging (MRI). These explorations have been with the brains of both "notorious" and "common" delinquents. Hypofrontality has been the mainstream focus of research models and hypotheses.

Deterioration in the controlling functions of the prefrontal lobe is not necessarily post-traumatic, but, nonetheless, the brain is best observed when trauma is present and anatomically observable. External signs of trauma provide the best verification of hypofrontality through the assessment of glucose metabolism using PET. In a study conducted by Raine (1994), twenty-two murderers had significantly lower glucose metabolism in the prefrontal cortex, when compared to controls. The author later hypothesized that excessive sub-cortical activity predisposes aggression, thus indicating insufficient prefrontal control of this subcortical excess, but only in impulsive perpetrators (Raine, 1998). Both studies by Raine (1998, 1994) were based on glucose metabolism as detected from positron emission tomography. The first objective proof of difference between an impulsive criminal, who acts in the moment, and a predatory perpetrator, whose crime is carefully planned, was offered in these two studies. A planned, "proactive" or "predatory" crime is perpetrated by a person whose forebrain shows no significant differences in metabolizing glucose from normal controls (see Raine, 1998).

Vignettes

1st case - At the end of 2010 the Albanian public was shocked by the case of a thirteen-year-old boy, arrested and charged with two killings. Both victims were females aged 40-50 years old, who were acquaintances of the young delinquent. Each woman was raped post-mortem. The police succeeded in arresting the boy as both crimes were non-professionally perpetrated and the respective crime scenes were full of clues. Nevertheless, it is worth mentioning that the second crime was perpetrated four months after the first. This time lapse was unexplained by the police, which meant the perpetrator was still at large. Treating a minor who was, beyond all doubts, guilty for the first, initially unresolved crime was eventually was perceived as a major investigative error.

A judicial controversy was raised immediately upon pre-detention, before the thirteen-year-old minor confessed to both crimes. The Albanian criminal code requires a minimum age of 14 years as a necessary age for a person to stand trial or, as occurred in this case, to be charged with a crime. In an obvious judicial impasse, the Court of Appeal in a Southern Albanian district freed the boy two months after his arrest, as the individual could not be prosecuted and stand trial, as he was a minor.

Meanwhile, a psychiatric forensic examination was performed during pre-detention by a team of infantile psychiatrists and psychologists. No obvious psychiatric diagnosis was available, but the psychological interview revealed several drawbacks in his childhood. Growing up in a separate family (although not divorced, the father had immigrated several years earlier in order to support the family), the boy's explosive behavior was admitted by the mother. The boy himself confessed to several previous and unreported acts of intra-familial violence. In one instance, he seriously beat his younger sister. Each incident was followed by a runaway period, when he would leave the family for two to eight days, during which time he committed small vagabond misdeeds in the suburban areas of his native city.

The boy was considered legally non-competent and his father was assigned the responsibility for his care. Immediately thereafter, however, the father again left the country, this time immigrating together with his son. No further acts of delinquency have been reported, although the two men actually live outside Albanian judiciary jurisdiction.

2nd case - A 43-year-old individual murdered a person after a car collision, during a futile quarrel and discussion that followed the accident. The person who committed the homicide was immediately arrested through a massive police operation in 2008. This individual was notorious for his impulsive acts and previous penal record, although none of his prior misdeeds was so severe. A psychiatric examination was immediately commissioned, owing to obvious signs of an anamnestic cranial trauma, and the fact that he was continuously under anti-epileptic treatment for refractory seizures. At the time he was taking Carbamazepine in therapeutic dosages.

The post-traumatic epilepsy and frontal trauma were incontestable. The plasma drug levels of Carbamazepine were within therapeutic range. The cranial trauma that the accused had suffered was caused by a bullet, which apparently was accidental, ten years before the more recent murder that he perpetrated. The Figure 1 illustrates the sequelae of the bullet and cicatrix ("scar") in the prefrontal right region of the individual.

An insanity defense was raised by the family attorney, but not successfully upheld in the Court of Appeal. The hypofrontality was considered a mitigating factor. The accused's inability to control impulses was classified as an insufficient presence of the *actus reus*. Because his aggression was reactive and uncontrolled, he was obviously unable to stop impulsivity. Since the other major factor, namely *mens rea*, was still present (he was considered able to produce intentionally criminal acts), and a successful insanity defense as a rule requires the loss of both elements (simultaneous insufficiency of the *actus reus* and the mens rea), he was found guilty with a mitigating sentence.

Forensic casuistics suggest that a syndrome provoked from lesions to the orbitofrontal cortex, where symptomatology is directly related to the "hypofrontality," will mirror its severity through sudden and unexpected explosive behavior, lack of emotional sensitivity, asocial and inadequate manners and labile affect (Grimes, 2000). The case that we described above, with obvious signs of prefrontal lesions, illustrates the major role the frontal lobe has in the generation of impulsivity and its control.

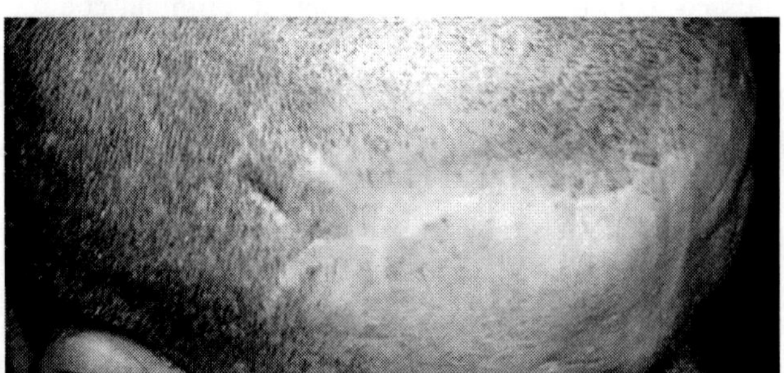

Figure 1. Wide right prefrontal cicatrix, caused from a bullet shot wound.

Pharmacological Approach

In an attempt to simplify the phenomenology of human aggression, treatment options offer an almost independent perspective of the entire criminological diagnostic field. The revised *Psychopathy-Checklist* (PCL-R) comprises a list of symptoms, but importantly, pharmacological options are offered and suggested, based on symptomatology (Hare, 1991). This symptom-oriented treatment focuses mainly on impulsivity and aggressive behavior. "Treatable" symptoms correspond to the so-called factor 2 of PCL-R (anti-social and impulsive life style). Thus, elements related to factor 2 in the frame of the so-called "psychopathy" are more compliant to treatment, in contrast to elements of the so-called Factor 1, such as inter-personal deficits that mainly include a lack of empathy, irresponsibility, among others. In fact, pharmacological interventions are much more effective toward "positive" or "productive" symptomatology, rather than improving social inadequacies of the aggressive individual.

Anecdotal treatments are widely suggested, but multi-centric, double-blind studies are scarce or non-existent. In fact, applying certain treatments to a precise target group, such as violent prisoners, involves major ethical and legal controversies in many countries, including Albania. Therefore it seems logical that the pharmacology of anti-social behavior and of the aggression (be it sexual or not), is far from being codified.

1. Serotonin and SSRI are the first pharmacological class that has been studied and applied. Since aggression and impulsivity are due to serotonin depletion inside the central nervous system, the inhibitors of its re-uptake have been tested in ability to control symptoms. It is suggested that SSRI drugs reduce irritability, impulsivity and anti-social behavior. These drugs might even normalize the perception of expressed fear in human faces (Harmer, 2003). In fact, fear perception is considered lacking in brutal perpetrators.
2. Lithium, anti-epileptics and mood stabilizers are some other pharmacological classes of agents that have been studied purposefully. Anti-epileptics (phenytoin) have been suggested to control aggressive behavior even among non-epileptic prisoners (Barratt, 1991). Levetiracetam and oxcarbazepine are other recently applied drugs in two successive studies from the anti-epileptic class (Mattes, 2012). It is worth mentioning that in all reports, the efficacy of the antiepileptics has been considered as limited, and studies have suffered serious biases.
3. If serotonin depletion is correlated to aggression, it seems that with dopamine we have the opposite balance. An increased dopaminergic activity is found in the frame of aggressive and impulsive behavioral models, where an individual searches pathologically for pleasure or inappropriate sensation-seeking. Newer anti-psychotics, such as clozapine, manifest their anti-aggressive effect, and it seems they do so, separately from their influencing on other positive psychotic symptoms (Citrome, 2001).
4. Benzodiazepines have been suggested as effective drugs for "smoothing" impulsivity, but due to their potential for creating dependence, their use is restricted to psychiatric emergencies. Much more important, several authors suggest that some criminals abuse benzodiazepines, just to "calm down" before perpetrating a crime (Dåderman, 2010).

5. Beta-blockers have been suggested as a second-line treatment in the case of agitation or aggression, following head injury (Fleminger, 2003).
6. Sexual hormones have been continuously scrutinized, especially testosterone, whose plasmatic levels correlate fairly well with violent and aggressive behavior, extraversion, sensation-seeking, delinquent recidivism and above all, with sexual violence. Appropriate medications that lower the plasmatic level of testosterone are available [TLM or testosterone-lowering medications], and their role has been reviewed (Turner, 2012). It seems that testosterone influences mainly the aggressive impetus; whereas serotonin (see point 1) has a primary role in aggravating impulsivity. The sexual hormone hypothesis has progressed to where some authors have documented the modulating or smoothing effects of estradiol (female hormone) for the negative inter-personal effects provoked from male alcoholism (Eriksson, 2003).
7. Low plasmatic levels of cholesterol have been found to be responsible for non-natural deaths, i.e., suicides, violent deaths and accidents. It might be possible that abnormally lower plasmatic cholesterol levels unfold through an endogenous serotonin insufficiency. Within this frame, a double-blind study offering alimentary supplements composed of fatty acids (omega-6 and omega-3) to a group of violent prisoners, Gersch (2002) observed a consistent decrease of assaults and violence within the detention facility. Very important, however, is the conclusion of Gersch that dietary interventions should be considered when addressing anti-social behaviors.

CONCLUSION

There must be a continuum in the temporal behavior of individuals starting from early infancy that leaves traces, even into adulthood. Nevertheless, models are not universally accepted and cases are shaped individually. Far from having a uniform effect, we are dealing with a panoply of developmental and eventually, criminological pathways that will not necessarily lead to a common final destination.

Aggressive behavior expressed during infancy and early childhood is not intrinsically pathological, as long as these behavioral models serve an evolving life, and the surrounding environment generates no problems manifested during these formative periods. Early expressions of aggression will help the child to confirm himself/herself to personal will and desires, thus permitting the child to shape an ego and, thereafter, to understand the responsibilities and limitations of a social life. If minor violence is unimportant and futile during the age span from one to four years of life, and considered as normal, especially in response to frustration, another issue is how to deal with this problem outside a family setting, mainly in schools, where teachers "stand-in" for parents and consistent discomfort might be created. A vicious circle of aggression will be formed once the home-based parental figure responds to any aggressive behavior performed by the infant or toddler with the same way of acting-out, whereby the child psyche will internalize a high level of anxiety.

The persistence of violent acts beyond the fourth year of age might be considered as equivalent to insufficiencies in affective investment, mainly from the mother toward her progeny, once other organic causes have been carefully ruled out for children with sensorial deficiencies, such as deafness, mental retardation, etc. These pathologies might easily provoke aggressive and explosive behaviors from the handicapped child.

When dealing with an oppositional-defiant disorder, medical professionals should consider that passive oppositional behavior, when persistent, frequently is a disguise for latent depression, and depressions usually are under-treated in childhood (Keller, 1991).

Other situations worth mentioning include parental and societal distress related to runaway kids and thieving, as both these phenomena have a developmental trajectory. Behaviors such as these finish almost inevitably by becoming a law enforcement issue with potential detainment and imprisonment for the adolescent. Familial dismemberment is an important etiological factor, and children living with a divorced parent frequently run away from home. Stealing in contrast is an act that often begins in the home. A very interesting issue is the continuity and chronology of acts of theft: initially the child steals within the family. Thereafter, the act is repeated outside the family, possibly with an accomplice acquaintance of the small (child) burglar. Quite often alimentary objects are among the first to get robbed. Later the child steals money or other symbolic objects which for him are very important; for young boys, for example, stealing female lingerie takes on special meaning. Stealing and thieving have their sub-categories. Some children might show high levels of anxiety and experience a sense of guilt following the misdeed. One important consideration is the observation that some children almost purposefully act through misdeeds with the aim of or need for their stealing to be uncovered. This is the so-called "self-punishing theft" postulated by Alexander and Staub (1929). These authors write "[…] exactly the theft of desserts will serve, to provoke the punishment" [*Eine Erinnerung seiner früheren Jugend gibt uns darüber Aufschluß, warum er gerade den Diebstahl von Süßigkeiten dazu benutzt, die Strafe zu provozieren*] (p. 92).

Concluding this wide argument for the roots of human aggression, we need to again raise the question, whether we are dealing with a mental disorder or the psychopathology of a criminal. Wakefield (1992) proposed a group of dual criteria in order to characterize mental disorders as such. First, a deviant behavior or an aberrant emotional model should create consistent harm and/or suffering to the individual and his/her environment. Second, the behavioral model has to be dysfunctional, a definition which aims to bypass the cultural uniqueness of some deviations. In defining this concept, Wakefield positioned an active dysfunction under an evolutionary point of view, wherein harming another human was viewed as a behavior that was inappropriate within civil society.

Current perspectives, however, are converging more and more to interrelationships among several risk factors that might lead to delinquency and thus enable practitioners to forecast anti-social activity in the years to come over an individual's lifetime. Children with ADHD (attention-deficit, hyperactivity disorder), and those with aggressive behavior and callous personality traits, will obviously be at high risk for manifesting overt psychopathology during adulthood. There is an ontological and evolutionary trend in the delinquent activity and wrongdoings of children of today and even for future adults. Solutions need to consider this continuum of lifetime phases, before acting at a single moment in time, thus restricting in an unfortunate and substantial way the success of an intervention designed for both immediate remedy and a lifetime of good health and social responsibility.

References

Alexander, F. & Staub, H. (1929). "Der Verbrecher und seine Richter. Ein psychoanalytischer Einblick in die Welt der Paragraphen," *Internationaler Psychoanalytischer Verlag Wien.*

Barratt, E. S., Kent, T. A., Bryant, S. G. & Felthous, A. R. (1991) "A controlled trial of phenytoin in impulsive aggression," *Journal of Clinical Psychopharmacology*, *11*(6), 388-389.

Barry, C. T., Frick, P. J., DeShazo, T. M., McCoy, M. G., Ellis, M. & Loney, B. R. (2000). "The importance of callous-unemotional traits for extending the concept of psychopathy to children," *Journal of Abnormal Psychology*, *109*(2), 335-340.

Boes, A. D., Tranel, D., Anderson, S. W. & Nopoulos, P. (2008). "Right anterior cingulate: a neuroanatomical correlate of aggression and defiance in boys," *Behavioral Neuroscience*, *122*(3), 677-684.

Bogousslavsky, J. (2003), "L"amour perdu de Gui et Madeleine" [The lost love of Gui and Madeleine] Emotional syndrome and right temporal behavior of Guillaume Apollinaire, *Revue Neurologique* (Paris), *159*(2), 171-179.

Cardasis, W., Huth-Bocks, A. & Silk, K. (2009). "Tattoos and anti-social personality disorder," Invited lecture delivered to Balkan Academy of Forensic Sciences, Scientific Session 4, June (Abstract book, Path., 109), Kavala, Greece.

Citrome, L., Volavka, J., Czobor, P., Sheitman, B., Lindenmayer, J. P., McEvoy, J., Cooper, T. B., Chakos, M. & Lieberman, J. A. (2001). "Effects of clozapine, olanzapine, risperidone, and haloperidol on hostility among patients with schizophrenia," *Psychiatric Services : A Journal of the American Psychiatric Association*, *52*(11), 1510-1514.

Cohn, M., van Domburgh, L., Vermeiren, R., Geluk, C. & Doreleijers, T. (2012), "Externalizing psychopathology and persistence of offending in childhood first-time arrestees," *European Child and Adolescent Psychiatry*, *21*(5), 243-251.

Cornell University School of Law > http://www.law.cornell.edu/wex/actus_reus (Last accessed November 18, 2012), see also: http://www.law.cornell.edu/wex/mens_rea. (Last accessed November 18, 2012).

Dåderman, A. M., Edman, G., Meurling, A. W., Levander, S. & Kristiansson, M. (2012). "Flunitrazepam intake in male offenders," *Nordic Journal of Psychiatry*, *66*(2), 131-140.

Damasio, H., Grabowski, T., Frank, R., Galaburda, A. M. & Damasio, A. R. (1994), "The return of Phineas Gage: Clues about the brain from the skull of a famous patient," *Science*, *264*(5162), 1102-1105.

Eriksson, C. J., von der Pahlen, B., Sarkola, T. & Seppä, K. (2003), "Oestradiol and human male alcohol-related aggression," *Alcohol and Alcoholism: International Journal of the Medical Council on Alcoholism*, *38*(6), 589-596.

Ferguson, D. M., Lynskey, M. T. & Horwood, L. J. (1996), "Factors associated with continuity and changes in disruptive behavior patterns between childhood and adolescence," *Journal of Abnormal Child Psychology*, *24*, 533-553.

Fleminger, S. (2003), "Managing agitation and aggression after head injury," *British Medical Journal*, *327*(7405), 4-5.

Fountas, K. N. & Smith, J. R. (2007), "Historical evolution of stereotactic amygdalotomy for the management of severe aggression," *Journal of Neurosurgery*, *106*(4), 710-713.

Gesch, C. B., Hammond, S. M., Hampson, S. E., Eves, A. & Crowder, M. J. (2002), "Influence of supplementary vitamins, minerals and essential fatty acids on the anti-social behavior of young adult prisoners: Randomized, placebo-controlled trial," *British Journal of Psychiatry*, *181*, 22-28.

Grimes, A. L., McCullough, L. B., Kunik, M. E., Molinari, V., Workman, R. H. Jr, (2000), "Informed consent and neuroanatomic correlates of intentionality and voluntariness among psychiatric patients," *Psychiatric Services: A Journal of the American Psychiatric Association*, *51*(12), 1561-1567.

Hare, R. D., Hart, S. D. & Harpur, T. J. (1991), "Psychopathy and the DSM-IV criteria for anti-social personality disorder," *Journal of Abnormal Psychology*, *100*(3), 391-398.

Harmer, C. J., Rogers, R. D., Tunbridge, E., Cowen, P. J. & Goodwin, G. M. (2003), "Tryptophan depletion decreases the recognition of fear in female volunteers," *Psychopharmacology*, *167*(4), 411-417.

Jensen, P. S., Martin, D. & Cantwell, D. P. (1997), "Comorbidity in ADHD: implications for research, practice, and DSM-V," *Journal of the American Academy of Child and Adolescent Psychiatry*, *36*(8), 1065-1079.

Goethe, Johann W. (1808). "Faust Eine Tragödie," *Tübingen*, Volume *I*, Verses 1224-1237.

Keller, M. B., Lavori, P. W., Beardslee, W. R., Wunder, J. & Ryan, N. (1991), "Depression in children and adolescents: New data on "under-treatment" and a literature review on the efficacy of available treatments," *Journal of Affective Disorders*, *21*(3), 163-171.

Kim, J. & Deater-Deckard, K. (2011). "Dynamic changes in anger, externalizing and internalizing problems: attention and regulation," *Journal of Child Psychology and Psychiatry*, *52*(2), 156-166.

Leblanc, J. C. (2001), "Bullying: It's not just a school problem," *Paediatrics and Child Health*, *6*(7), 411-413.

Lilly, R., Cummings, J. L., Benson, D. F. & Frankel, M. (1983), "The human Klüver-Bucy syndrome," *Neurology*, *33*(9), 1141-1145.

Loeber, R. & Stouthamer-Loeber, M. (1998). "Development of juvenile aggression and violence: Some common misconceptions and controversies," *American Psychologist*, *53*(2), 242-259.

Lombroso, C. (1887), "L"homme criminel," Atlas. XXXII Planches, Paris, Ancienne Librairie Germer Baillière; Félix Alcan (Ed.), pp. 1-44. Available at: http://www2.biusante.parisdescartes.fr/livanc/?cote=20073&do=livre. (Last accessed November 20, 2012).

Lombroso, C. (1887). "L"homme criminel. Criminel-né - fou moral - épileptique (Étude anthropologique et médico-légale), Paris, Ancienne Librairie Germer Baillière; Félix Alcan (Ed.), 122-163.

McBurnett, K., Lahey, B. B., Rathouz, P. J. & Loeber, R. (2000). "Low salivary cortisol and persistent aggression in boys referred for disruptive behavior," *Archives of General Psychiatry*, *57*(1), 38-43.

Mc Curley, C. (2006), "Self-reported law-violating behavior from adolescence to early adulthood in a modern cohort," pp. 5-12. Available at: www.ncjrs.gov/pdffiles1/nij/grants/217588.pdf (Last accessed Nov. 15th, 2012).

Macmillan, M. (1992), "Inhibition and the control of behavior: From Gall to Freud via Phineas Gage and the frontal lobes," *Brain and Cognition*, *19*, 72-104.

Macmillan, M. (1996). "Phineas Gage's contribution to brain surgery," *Journal of the History of the Neurosciences*, *5*(1), 56-77.

Mattes, J. A. (2012). "Medications for aggressiveness in prison: Focus on oxcarbazepine," *Journal of the American Academy of Psychiatry and the Law*, *40*(2), 234-238.

Matthies, S., Rüsch, N., Weber, M., Lieb, K., Philipsen, A., Tuescher, O., Ebert, D., Hennig, J., van Elst, L. T. (2012), "Small amygdala-high aggression? The role of the amygdala in modulating aggression in healthy subjects," *World Journal of Biological Psychiatry*, *13*(1), 75-81.

Mehta, P. H., Jones, A. C. & Josephs, R. A. (2008). "The social endocrinology of dominance: Basal testosterone predicts cortisol changes and behavior following victory and defeat," *Journal of Personality and Social Psychology*, *94*(6), 1078-1093.

Meloy, J. R. (2001). *The Mark of Cain: Psychoanalytic Insight and the Psychopath*, The Analytic Press, Inc., Publishers, 91-112.

Menicocci, M. (2012), "Dream-land. The Mythical Skinheads" Communitarianism," *Antrocom Online Journal of Anthropology*, *8*(1), 265-272.

Miczek, K. A., de Almeida, R. M., Kravitz, E. A., Rissman, E. F., de Boer, S. F. & Raine, A. (2007), "Neurobiology of escalated aggression and violence," *Journal of Neuroscience*, *27*(44), 11803-11806.

Moffitt, T. E. (1993). "Adolescence-limited and life-course-persistent anti-social behavior: A developmental taxonomy," *Psychology Review*, *100*, 674-701.

Montoya, E. R., Terburg, D., Bos, P. A. & van Honk, J. (2012), "Testosterone, cortisol, and serotonin as key regulators of social aggression: A review and theoretical perspective," *Motivation and Emotion*, *36*(1), 65-73.

Morgane, P. J. & Kosman, A. J. (1957), "Alterations in feline behavior following bilateral amygdalectomy," *Nature*, *180*(4586), 598-600.

Ollendick, T. H., Seligman, L. D. & Butcher, A. T. (1999), "Does anxiety mitigate the behavioral expression of severe conduct disorder in delinquent youths?" *Journal of Anxiety Disorders*, *13*(6), 565-574.

Parke, R. D. & Slaby, R. G. (1983), "The development of aggression," In P Mussen and EM Hetherington (Eds.), *Handbook of Child Psychology* Vol. *4*, Socialization, Personality, and Social Development" (4th Edition) 547-641, New York, NY: Wiley.

Pauly, P. J. (2005). "The political structure of the brain: cerebral localization in Bismarckian Germany," *Electroneurobiología*, *14*(1), 25-32.

Peterson, J. B. & Shane, M. (2004). "The functional neuroanatomy and psychopharmacology of predatory and defensive aggression," In J McCord (Ed.), *Beyond Empiricism: Institutions and Intentions in the Study of Crime*, Series: Advances in Criminological Theory, Vol. *13*, 107-146, Piscataway, NJ: Transaction Books.

Raine, A., Buchsbaum, M. S., Stanley, J., Lottenberg, S., Abel, L. & Stoddard, J. (1994), "Selective reductions in prefrontal glucose metabolism in murderers," *Biological Psychiatry*, *36*(6), 365-373.

Raine, A., Meloy, J. R., Bihrle, S., Stoddard, J., LaCasse, L. & Buchsbaum, M. S. (1998), "Reduced prefrontal and increased subcortical brain functioning assessed using positron emission tomography in predatory and affective murderers," *Behavioral Sciences and the Law*, *16*(3), 319-332.

Raleigh, M. J., McGuire, M. T., Brammer, G. L., Pollack, D. B. & Yuwiler, A. (1991). "Serotonergic mechanisms promote dominance acquisition in adult male vervet monkeys," *Brain Research*, *559*(2), 181-190.

Remschmidt, H. & Walter, R. (2010), "What becomes of delinquent children? Results of the Marburg child delinquency study," *Deutsches Ärzteblatt international*, *107*(27), 477-483.

Sadock, B. J., Sadock, V. A. & Kaplan, H. I. (2008), *Kaplan and Sadock's Concise Textbook of Child Psychiatry* (First Edition) Lippincott Williams and Wilkins.

Schwartzbaum, J. S. & Pribram, K. H. (1960). "The effects of amygdalectomy in monkeys on transposition along a brightness continuum," *Journal of Comparative Physiological and Psychology*, *53*, 396-399.

Spriggs, A. L., Iannotti, R. J., Nansel, T. R. & Haynie, D. L. (2007), "Adolescent bullying involvement and perceived family; peer and school relations: Commonalities and differences across race/ethnicity," *Journal of Adolescent Health*, *41*(3), 283-293.

Stevenson, J. & Goodman, R. (2001). "Association between behavior at age 3 years and adult criminality," *British Journal of Psychiatry*, *179*, 197-202.

Turner, D., Basdekis-Jozsa, R. & Briken, P. (2012). "Prescription of testosterone-lowering medications for sex offender treatment in German forensic-psychiatric institutions," *Journal of Sexual Medicine*, October 22, [ahead of print], Doi: 10.1111/j.1743-6109.2012.02958.x.

Ulzen, T. P. & Hamilton, H. (1998). "The nature and characteristics of psychiatric comorbidity in incarcerated adolescents," *Canadian Journal of Psychiatry*, *43*(1), 57-63.

Vervoort, M. H., Scholte, R. H. & Overbeek, G. (2010), "Bullying and victimization among adolescents: The role of ethnicity and ethnic composition of school class," *Journal of Youth and Adolescence*, *39*(1), 1-11.

Wakefield, J. C. (1999). "Evolutionary versus prototype analyses of the concept of disorder," *Journal of Abnormal Psychology*, *108*(3), 374-399.

Whittle, S., Yap, M. B., Yücel, M., Fornito, A., Simmons, J. G., Barrett, A., Sheeber, L. & Allen, N. B. (2008). "Prefrontal and amygdala volumes are related to adolescents' affective behaviors during parent-adolescent interactions," *Proceedings of the National Academy of Sciences of the United States of America*, *105*(9), 3652-3657.

Wiecko, F. M. (2012). "Late-onset offending: Fact or fiction," *International Journal of Offender Therapy and Comparative Criminology*, September 26, [ahead of print] Doi: 10.1177/0306624X12458503.

Zara, G. & Farrington, D. P. (2009). "Childhood and adolescent predictors of late onset criminal careers," *Journal of Youth and Adolescence*, *38*(3), 287-300.

Zoccolillo, M. (1992), "Co-occurrence of conduct disorder and its adult outcomes with depressive and anxiety disorders: A review," *Journal of the American Academy of Child and Adolescent Psychiatry*, *31*(3), 547-356.

In: Assaults
Editor: Keith V. Bletzer

ISBN: 978-1-62808-051-3

Chapter 2

PEER ASSAULT: PROBLEMS ASSOCIATED WITH BULLYING

Caleb McCoy, Brian Johnson, Yinan Zhao, Emily Salyer and Cliff McKinney*

Department of Psychology, Mississippi State University, Mississippi State, MS US

ABSTRACT

Bullying is a risk factor that can impede children's physical and psychological health. The act of bullying is often described as physically aggressive behaviors and/or verbal aggression toward someone who is portrayed as socially and emotionally weak and/or defenseless. The occurrence of bullying might seem to take place without specific reasons. Verbal bullying is expressed through insults and/or aggressive language to harm the victim, whereas physical bullying involves actual bodily harm through aggressive acts. Bullying happens within various settings including families, educational settings, work places, and over the Internet and other electronic media (i.e., cyber bullying). Specific types of bullying across various settings are discussed within the context of prevention efforts to reduce their occurrence as well as their negative psychological impacts. Overall, bullying is associated with both short-term and long-term negative effects that impact the development of children, adolescents and adults. These effects range from having low self-esteem to the possibility of suicide. However, the presence of programs in schools and involvement of the parents in the educational system can help to reduce bullying and its associated consequences.

Keywords: Bullying, psychological effects, prevention, school/family/ workplace, cyber-bullying

* Corresponding author: Email: CMcKinney@psychology.msstate.edu.

INTRODUCTION

Although public awareness seems to have increased in recent years, bullying has been a common phenomenon among children and teenagers for a long period of time. Based on a study in the United States, 17% of children from grades six to ten have experienced an act of being bullied, and 19% of them are reported to be "bullies" (Jimerson, Swearer & Espelage, 2010). This high percentage of bullying in the United States has already drawn considerable attention, as it relates to children's development. Bullying can produce seriously negative effects on children's physical and psychological health.

Bullying is an omnipresent phenomenon. However, it is predominantly witnessed in the halls of the educational systems. Bullying is a devastating occurrence that all people have either seen or themselves been a victim. *Bullying* can be defined as any form of aggressive behavior distinguished by repeated exposure over time, which results in injury and/or discomfort against vulnerable victims who cannot easily defend themselves against one or more other people (Ahmed, Braithwaite, 2006; Richard, Schneider & Mallet, 2011). Exposure to bullying is common in countries worldwide. Bullying can take place in multiple places, which usually include but are not limited to, educational systems and work places, online social networks, and through "texting" by means of cell phones. It takes place among siblings and family members, friends and acquaintances, and co-workers and classmates. These behaviors involve intentionally harmful, physical and social aggression in a milieu of authority or power imbalance between the bully and his/her victim. Bullying can be overt, which involves the action of a direct physical or verbal attack, but it can also be covert, which involves the perpetrator(s) secretly encouraging other children to "pick on" or "to ignore" a specific person or classmate. The act of bullying can involve as few as two people, where this relationship is labeled *bully versus victim engagement.* Bystanders to the bullying act are those who witness the act and do nothing about it. Thus, they are indirectly involved. Bullying aggression also can involve a group of people where there may be multiple bullies, victims and bystanders. In some prevention programs, the "bystander" is the key link in teaching young people the foundations of managing bullying.

It is estimated that one in five school children experience the effects of bullying (Ttofi & Farrington, 2008). Of these children, four sub-types of students may be directly or indirectly involved. The "bully" is easily recognized as the person who directly causes the harm against another person(s). The "bullied" is directly harmed by the bully. These roles are not absolute. Specifically, some children can take on both roles in what is termed as the "bully-victim," defined as someone who has been bullied themselves and who becomes a "bully" by projecting their past involvement as the "bullied" onto others. The fourth and final sub-type is the individual who is classified as "uninvolved." They tend to be bystanders who witness the bullying but choose to do nothing about it and often have the idea that someone else knows how to better handle the situation (Goldweber, Waasdorp & Bradshaw, 2012).

WHO IS THE BULLY?

Traditional views of bullies have stereotyped them as having low self-esteem and taking out their insecurities on victims. Recent findings have shown this to not be the case. Instead, research has shown that bullies tend to have high but unstable self-esteem, high aggression, and low social competency (Matthiesen & Einarsen, 2007). It also has been found that children who are victims of bullying or child abuse are much more likely to become adult bullies (Harvey et al, 2006).

Boys typically use the overt type of engagement to directly confront, harass, taunt and belittle peers and others, both physically and emotionally, in order to express and protect their power or authority in the social environment where they are present (Hutzell & Payne, 2012). Boys who express social dominance and persuasiveness in this fashion typically have had a prior experience of being victims themselves and are usually able to get peer support for this behavior. Across their educational experience from pre-school to college, continuation of these roles occurs. Males are more commonly the perpetrator of overt bullying in elementary, high school and college. However, girls are typically the victim and perpetrator of covert bullying from pre-school to college with a peak in middle school (Chapell et al, 2006). Females characteristically gossip, start rumors, turn friends against each other, and ostracize others to avoid and conceal direct confrontation, but they are not at all exempt from using external aggression. Both males and females use aggression in various forms to gain and hold power in social networks and to cover insecurities that they may have, which commonly develop from being bullied in the past (Farmer, Farmer, Estell & Hutchins, 2007). The progression of these relationships continues through educational settings. Typically the roles do not change from high school to college. After establishing their role as a bully or victim, little change occurs due to the social harm and deprivation that has occurred. These roles often are reinforced by attracting attention; encouragement often comes from bystanders who are peers (Richard et al, 2011). Although their trajectory of involvement is longer, girls at times are more likely to aid those who are being bullied, unlike their male counterparts.

The role of a bully is not limited to just students. These actions also can be performed by administrative positions in schools as well. Although bullying by administrators can happen throughout the school years, this role is more common among college instructors and coaches. Bullies who are peers often use physical confrontations, whereas this type of action is highly unlikely among coaches and even rarer among instructors. Those who are in a position of authority often use ways that cannot be traced by those of higher authority but it can be witnessed by other students (Chapell et al, 2006).

Who Is Being Bullied?

In many cases, it is easy to mistake bullying as teasing. Thus, a lot of bullying behaviors are treated as mild teasing by teachers and parents. Teasing happens very frequently among children and does not produce the severe effects associated with bullying. Instead of serious aggressive behaviors, teasing usually includes playful name-calling and put-downs without aggression. Further, teasing usually happens once rather than in a repetitive pattern, which is characteristic of bullying (Drew, 2010). The purpose of teasing is to make jokes rather than intentional harming. On the contrary, bullying is more than making jokes on others; it is a repetitive pattern of intentionally harming others that can include anti-social behaviors. Sometimes when children complain about being bullied by peers in school, parents may just treat it as teasing among children. Under such circumstances, parents and teachers might be ignoring bullying behavior. When parents and teachers cannot clearly identify between the two, children who are experiencing bullying might not receive immediate help. Over the long-term, their development may be seriously threatened.

Few studies have been done on the reasons why specific students are targeted and victimized by bullying. Some have shown mixed correlations between race of victim and offender. These correlations have shown that in some areas of society, African Americans are less likely to be bullied than Caucasian and Hispanic youth, but in other areas frequented by same-race peers, they are at higher risk. In regards to a general rate of bullying, statistics have shown that African American youth are more likely to participate and be labeled by teachers and peers in the bullying sub-group as a perpetrator and less likely as the victim. In regard to associations of bullying with race, the context and environment must be taken into consideration when trying to examine predictors of bullying.

Urban areas tend to be viewed with a more negative image of their social environment with the assumption of increasing victimization rates of bullying toward African Americans than in non-urban areas. In fact, ‘urbanicity’ has a direct effect on who is bullied. Little differences are found in bullying toward specific races, when household income is controlled. In these cases, when household income is comparable between groups, both Caucasians and African Americans have equal risks of being victimized by bullies. This victimization comes from direct discrimination based on gender, race, religion, sexuality or socio-economic status. Other studies have shown that a student’s physical representation, such as the way of talking, the way that one dresses and “the look” one chooses to portray are among the highest predictors to whether they are bullied or not (Goldweber, Waasdorp & Bradshaw, 2012).

Sexuality also plays an enormous role in who is victimized by bullies. Those who do not conform to the social norms of heterosexuality and gender roles are at high risks of being bullied (Toomey, Ryan, Diaz, Card & Russell, 2010). Males who tend to be effeminate and females who are perceived as being masculine tend to be targeted by bullies, regardless of their actual sexual orientation. Refusal to comply with these societal norms and/or openly expressing their sexuality often leads to negative responses from peer groups including physical assault, social ostracizing and verbal aggressions (Toomey et al, 2010).

Overall, victims of bullying are often those perceived as weaker or in some way different from other students. Those who are given a stereotypical name such as “nerd” or “geek” are typically more likely to be victimized across educational settings. Because of labels, some students are unable to acquire social prominence within the school and often are not able to gain the social support that other students have. Students labeled as popular are generally unlikely to be victimized and are more likely to be the bully. Although some youth labeled as a bully may not be popular, they seek to gain a dominant position over other students. Research has shown that those who use aggression to declare their power in the school system often use manipulation to control their peers and social world (Farmer et al, 2012). Those who use this technique are often using aggression and manipulation to fulfill their own needs and insecurities.

Authoritative Roles and the School Environment

The social progression of bullying is not limited to the influence of other students but also includes the influence of parents and other authority figures. These adults (e.g. teachers, coaches, parents) can either increase or decrease the negative effects of bullying by either acknowledging the problem and intervening or over-looking the incident and choosing to ignore the situation. In actuality, bullying is a group effort and is never the fault of one child (Richard et al, 2011). The influence that parents, teachers and coaches play has a direct role in whether a student becomes a bully or not. A child who does not receive the proper attention to become socially and emotionally adept as a student often lashes out and projects anger onto other students. By making the classroom a positive environment for all students, where the teacher believes in each student's potential and gives them a sense of appreciation, bullying is likely to decrease among students (Richard et al, 2011). The goal in each school is to sustain a bully-free environment and make the learning environment a positive place to be educated and learn key social abilities that each student will be able to use as they progress into later adolescence and adulthood.

Teachers' roles are more important than any bully prevention policy that schools can offer (Richard et al, 2011). By creating a positive learning environment and by making the material interesting, both teachers and students experience less stress, which results in decreased bullying. Thus, school policies are important and must be clarified to sustain a well-structured educational environment. This social structure and the academic program the school offers are thought to be linked with the severity of bullying in the educational system (Richard et al, 2011). Students with low interest in school are more likely to display aggressive behaviors in school, unlike schools with committed teachers and school administration. Bullying within the school system is amplified with today's technology. Because of the increased usage of cell phones and online social media networks, bullying takes place in more environments than ever before.

Cyber Bullying

The past few decades have seen huge technological shifts, including computers, the internet and cell phones. These advances have vastly altered the way that we communicate. Some of these new modes of communication include interactive possibilities such as texting, blogs and social media. One study reported that 93% of teens actively use the internet and 75% have a cell phone (Schneider, O'Donnell, Stueve & Coulter, 2012). These new platforms for communication and connectivity have created a new delivery method for bullying. This new form of bullying is called *cyber bullying*, which can be defined as the use of e-mails, cell phones, instant messenger, chat rooms, and/or social networking websites to scare, harass or intimidate someone. This can include directly harassing or targeting by using social media to exclude or torment, including the misuse of pictures or video (Menesini & Nocentini, 2009).

Prevalence rates for cyber bullying vary depending on the method and the definition that the researchers used to identify what constitutes cyber bullying. Studies shows anywhere between four to 36 percent of people have experienced cyber bullying (Barlett & Gentile, 2012). The two main electronic devices through which cyber bullying can occur are computers and cell phones (Privitera & Campbell, 2009). These devices allow for remoteness and anonymity, the two things that researchers believe may make cyber bullying an easier mode of bullying than traditional ways (Dooley, Pyżalski & Cross, 2009). Remoteness allows the bully not to have to see the pain which he/she has inflicted because it avoids face-to-face confrontation. Anonymity and remoteness also give bullies a better chance at avoiding conflict and/or negative consequence that might arise. Many believe that they can avoid getting into trouble from this form of bullying because they believe that what they say online will not be found or taken the wrong way, and if it is, they can say that they were "just joking" (Barlett & Gentile, 2012).

When it comes to cyber bullying, many underlying factors play a role in who is victimized. Smith and associates (2008) suggest that evidence as to which sex is more likely to be the transgressor of cyber bullying is mixed. Most studies suggest that males and females are equally likely to be a cyber-bully, whereas a few suggest that one sex is more likely to be a cyber-bully than the other. When asked who students thought would be more likely to use technology to bully, students were more likely to report that females were. They stated that because females use social technology more they are more prone to certain forms of social bullying, so they would be more likely to be a cyber-bully. Students further stated that males are more likely to be physical, and they believed their bullying would not go beyond that. Despite these perceptions, no significant gender differences between girls and boys have been found (Smith et al, 2008).

Research has indicated a crossover between traditional bullying and cyber bullying. Those who are bullies in a traditional sense are more likely to be cyber bullies. The same is true for the victims of traditional bullying. They also are more likely to be the victim of cyber bullies. A power imbalance is still present when cyber bullying occurs. In both forms of bullying a powerful perpetrator bullies a weaker victim. However, the anonymity offered by technology erases typical physical or social power imbalances and creates a new power imbalance (Barlett & Gentile, 2012; Dooley et al, 2009).

Cyber bullying, like traditional bullying, is not limited to childhood and adolescence. Technological advances in the workplace have allowed cyber bullying to follow the same trend. Depending on the strictness of the definition, the prevalence of cyber bullying in the work place ranges from 11 to over 50 percent. A notable difference between cyber bullying at work and during childhood and adolescence is that cyber bullying at work is more likely to be accompanied by traditional bullying practices, whereas children and adolescents often report that they have only experienced cyber bullying (Privitera & Campbell, 2009).

Like traditional bullying, cyber bullying can lead to increased psychological distress such depression, anxiety, and suicide for those who are victimized. One study of Pacific Islander high school students reported the incidence of binge drinking tripled for those who had been victims of cyber bullying (Goebert, Else, Matsu, Chung-Do & Chang, 2011). Reports in another study indicate that those who were only cyber bullied experienced more distress than those who are only bullied in the more traditional social form (Schneider et al, 2012). Finally, another study asked students to indicate which style of bullying they felt was more harmful. Most forms were rated as equally harmful, but picture/video bullying was rated as the worst. Many students commented on the added anxiety of not knowing who you are facing could sometimes make cyber bullying more frightening (Smith et al, 2008).

Cyber bullying is a relatively new phenomenon and researchers agree that it has yet to be addressed in an appropriate manner. When asked about how they feel it should be handled, students responded that it was something that could be stopped without ridding the world of these means of technological communication. However, they did suggest that victims tell someone and that campaigns be aimed to alert the bully of the consequences of his or her actions (Smith et al, 2008). Most states now mandate that schools address the issue of cyber bullying, although little consistency exists in how much emphasis schools place on it. Schools can only do so much because the acts of cyber bullying mostly occur outside of schools (Schneider et al, 2012) even if results appear during school hours when social media is accessed. Prevention and early intervention are the best ways to curtail such activities. It is important for parents and teachers to be aware of the signs of cyber bullying and to keep open the channels of communication. Several websites are available, such as www.stopcyberbullying.org and www.cyberbullyhelp.com that can serve as a good first step in addressing the issue of cyber bullying (Goebert et al, 2011).

SIBLING BULLYING

School bullying is the type that is most commonly reported. It has become a serious public concern. Research on sibling bullying or bullying at home seems scant. The lack of reports of family bullying does not mean that it produces less harmful effects. In reality, similar to the effects of school bullying, family bullying can bring lifetime negative consequence for the victims.

Bullying among siblings is one of the most common types of bullying. It can be recognized when one child in the family constantly produces insulting words or aggressive behaviors towards siblings. A variety of factors are associated with bullying among siblings. Birth order is one of the most important contributors. The first-born child or the older child is usually physically stronger than the younger one, and the physical advantages may be the prerequisite to produce aggressive behaviors towards younger siblings (Menesini, 2010). In addition, the first-born child may be the focus of the family and is likely to obtain special care and attention from parents before the siblings are born (Menesini, 2010). It is easy for older children to apply authority and other aggressive behaviors to younger siblings (Menesini, 2010). Gender differences are another factor, which may be involved in bullying among siblings. Studies report that sisters generally exhibit more affection towards other siblings. Thus, sisters have a lower potential to produce bullying behavior compared to brothers (Menesini, 2010). Additionally, children with conduct disorder (CD) can have a higher potential to produce aggressive behaviors and often project this aggression onto siblings. Children diagnosed with CD usually exhibit repetitive serious aggression and anti-social behaviors, which include threatening others and their property (Mash & Wolfe, 2010).

Prevention of bullying among siblings has equal urgency to those in public settings described above. Parental discipline practices play an essential role in reducing bullying behaviors within the family (Kokkinos & Panayiotou, 2007). Adopting the methods of behavior modification can be effective in eliminating bullying behaviors. In some cases, when parents notice bullying behaviors at home, they might seriously punish their child or children with corporal punishment, such as spanking. Although corporal punishment can produce short-term effects on eliminating children's bullying behaviors (see related chapter, this volume), it leads to long-term increases in bullying behavior (Kazdin, 2001). When parents physically punish the bully, the punishing behaviors provide a model for the child to imitate. Furthermore, punishment from parents can also lead to a strong reaction on the part of the child. Specifically, defiance theory suggests that if children perceive the punishment as reasonable, they are likely to be compliant; on the other hand, when children perceive the punishment as unfair, they might become offensive and aggressive (Ttofi & Farrington, 2008).

Compared with corporal punishment, positive reinforcement and time-out procedures are more successful at preventing bullying. Parents need to establish the rules for the bullying behavior in the family. If the child does not produce aggressive behaviors towards siblings for a certain period of time, he or she may be rewarded appropriately. Positive reinforcement and time-out are more likely to shape a child's desired behavior than physical forms of punishment in the long-term.

Multi-systemic therapy (MST) also can be considered an effective method to prevent bullying between/among siblings. Instead of relying solely on parents' supervision, MST expands the sphere to a larger social system, including family, school, clinic and associated social organizations (Swenson, Henggeler, Taylor & Addison, 2009). A child with bullying behaviors should be supervised by parents at home as well as teachers and peers at school. Through learning appropriate coping skills from teachers and through peer interactions, a child can be more adaptive in the surrounding social environment. If necessary, children who have expressed themselves through bullying behaviors might require counseling and/or treatment by professional clinicians. A great number of studies have indicated that MST is highly effective in reducing children's aggressive behaviors and improving family relations (Mash & Wolfe, 2010). These behaviors among children, whether at home, in school, or over the Internet, often progress through the child's life. This can carry over into the workplace.

WORKPLACE BULLYING

Bullying is traditionally a concept that people relate to scenarios of childhood and school. This is not the only place that bullying occurs. Workplace bullying is not a new phenomenon but it is one that has recently become the focus of research and public attention. We can extend the definition of bullying at school and home to *workplace bullying*, which is any behavior, conscious or unconscious, that causes another person to feel victimized, humiliated or distressed (Hauge, Skogstad & Einarsen, 2010). Unlike the playground or hallways, however, bullying behaviors in the workplace very rarely are physical but they can cause a drop in job performance (Harvey, Heames, Richey & Leonard, 2006).

Harvey and associates (2006) identified seven different types of bullying behavior found in the workplace and include the following: (a) stigmatizing the victim or pointing out differences between the victim and the bully or the bullies in-group; (b) blaming failures of any kind on the victim, either as an act to humiliate the victim or to simply protect the bully from blame of failure; (c) sexually harassing the victim; (d) singling out someone and placing unreasonable pressure and/or deadlines on one person unequally in comparison to others; (e) isolating the victim by withholding information or opportunities that may be afforded to others; (f) setting up the victim to fail, constantly reminding the victim of past failures and avoiding giving credit to the victim when credit is due; (g) and physically abusing the victim.

Prevalence rates for workplace bullying have been found in one study to be as high as 53% of the respondents who reported being bullied and 77% witnessed bullying during their working career (Rayner, 1997), although most numbers are more conservative and vary between 7 to 10 percent. Research has shown that both sexes are almost equally as likely to be bullied, whereas some studies show women to have a slightly higher prevalence rate of victimization as men (Rayner, 1997; Harvey et al, 2006). Victims often are in staff positions, as opposed to managerial or executive positions, or they are new to their position or location within the company or new management has recently been put into place (Rayner, 1997). Youth is another characteristic that victims of workplace bullying often share, as the bullied victims are usually relatively young, compared to their coworkers (Rayner, 1997).

Among most victims in the worksite, low self-esteem seems to be a common factor. Victims appear to be less socially confident and competent (Harvey et al, 2006). They are usually more submissive and passive as well. In some cases, they may even be combative when put under social pressure. These factors can combine to make them appear weak or as easy targets for bullies. Because these traits are relatively stable over their lifetime, those who are victims of bullying in school are at higher risk for being victims of bullying in the workplace (Harvey et al, 2006; Matthiesen & Einarsen, 2007). In a small number of situations, victims might actually become an equal rival to the bully. In these cases, the situation is more of a fight for dominance rather than a traditional bully/victim situation (Harvey et al, 2006).

Although it appears that both sexes are equally victimized by bullying in the workplace, the sex of the bully seems to be dependent on the sex of the victim. Women report being bullied equally by both sexes, whereas men rarely report being bullied by women (Rayner, 1997). One explanation for this finding can be found within the definition of bullying. For an act to be considered bullying, the victim must feel like they have little or no control and/or feel threatened. Traditionally, men might not see women as threatening, and those who do might be reluctant to report it as such, because of socialized gender norms where “reporting” would be perceived as a weakness (Rayner, 1997).

Bullying in the workplace has consequences that are similar to those experienced by the victims of childhood incidents with a few exceptions. Experiencing bullying within the workplace can lead to depression and anxiety and in severe cases post-traumatic stress disorder (Hauge, Skogstad & Einarson, 2010). Workplace bullying also has been found to be related to later long-term sickness and work absenteeism (Ortega, Christensen, Hogh, Rugulies & Borg, 2011). Although these impacts affect people on an individual level, they also have a strong connection to the organization in which they are occurring. All of these things can lead to more frequent sick-days, lower job satisfaction, and decreased productivity. These are all important reasons for organizational leaders to take notice of workplace bullying behaviors and work to reduce or eliminate them. Regardless of where the bullying takes place, multiple problems are associated with the act of bullying.

PROBLEMS CAUSED BY BULLYING

Victims of bullying often come into contact with short-term and/or long-term negative effects, which can range from physical and psychological health problems; at the extreme they can become fatal (Ttofi & Farrington, 2008). Bullying causes serious harm to a student's social life. Pre-school and elementary environments tend to be the place where children are first labeled as being a bully or a victim. Serious physical harm is rare among elementary students but becomes more common in middle school and high school. Middle school is often the time period when students start to discover self-identity and identify the social groups that may continue throughout their experiences in the education system and as an adult. These social relationships can develop a significant sense of group affiliation and is crucial among teens because these social circles can help to defend against anxiety caused by social rejection or isolation (Carney, Jacob & Hazler, 2011).

Psychological problems caused by bullying are not limited to only the person persecuted but also are found in bullies themselves, who often suffer from more psychiatric symptoms than other students of the same age. Studies have shown that bullies have a higher rate of psychosomatic symptoms, are more likely to say that school is not an enjoyable place to be, and continue to dislike the environment they encounter in future educational settings (Ttofi & Farrington, 2008). Victims are likely to say that they are unhappy and feel as if they are not safe at school. They are more likely to have higher rates of absences and poor academic success (Hutzell & Payne, 2012). Both male and female bullies and the bullied are likely to suffer from higher risk of depression, anxiety and suicidal ideation. Female victims often have eating disorders as well as depression and feelings of self-worthlessness (Chapell et al, 2006). These risks have a direct impact on the students' physical and emotional health in multiple ways. Symptoms of feeling nervous, sleep deprivation, loneliness, helplessness and agitation are very common among bullied victims and can lead to themselves becoming the bully-victim. Those who suffer from these symptoms are more likely to be submissive, withdrawn, and isolated when compared to other youth their own age (Ttofi & Farrington, 2008).

Bullying can result in long-term social, emotional and psychological effects that can continue throughout the victims' lives. They tend to have poorer social skills, which makes it harder for them to adapt to new situations and environments as they progress forward within an educational system (Farmer et al, 2007). Both the persecutor and the victim involved are more likely to start smoking, have poorer academic standings and display a stronger requisite for social acceptance, unlike those who are not involved (Richard et al, 2011). Bullies with psycho-social deficiencies who show a clear need are often referred to programs that offer assistance. These programs can help by providing counseling and psychotherapy to address problems and to prevent aggressive behaviors (Hutzell & Payne, 2012).

Recommendations to Reduce Bullying and Its Effects

Throughout the years, bullying has expanded from schoolyard scuffles to online harassment and it can even follow one into professional worlds. With current variations in the forms of bullying that take place, many prevention programs have been established to help guide individuals and to expunge inappropriate or threatening behaviors. These programs also have been developed to not only purge negative behaviors but to also help individuals to learn correct conduct or to learn how to handle negative situations in better ways. These programs are allowing people to not only prevent bullying but also to be prepared for whatever might come their way in all aspects of life.

As bullying increases in hallways and on playgrounds, many schools have set-up programs to make the environment safer for students. These programs have been implemented to control and reduce school bullying. In 1983, Norway created the first national anti-bullying program implemented anywhere in the world. Evaluation of the program showed a dramatic decrease of about one-half the cases of victimization after the intervention (Ttofi & Farrington, 2011). Many other nations then started to develop their own programs for training individuals, based on publicized success rates.

Ttofi and Farrington (2011) have reviewed the KiVa Program developed in Finland, which used Internet and visual learning platforms to change student attitudes about bullying. KiVa included devices that allowed an enhancement of their anti-bullying education program, including the use of role-playing exercises, short films on bullying, classroom discussions and group work. Another plus was that teachers were given vests that enhanced their visibility, while they were watching students in the schoolyard. Ttofi and Farrington (2011) also stated that the program included peer support groups for victims of bullying and cooperative group work among experts in dealing with children involved in bullying. Parents were given information and advice about bullying. This program proved that taking simple steps, such as involving teachers and parents, in preventing bullying can cause effective outcomes.

Another recommendation to help with bullying is that children should always have someone to turn to, including psychologists and school nurses. Although school psychologists are limited and have historically focused on assessment and individual treatment in the schools, an incredible opportunity exists for them, as well as others, to function as prevention specialists to help schools determine appropriate assessment tools and to guide intervention planning, implementation and evaluation (Leff, 2007). Another prevention program is the Solving Problems Together Foundation, which provides students with an opportunity to increase critical thinking and problem-solving skills while they work simultaneously toward a solution in dealing with problems (Hall, 2006). This model provides students with a sense of empowerment and allows them to take charge of their own problems. The process behind the program is that students analyze their situations and problems and then seek appropriate resources to help them. Hall (2006) stated that the main purpose of this program is to allow students identified as victims of bullying to develop effective strategies for responding to this behavior. The main goal of this program is for students to go through the problem-solving process so that they can determine strategies that can use when they are facing a difficult situation and/or bullying behavior. This program has many positive effects associated with it, including the development of better problem solving techniques.

With competition in the workplace becoming harder, individuals will resort to anything to get ahead, including lying, wrongfully blaming others and even physical violence. With many of these problems becoming more and more prominent in the workplace, companies and individuals have resorted to developing and implementing programs that will help make their businesses not only happier places to work, but also stronger businesses in general. One prevention step being developed and implemented in workplaces is Anti-bullying Policies. These programs are being implemented in hopes of producing a positive, high-care workplace environment. A bill informally referred to as "The Healthy Workplace Bill" has been introduced across the United States in 16 states since 2003 (Duffy, 2009). This bill has different versions depending on the state, but the bill holds both individual employees and their employers liable for any form of demonstrated workplace harm. Duffy (2009) stated that the bill provides for employer incentives to develop preventive measures and respond adequately and promptly to allegations of workplace bullying. In the long run, this discourages the likelihood of frivolous law-suits. As supported by the bill, placing more programs into the workplace allows not only the employees to benefit from the positive aspects of it, but also the employers because awards they will benefit from when they implement measures that have been supported and specified in this bill.

Another prevention program developed for the workplace is the Three-Step Strategic Program (Namie & Namie, 2009). This program consists of moderation/mediation, coaching and organizational development. The moderation stage is used to allow parties to move beyond any kind of misunderstanding or misperceptions, while mediation is the conflict resolution process. The second part of the program consists of a coaching strategy. This part is mainly supportive, which can fall into inter-personal emotional, career development, or skills enhancement. The third intervention strategy is organization development. Many sources of bullying can be found in attributes of the organization, including reporting relationships, layers in the hierarchy and equitable processes that match rewards to performance. Organizational development defines problems as systemic and suggests that solutions must necessarily affect all people at all levels of the organization. The three-step program has many positive aspects that can result in controlling many kinds of negative problems in the workplace. The first stage allows for affected individuals with the opportunity to explain their perception of the situation, which can prevent rumors and other problems from spreading. The second stage allows individuals to seek support, which helps individuals to work through tough situations. The last stage allows for equal treatment among all employees no matter the status or position that they may hold.

CONCLUSION

Bullying is a devastating occurrence that almost everybody has experienced and/or witnessed at least once in their lifetime. Its presence can be seen in schools, within the home between family members, on the Internet and media devices, and even in the workplace. This aggressive behavior is not prone to any specific individual, but it is often shown to be aimed at people with specific characteristics and lifestyles. Often those who are bullied are seen as being weak or frail, and those who committing the act of bullying are often seen as dominant, powerful and frightening. Both the bully and the bullied might suffer from negative physical and/or psychological consequences associated with their acts, which can have both short-term and long-term effects. Some of these effects range from depression, anxiety and low self-esteem to life-threatening physical damage and even suicide. Although effective programs have been implemented and are successful in reducing bullying within these settings, its variable practices still occur daily worldwide.

The presence of programs within educational systems works, not only as a way to stop bullying on jurisdictional school property, but also to prevent it from occurring after the students have departed from school and are in a working environment or when they have children of their own. As bullying often goes unnoticed, those who are bullied do not know how to deal with their situation. They tend to have feelings of being alone and shy away from any help that is offered. Prevention programs are working to reach out and offer help to any individual or group that feels threatened in any environment. Overall, bullying is a treacherous occurrence that is hard to stop. It is slowly decreasing due to these specialized programs within the educational settings, home and workplace. Parents are becoming more involved, as well as faculty and administrators in schools and administrators on college campuses, to help stop bullying from occurring. Positive attitudes and active reinforcements are the key in producing a more successful and progressive environment for all those involved in bullying.

REFERENCES

Ahmed, E. & Braithwaite, V. (2006), "Forgiveness, reconciliation, and shame: Three key variables in reducing school bullying," *Journal of Social Issues*, *62*, 347-370.

Barlett, C. P. & Gentile, D. A. (2012), "Attacking others online: The formation of cyberbullying in late adolescence," *Psychology of Popular Media Culture*, *1*, 123-135.

Carney, J. V., Jacob, C. J. & Hazler, R. J. (2011), "Exposure to school bullying and the social capital of sixth-grade students," *Journal of Humanistic Counseling*, *50*, 238-253.

Chapell, M. S., Hasselman, S. L., Kitchin, T., Lomon, S. N., MacIver, K. W. & Sarullo, P. L. (2006), "Bullying in elementary school, high school, and college," *Adolescence*, *41*, 633-648.

Dooley, J. J., Pyżalski, J. & Cross, D. (2009), "Cyberbullying versus face-to-face bullying: A theoretical and conceptual review," *Journal of Psychology*, *217*, 182-188.

Drew, N. (2010), "*No Kidding about Bullying: 125 Ready-to-use Activities to Help Kids Manage Anger, Resolve Conflicts, Bullying Empathy, and Get Alone, Grades 3-6,"* Minneapolis, MN: Free Spirit Publishing Inc.

Duffy, M. (2009), "Preventing workplace mobbing and bullying with effective organizational consultation, policies, and legislation." *Consulting Psychology Journal: Practice and Research*, *61*, 242-262.

Farmer, T. W., Farmer, E. M. Z., Estell, D. B. & Hutchins, B. C. (2007), "The developmental dynamics of aggression and the prevention of school violence," *Journal of Emotional and Behavioral Disorders*, *15*, 197-208.

Goebert, D., Else, I., Matsu, C., Chung-Do, J. & Chang, J. Y. (2011). "The impact of cyberbullying on substance use and mental health in a multiethnic sample," *Maternal and Child Health Journal*, *15*, 1282-1286.

Goldweber, A., Waasdorp, T. E. & Bradshaw, C. P. (2012), "Examining associations between race, urbanicity, and patterns of bullying involvement," *Journal of Youth and Adolescence*. doi: 10.1007/s100964-012-9843-y

Hall, K. R. (2006), "Solving problems together: A psychoeducational group model for victims of bullies," *Journal for Specialists in Group Work*, *31*, 201-217.

Harvey, M. G., Heames, J. T., Richey, R. & Leonard, N. (2006). "Bullying: From the playground to the boardroom," *Journal of Leadership and Organizational Studies*, *12*, 1-11.

Hauge, L., Skogstad, A. & Einarsen, S. (2010). The relative impact of workplace bullying as a social stressor at work," *Scandinavian Journal of Psychology*, *51*, 426-433.

Hutzell, K. L. & Payne, A. A. (2012), "The impact of bullying victimization on school avoidance," *Youth Violence and Juvenile Justice*, *10*, 370-385.

Jimerson, S., Swearer, S. & Espelage, D. (2010). "International scholarship advances science and practicing addressing bullying in schools," In Jimerson S, Swearer S, Espelage D (Eds.), *Handbook of Bullying in School: An International Perspective* (1-6), New York, NY: Routledge.

Kazdin, A. E. (2001). "Behavior modifications in applied settings (6th ed.)," Belmont, CA: Wadsworth/Thomson Learning.

Kokkinos, C. M. & Panayiotou, G. (2007). "Parental discipline practices and locus of control: Relationship to bullying and victimization experiences of elementary school students," *Social Psychology of Education*, *10*(3), 281-301.

Leff, S. S. (2007). "Bullying and peer victimization at school: Considerations and future directions," *School Psychology Review*, *36*, 406-412.

Mash, E. & Wolfe, D. (2010), "*Child Abnormal Psychology*" (4th ed.), Belmont, CA: Wadsworth.

Matthiesen, S. & Einarsen, S. (2007), "Perpetrators and targets of bullying at work: Role stress and individual differences," *Violence and Victims*, *22*, 735-753.

Menesini, E. (2010), "Bullying among siblings: The role of personality and relational variables," *British Journal of Developmental Psychology*, *28*, 921-939.

Menesini, E. & Nocentini, A. (2009). Cyberbullying, definition and measurement: Some critical considerations," *Journal of Psychology*, *217*, 230-232.

Namie, G. & Namie, R. (2009). "U.S. Workplace bullying: Some basic considerations and consultation interventions," *Consulting Psychology Journal: Practice and Research*, *61*, 202-219.

Ortega, A., Christensen, K. B., Hogh, A., Rugulies, R. & Borg, V. (2011). "One-year prospective study on the effect of workplace bullying on long-term sickness absence," *Journal of Nursing Management*, *19*, 752-759.

Privitera, C. & Campbell, M. (2009), "Cyberbullying: The new face of workplace bullying?," *Cyberpsychology and Behavior*, *12*, 395-400.

Rayner, C. (1997), "The incidence of workplace bullying," *Journal of Community and Applied Social Psychology*, *7*, 199-208.

Richard, J. F., Schneider, B. H. & Mallet, P. (2011). "Revisiting the whole-school approach to bullying: Really looking at the whole," *School Psychology International*, *33*, 263-284.

Schneider, S. K., O'Donnell, L., Stueve, A. & Coulter, R. S. (2012), "Cyberbullying, school bullying, and psychological distress: A regional census of high school students," *American Journal of Public Health*, *102*, 171-177.

Smith, P. K., Mahdavi, J., Carvalho, M., Fisher, S., Russell, S. & Tippett, N. (2008). "Cyberbullying: Its nature and impact in secondary school pupils," *Journal of Child Psychology and Psychiatry*, *49*, 376-385.

Swenson, C., Henggeler, S., Taylor, I. & Addison, O. (2009). "*Multisystemic Therapy and Neighborhood Partnerships: Reducing Adolescent Violence and Substance Abuse,*" New York, NY: Guilford.

Toomey, R. B., Ryan, C., Diaz, R. M., Card, N. A. & Russell, S. T. (2010). "Gender-nonconforming lesbian, gay, bisexual, and transgender youth: School victimization and young adult psychosocial adjustment," *Developmental Psychology*, *46*, 1580-1589.

Ttofi, M. M. & Farrington, D. P. (2008). " Bullying: Short-term and long-term effects, and the importance of defiance theory in explanation and prevention," *Victims and Offenders*, *3*, 289-312.

Ttofi, M. M., Farrington, D. P. (2011)," Effectiveness of school-based programs to reduce bullying: A systematic and meta-analytic review," *Journal of Experimental Criminology*, *7*, 27-56.

In: Assaults
Editor: Keith V. Bletzer
ISBN: 978-1-62808-051-3

Chapter 3

INTERPERSONAL VIOLENCE AND WOMEN'S REPRODUCTIVE HEALTH: CURRENT RESEARCH AND FUTURE DIRECTIONS

Nicole M. Heath * ***and Natalie R. Stevens***
Department of Behavioral Sciences, Center for Women's Behavioral and Mental Health, Rush University Medical Center, Chicago, IL, US

ABSTRACT

Commonly called "IPV," interpersonal violence (i.e., physical and/or sexual assault) perpetrated on women is a major public health concern. A considerable number of studies have demonstrated the devastating effects it can have on both the psychological and physical health of women who have been harmed. This is especially true when we consider the harmful consequences that physical and sexual assault can have on women's reproductive health. Although the prevalence of such assault on women in the general population is unfortunately high, ethnic minority women living in low socio-economic, urban neighborhoods are at even greater risk of being victims of IPV, when compared to women who do not have these socio-demographic risk factors. Assault experiences confer a greater likelihood of obstetric and gynecological health problems, such as sexually transmitted infections, pelvic pain, sexual dysfunction, unintended pregnancy, infertility, miscarriage, cervical cancer, and maternal and fetal complications during pregnancy and birth. In addition, women who have been assaulted report greater fear and avoidance of obstetric and gynecological exams and are less likely to receive preventive health care services, which increases risk for medical complications that go undetected. The aim of this chapter is to review the known literature on the association between women's reproductive health and both physical and sexual assault, with specific attention to pregnancy outcomes for mother and baby. We present preliminary descriptive data from a prospective study of female patients who sought both obstetric/gynecologic and psychological care from a major, urban medical center. We discuss the implications of these associations on psychological treatment and obstetric care, and highlight the need for multi-disciplinary interventions for pregnant survivors of IPV.

Keywords: Women; reproductive health; PTSD; pregnancy; interpersonal violence

* Corresponding author: Email: Nicole_Heath@rush.edu.

INTRODUCTION

Women who have histories of interpersonal violence (IPV), abuse, or trauma are more likely to be burdened by significant psychological and physical health problems than women without these histories. The deleterious effects of IPV have been widely documented with a great deal of research, which attends to mental health consequences and demonstrates that posttraumatic stress disorder (PTSD) is among the most common subsequent disorders (Foa & Rothbaum, 1998; Keane & Barlow, 2004; Resnick, Kilpatrick, Dansky, Saunders & Best, 1993; van der Kolk et al, 1996). Depression has been further demonstrated to be highly comorbid with PTSD following IPV (Foa & Rothbaum, 1993; Kessler, Sonnega, Bromet, Hughes & Nelson, 1995; Schumm, Briggs-Phillips & Hobfoll, 2006). However, the negative impact of IPV is far more multi-faceted, affecting health behaviors and physiology as well as psychological symptoms.

Although PTSD and depression are common consequences of IPV, the broader sequelae are quite complex, given that many instances of IPV are perpetrated by a known person and tend to involve repeated acts of violence, sometimes over long periods of time (Courtois, 2004; Herman, 1992; van der Kolk, Roth, Pelcovitz, Sunday & Spinazzola, 2005). Thus, women survivors of IPV often experience feelings of shame surrounding their general self-concept as well as their sexuality specifically. Survivors of IPV are also more likely to develop physical health problems, which can sometimes be difficult to diagnose and treat. Numerous studies have reported associations between IPV and somatization, demonstrating that the consequences of IPV manifest in physical as well as psychological symptoms (Courtois, 2004; Herman, 1992; van der Kolk, 2005). Independent of somatoform disorders, IPV is known to directly impact physical health, such as a higher BMI, an increased risk for cardiovascular disease, immune dysfunction, and inflammation (Black, 2006; Campbell, 2002; Elenkov, Iezzoni, Daly, Harris & Chrousos, 2005; McEwen, 2003). Among child-bearing women specifically, the psychological and physical consequences associated with histories of IPV can pose a threat to the health of the infant as well as the mother.

Although rates of IPV are startlingly high in the general population (see Tjaden & Thoennes, 1998), they are even higher among vulnerable populations, such as low-income, ethnic minority women, where prevalence rates range from a low of 47% (Stevens et al, 2012) to a high of 70 to 71% (Heath, Chesney & Hobfoll, 2012; Schumm et al, 2006) and varied percentages in-between (Schumm, Stines, Hobfoll & Jackson, 2005; Sutherland, Sullivan & Bybee, 2001). Such discrepancies in IPV rates create a disproportionate health challenge for women living in these at-risk conditions, as they often have less access to mental health care services. The following sections briefly review the broad impact that IPV can have on obstetric and gynecologic health through psychological functioning and other health behaviors.

IPV and Gynecologic/Sexual Health

A large body of research demonstrates that women with histories of IPV experience more gynecological health problems, including chronic pelvic pain (Campbell, Lichty, Sturza & Raja, 2006; Coker, Smith, Bethea, King & McKeown, 2000); sexual dysfunction (Coker,

2007; Weaver, 2009); human papillomavirus, which is the leading known cause of cervical cancer (Coker, Hopenhayn, DiSimone, Bush & Crofford, 2009; Farley, Golding & Minkoff, 2002; Kahn, Huang, Rosenthal, Tissot & Burk, 2005); and higher utilization of health care services for physical complaints in general (Grimstad & Schei, 1999; Koss, Koss & Woodruff, 1991; Resnick, Acierno & Kilpatrick, 1997). However, health care services that are necessary for prevention of illness, such as cervical cancer screenings, and consistent routine care, are more commonly avoided among women with histories of sexual violence (Farley et al, 2002; Pedersen & Cohen, 2010). Research demonstrates that this avoidance of gynecological care is due to fear of or discomfort during pelvic exams (Weitlauf et al, 2008; Weitlauf et al, 2010) and perception that these services are unnecessary or even unsafe, compared to patients who are not survivors of violence (Farley et al, 2002; Weitlauf et al, 2010).

In addition to being less likely to seek or obtain gynecologic health care, high-risk sexual activity is more common among women who have experienced past violence (Coker, 2007; Kendall-Tackett & Giacomoni, 2007; Moore, 1999; Weaver, 2009). Sexual violence increases the likelihood of engaging in consensual sexual activity at earlier ages (Farley et al, 2002), as well as having more sexual partners (Farley et al, 2002; Hoffman, Exner, Leu & Ehrhardt, 2003; Weaver, 2009) and failing to use contraceptives and condoms (Raj, Silverman & Amaro, 2000; Wingood & DiClemente, 1997). These risky sexual behaviors place younger women at increased risk of sexually transmitted infections (Beadnell, Baker, Morrison & Knox, 2000; Coker et al, 2000; Coker, 2007; Mahapatro, Gupta, Gupta & Kundu, 2012; Moore, 1999), unwanted pregnancy (Coker, 2007; Dietz et al, 1999; Moore, 1999), and delayed or inadequate access to prenatal care (Bohn, 2002; Bohn & Parker, 1993; Dietz et al, 1997; McFarlane, Parker, Soeken & Bullock, 1992).

IPV, Obstetric Health, and Birth Outcomes

During pregnancy, when women might be more motivated to undergo prenatal exams and screenings to ensure the health of their infants, they are still likely to experience distress and discomfort during prenatal exams (Weitlauf et al, 2008; Weitlauf et al, 2010). This discomfort and fear can be exacerbated by lack of provider awareness or sensitivity to the woman's distress (Seng et al, 2010; Seng, Sparbel, Low & Killion, 2002). Psychological distress symptoms during pregnancy, including those related to IPV, place pregnant women at increased risk of obstetric complications and negative birth outcomes.

One possible route to worse birth outcomes is using maladaptive coping strategies such as consumption of alcohol, tobacco and illicit drugs (Bohn & Parker, 1993; Brady, Back & Coffey, 2004; Chilcoat & Breslau, 1998; Herman, 1992). Abuse-related posttraumatic stress symptoms are associated with higher use of tobacco even during pregnancy, which places women at higher risk of impaired fetal growth and obstetric complications (Lopez, Konrath & Seng, 2011). Women with PTSD symptoms related to past violence often experience more complications early in pregnancy, including higher rates of spontaneous abortion, ectopic pregnancy, and hyperemesis (Seng et al, 2001). Recent research has built on prior findings and strengthened our knowledge that increased exposure to stress, traumatic events such as terrorist attacks and natural disasters, and/or PTSD are associated with pre-term birth, low-birth weight, and smaller head circumference (Dominguez, Dunkel-Schetter, Mancuso, Rini

& Hobel, 2005; Engel, Berkowitz, Wolff & Yehuda, 2005; Xiong et al, 2008). For example, a study of a diverse sample of 1,581 women (45% of whom were African-American) revealed that those who had been exposed to IPV and subsequently developed PTSD were more likely to deliver low birth weight infants and to have shorter gestational periods than those in the sample who had not experienced such violence and did not have PTSD symptoms during pregnancy (Seng, Low, Sperlich, Ronis & Liberzon, 2011). Histories of violence and abuse also have been associated with an increased likelihood of psychological distress during and after childbirth.

Survivors of IPV may confront greater challenges when it comes to preparing for childbirth and postpartum adjustment. In particular, significant fear of the childbirth process, including pain, injury, loss of control, and negative birth outcomes, is more common among women who have violence histories (Schroll, Tabor & Kjaergaard, 2011). Moreover, survivors of abuse and violence are more likely to experience psychological trauma during childbirth as well as PTSD symptoms as a result of a traumatic birth experience (Soet, Brack & Dilorio, 2003). Finally, research has found that symptoms of postpartum depression are more common, even up to eight months postpartum, among women with violence histories compared to women with no prior exposure to violence (Records & Rice, 2009).

IPV and Obstetric Disparities

Low income, ethnic minority women living in urban settings tend to be at greater risk for experiencing more instances of IPV which, in turn, places them at greater risk for the many psychological, gynecologic, and obstetric complications reviewed above. Specifically, a recent study found that African-American women had higher lifetime prevalence of violence and a four-fold higher rate of PTSD symptoms (in addition to more substance use) during pregnancy than non-African-American women (Seng, Kohn-Wood, McPherson & Sperlich, 2011). This study also demonstrated that the onset of abuse-related PTSD symptoms among African-American women occurs closer to the time of pregnancy than among non-African-American women, resulting in an increased likelihood that African-American women will be burdened by PTSD symptoms during pregnancy. Given that low-income African-American women are also at greater risk for complications such as preeclampsia and poor birth outcomes such as pre-term birth and having a low birth-weight infant (Eskanazi, Fenster & Sidney, 1991; Healy et al, 2006; Rosenberg, Garvers, Chavkin & Chiasson, 2003), addressing histories of IPV and abuse-related psychological distress during pregnancy may be a modifiable risk factor for poor birth outcomes.

Unfortunately, these vulnerable groups of women are also less likely to receive mental health treatment, despite higher rates of psychological symptoms (Azocar, Miranda & Dwyer, 1996; Grote, Swartz & Zuckoff, 2008; Grote, Zuckoff, Swartz, Bledsoe & Geibel, 2007). Thus, addressing the psychological needs of at-risk women who have been exposed to IPV could significantly impact obstetric and gynecologic health outcomes and reduce problematic disparities among vulnerable groups of women.

Preliminary Research Goals

Research in the area of obstetric/gynecologic health implications of IPV is still in its early stages. Prospective designs that could elucidate temporal ordering of the associations among IPV, psychological symptoms, and reproductive health would be beneficial to development of more comprehensive health care for women via appropriate treatment options to improve a variety of psychological and physical health outcomes. To begin to address these questions, we present some preliminary data from a prospective investigation of patients who were referred for psychotherapy treatment by their obstetricians and gynecologists.

METHODS

Participants

Participants in this study were 20 female patients receiving psychotherapy through a women's behavioral health program, housed in a large urban hospital in the Midwest; an additional three women were invited to participate, but declined. This sample was diverse (Table 1). Their mean age was 33.25 (*SD* = 8.83; range = 19-49). The ethnic distribution was 40% Black/African American, 30% White, 20% Hispanic, and 10% multi-ethnic. Sixty five percent had attained at least some college (e.g., trade certificate or higher) and 35% were unemployed at the time of their initial psychological intake evaluation. The majority of the sampled patients (55%) received public aid insurance or the hospital's charity care insurance; only 45% were privately insured.

Procedures

Patients were referred by obstetricians and gynecologists to the women's behavioral health service for psychological care (reasons for referral are presented below). For an intake evaluation to begin psychotherapy, these patients met individually with a clinician who was either a licensed clinical psychologist or a post-doctoral psychology trainee. Evaluation for this service included a semi-structured clinical interview to develop diagnostic impressions and self-report measures of symptom levels. Based on these results, the clinician and patient developed a treatment plan for individual psychotherapy. For all cases of treatment that lasted longer than 12 sessions, symptom levels were periodically re-assessed at the discretion of the clinician and based on the individualized treatment plan.

Following intake, patients recruited for this study were assured that, whether or not they chose to participate, it would not have any impact on their psychological or medical treatment. All participants consented for their de-identified demographic data, IPV histories, psychological diagnoses, and psychological testing data to be used in this study, which was approved by the university's institutional review board. No compensation was offered for participation in this study other than receipt of the designated services.

Measures

Semi-structured clinical interview

During the first visit to the women's behavioral health service, patients participate in a semi-structured interview in which trained clinicians (either post-doctoral fellows or a licensed clinical psychologist) gather information regarding the history of the presenting complaint, boundary conditions under which symptoms are present, and potential differential diagnoses. In addition, all patients are asked about their educational and occupational histories, social and developmental histories including any experiences of traumatic events, and medical history. Through this interview, psychologists determine patient diagnoses and assign global assessment of functioning (GAF) scores. Three or fewer Axis I conditions (i.e., all clinical disorders, excluding personality disorders or mental retardation, which are the focus of clinical attention; APA, 2000) are coded for the purposes of this data set.

Table 1. Sample Demographics

Demographic Variables			
Variable	**%**	***Mean (SD)***	**Range**
Age	-	33.25 (8.83)	19 – 49
Children	-	1.25 (1.37)	0 – 5
Ethnicity			
African American	40%	-	-
White	30%	-	-
Hispanic	20%	-	-
Multi-ethnic	10%	-	-
Education		14.4 (3.25)	8 – 20
Less than HS	10%	-	-
High School	25%	-	-
Trade Certificate	10%	-	-
Associate's	15%	-	-
Bachelor's	15%	-	-
Post-graduate	25%	-	-
Employment Status			
Unemployed	35%	-	-
Part-time	30%	-	-
Full-time	35%	-	-

Beck Depression Inventory II

BDI-II (Beck, Steer & Brown, 1996): The BDI-II is a widely used 21-item measure that assesses the symptom severity of depression. Items are rated on a scale from zero to three, with anchors that vary across specific symptoms assessed. Total scores are calculated by summing answers to individual items, with higher scores reflecting greater levels of depressive symptoms. Beck and colleagues noted that BDI-II demonstrates high test-retest reliability and adequate convergent and discriminant validities when used in clinical settings (Beck et al, 1996; Beck, Steer, Ball & Ranieri, 1996).

State-Trait Anxiety Inventory

STAI (Spielberger, Gorsuch, Lushene, Vagg & Jacobs, 1983): The STAI is a 40-item self-report assessment of anxiety that contains two subscales: one measures current levels of anxiety (i.e., state anxiety) and one measures chronic levels of anxiety (i.e., trait anxiety). Respondents rate each item on a four-point scale, from 1 ("not at all") to 4 ("very much so"). Items are summed to yield total scores for each subscale, with higher scores reflecting higher levels of state and trait anxiety. Internal consistency, test-retest reliability, and convergent validity have been shown to be adequate across a variety of populations (Roemer, 2001; Spielberger et al, 1983).

PTSD Checklist – Civilian Version

PCL (Weathers, Litz, Huska & Keane, 1994): The PCL is a 17-item measure that assesses the level of reexperiencing, avoidance, and hyperarousal symptoms associated with PTSD. Participants report the extent to which they have been distressed by each listed symptom in the past 30 days on a 5-point scale from "not at all" to "extremely." Items are summed to create a total score. Higher scores demonstrate more severe PTSD symptoms. Several psychometric studies have proposed varied "cut-off scores" to indicate a PTSD diagnosis, including 44, 45, and 50 (Andrykowski, Cordova, Studts, and Miller, 1998; Blanchard, Jones-Alexander, Buckley & Forneris, 1996; Ruggiero, Ben, Scotti & Rabalais, 2003). The PCL has demonstrated high internal consistency as well as convergent validity in psychometric research (Ruggiero et al, 2003).

RESULTS

Of the 20 women recruited to date, it was clear that this was a highly traumatized sample. Sixty percent reported at least one type of IPV (e.g., physical or sexual abuse) in childhood, 50 percent reported at least one type of IPV in adulthood, and 80 percent reported at least one type of traumatic event (Figure 1).

Despite the high prevalence of trauma exposure and PTSD in this sample, we found that only 25% self-reported that addressing the trauma was one of their presenting concerns, corroborating the reluctance to receive services found in previous studies. The most prevalent presenting complaint was depression or mood changes (60% of the sample), followed by parenting and postpartum adjustment concerns (55%), anxiety-spectrum symptoms (30%), and pregnancy-related stressors such as adoption, abortion, or miscarriage (25%). Because we coded up to three presenting complaints in our database, these percentages were not orthogonal in that patients were able to identify multiple complaints (Table 2).

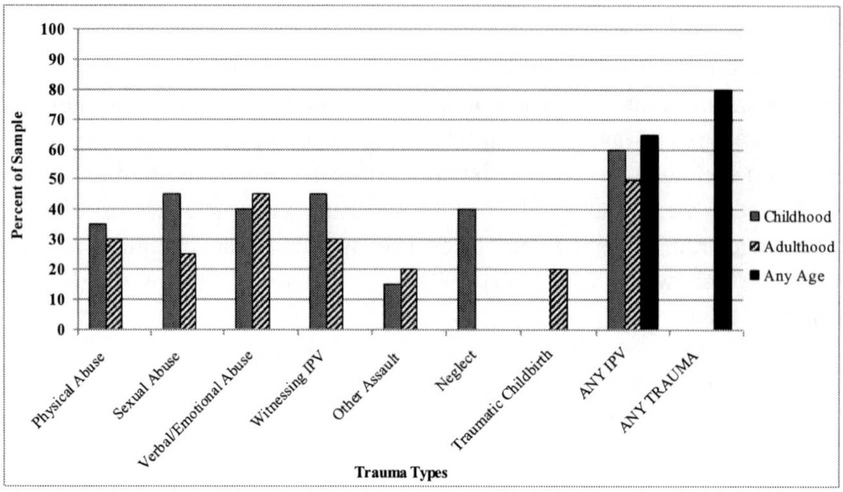

Figure 1. Prevalence of IPV and Other Trauma Types.

Table 2. Statistical Properties of Study Variables

Study Variables			
Variable	**%**	***Mean* (*SD*)**	**Range**
BDI	-	26.5 (12.15)	5 – 46
STAI-state	-	48.2 (12.64)	31 – 72
STAI-trait	-	52.0 (14.12)	29 – 73
PCL	-	49.2 (18.85)	17 – 74
GAF score	-	55.7 (7.50)	40 – 68
Presenting Complaints			
Depression	60%	-	-
Postpartum/Parenting	55%	-	-
Anxiety	30%	-	-
Pregnancy Stress	25%	-	-
IPV/PTSD	25%	-	-
Relationships	15%	-	-
Premenstrual Dysphoric Disorder	15%	-	-
Other	20%	-	-
Diagnostic Categories			
PTSD	45%	-	-
Major Depression	40%	-	-
Other Anxiety	25%	-	-
Adjustment Disorder	20%	-	-
Other Depression	15%	-	-

Table 3. Study Variables by Obstetric/Gynecologic Status

	Non-Pregnant (*n* = 8)			Pregnant (*n* = 4)			Postpartum (*n* = 8)		
Variable	**%**	***Mean* (*SD*)**	**Range**	**%**	***Mean* (*SD*)**	**Range**	**%**	***Mean* (*SD*)**	**Range**
BDI	-	23.5 (13.8)	5 – 39	-	32.75 (9.6)	23 – 46	-	23.4 (11.7)	11 – 43
STAI-state	-	43.6 (11.5)	31 – 64	-	52.0 (6.7)	43 – 59	-	50.9 (15.6)	32 – 72
STAI-trait	-	46.4 (15.0)	29 – 70	-	61.5 (10.1)	49 – 73	-	52.9 (13.6)	31 – 71
PCL	-	44.4 (21.7)	17 – 72	-	60.7 (14.7)	44 – 72	-	49.0 (17.7)	26 – 74
GAF score	-	57.6 (7.2)	50 – 68	-	51.3 (10.3)	40 – 60	-	56.0 (6.3)	50 – 65
IPV Types									
Childhood IPV	37.5%	-	-	100%	-	-	62.5%	-	-
Adulthood IPV	50%	-	-	50%	-	-	50%	-	-
Any IPV History	50%	-	-	100%	-	-	62.5%	-	-
Any Trauma History	75%	-	-	100%	-	-	75%	-	-
Diagnostic Categories									
PTSD	50%	-	-	75%	-	-	25%	-	-
Major Depression	37.5%	-	-	50%	-	-	25%	-	-
Other Anxiety	37.5%	-	-	---	-	-	25%	-	-
Adjustment Disorder	12.5%	-	-	---	-	-	37.5%	-	-
Other Depression	25%	-	-	25%	-	-	---	-	-

Baseline measures of self-reported functioning were expected. The sample had a mean BDI-II score of 26.5 (*SD* = 12.15), which falls in the moderate level of depression symptoms (Beck et al, 1996). Anxiety levels were similarly elevated, as women's STAI-state scores (*M* = 48.20, *SD* = 12.64) were one standard deviation above the mean as compared to the normative sample for this measure (Roemer, 2001; Spielberger et al, 1983). This anxiety elevation was more pronounced on the STAI-trait aspect of this measure, as our sample's average scores (*M* = 52.00, *SD* = 14.12) were nearly two standard deviations higher than the mean for the normative sample (Roemer, 2001; Spielberger et al, 1983). Baseline PTSD levels were elevated for this sample (M_{PCL} = 49.18, SD_{PCL} = 18.85), as average scores on the PCL exceeded two of the recommended clinical cutoffs for PTSD and approached the third and highest reported cutoff score. It should be noted that the most prevalent disorder treated in this specialty clinic is PTSD; 45% of the sample met the diagnostic criteria, followed closely by diagnoses of several from the major depressive disorder spectrum (40%; Table 2). Finally, participants in this research obtained an average GAF score of 55.7 (*SD* = 7.50), which falls in the range of moderate symptom levels (APA, 2000).

Compared to women who were not pregnant and presented with other gynecological concerns, and to the postpartum women who had recently given birth, patients who presented for therapy in this clinic, while pregnant, reported higher levels of depression, both state and trait anxiety, PTSD symptoms, and lower GAF scores. A higher percentage of pregnant women in this clinic have experienced childhood IPV and were diagnosed with PTSD than their non-pregnant and postpartum counterparts (Table 3).

CONCLUSION

The preliminary study data presented above demonstrates that women being treated in the women's behavioral health service are similar to samples reported in other studies in terms of their overall rate of exposure to IPV. The overall exposure to IPV was quite high in this sample and thus PTSD was the most prevalent disorder being treated, followed by major depression. Despite such a high exposure to trauma, the majority of women did not identify traumatic events as their main presenting complaint. Rather, many women reported the most problematic issues for them were depressed mood, postpartum depression, parenting stress, general anxiety symptoms, and pregnancy-related stress. This suggests that women survivors of IPV may be unaware of the breadth of impact that such IPV events can have on their mental and physical health, given that their scores on the PCL suggest that PTSD symptoms were, on average, very distressing for these women. Further, women who were pregnant at intake appear to be the most distressed as evidenced by their higher depression, anxiety, and PTSD scores and lower GAF scores. Pregnant women also reported the highest rate of histories of IPV exposure.

These data represent the early stages of an important line of prospective research that will investigate temporal links among IPV, psychological symptoms, and obstetric and gynecologic health. Future goals for this project include continuing to re-assess patient psychological symptoms as well as gather medical information on labor and delivery outcomes for those women who are pregnant during psychological treatment. At present, this study is limited by a small sample size and its cross-sectional nature that precludes most statistical analyses, given that most participants in the project have not yet provided multiple waves of data, which characterize a prospective investigation.

Given the unique needs of pregnant women in at-risk populations, an important trajectory for future research is to investigate potential interventions that simultaneously target IPV histories, psychological symptoms, and obstetric health care. Many effective interventions exist to address the psychological sequelae of IPV, including *Dialectical Behavior Therapy* (Robins, Schmidt & Linehan, 2004), *Seeking Safety* (Najavits, 2002), *Trauma Adaptive Recovery Group Education and Therapy*, (Ford & Russo, 2006), and *Skills Training in Affect and Interpersonal Regulation/Prolonged Exposure* (Cloitre, Koenen, Cohen & Han, 2002), and other exposure therapies. However, these treatments intervene only on the psychological level and access to psychological treatment among pregnant women is low (Seng et al, 2010; Seng et al, 2011; Seng, Sperlich & Low, 2008). Moreover, pregnant women struggling with past IPV (particularly sexual assault) and related post-traumatic stress are simultaneously confronted with sexual trauma 'triggers' in the context of their obstetric and gynecologic care, which when they appear can exacerbate psychological symptoms.

Obstetric care is, by its nature, a traumatic stimulus for female survivors of sexual abuse. This is particularly true because obstetric care involves direct and indirect reminders of sexual abuse, including that of being in a prone, exposed sexual position during pelvic exams, insertion of objects in the vagina, and loss of control of one's body. Indeed, for many women, pregnancy itself is associated with sex and sexuality, which can be a traumatic reminder. Even though modern obstetric care is sensitive to women, the greatly increased fears of sexual abuse survivors demand a much higher level of trauma-sensitive obstetric care for women with trauma histories.

Thus, interventions that directly involve training obstetric providers to respond to patients that disclose IPV histories in a trauma-sensitive manner would be further beneficial to reducing patients' symptoms and increasing their engagement in medical care. Interventions that are multi-level, with mutually reinforcing psychological and obstetric-gynecologic care should be a focus of future research to reduce psychological distress and improve the health of women who are survivors of sexual assault.

REFERENCES

American Psychiatric Association (2000). *Diagnostic and Statistical Manual of Mental Disorders* (4th Edition, text revision), Washington, DC: Author.

Andrykowski, M. A., Cordova, M. J., Studts, J. L. & Miller, T. W. (1998), "Posttraumatic stress disorder after treatment for breast cancer: Prevalence of diagnosis and use of the PTSD Checklist-Civilian Version (PCL-C) as a screening instrument," *Journal of Consulting and Clinical Psychology*, *66*, 586–590.

Azocar, F., Miranda, J. & Dwyer, E. V. (1996). "Treatment of depression in disadvantaged women," *Women and Therapy*, *18,* 91-105.

Beadnell, B. U., Baker, S. A., Morrison, D. M. & Knox, K. (2000). "HIV/STD risk for women with violent male partners," *Sex Roles*, *42*, 661-689.

Beck, A. T., Steer, R. A., Ball, R. & Ranieri, W. F. (1996), "Comparison of Beck Depression Inventories-IA and II in psychiatric outpatients," *Journal of Personality Assessment*, *67*, 588-597.

Beck, A. T., Steer, R. A. & Brown, G. K. (1996). *Manual for the Beck Depression Inventory-II* (2nd edition), San Antonio, TX: Psychological Corporation.

Black, P. (2006). "The inflammatory consequences of psychologic stress: Relationship to insulin resistance, obesity, atherosclerosis and diabetes mellitus, type II," *Medical Hypotheses*, *67*, 879-891.

Blanchard, E. B., Jones-Alexander, J., Buckley, T. C. & Forneris, C. A. (1996), "Psychometric properties of the PTSD Checklist (PCL)," *Behaviour Research and Therapy*, *34,* 669–673.

Bohn, D. K. (2002), "Lifetime and current abuse, pregnancy risks, and outcomes among Native American women," *Journal of Health Care for the Poor and Underserved*, *13*, 184-198.

Bohn, D. K. & Parker, B. (1993). "Domestic violence and pregnancy: Health effects and implications for nursing practice," In JC Campbell, J Humphreys (Eds), *Nursing Care of Survivors of Family Violence* (2nd edition, 156-172), St. Louis, MO: C.V. Mosby Co.

Brady, K. T., Back, S. E. & Coffey, S. F. (2004), "Substance abuse and posttraumatic stress disorder," *Current Directions in Psychological Science*, *12*, 206-209.

Campbell, J. C. (2002), "Health consequences of intimate partner violence," *Lancet*, *359*, 1331-1336.

Campbell, R., Lichty, L. F., Sturza, M. & Raja, S. (2006). "Gynecological health impact of sexual assault," *Research in Nursing and Health*, *29*, 399-413.

Chilcoat, H. D. & Breslau, N. (1998). "Investigations of causal pathways between PTSD and drug use disorders," *Addictive Behaviors*, *23*, 827-840.

Cloitre, M., Koenen, K. C., Cohen, L. R. & Han, H. (2002), "Skills training in affective and interpersonal regulation followed by exposure: A phase-based treatment for PTSD related to childhood abuse," *Journal of Consulting and Clinical Psychology*, *70*, 1067-1074.

Coker, A. L. (2007). "Does physical intimate partner violence affect sexual health?: A systematic review," *Trauma, Violence, and Abuse*, *8*, 149-177.

Coker, A. L., Hopenhayn, C., DiSimone, C. P., Bush, H. M. & Crofford, L. (2009). "Violence against women raises risk of cervical cancer," *Journal of Women's Health*, *18*, 1179-1185.

Coker, A. L., Smith, P. H., Bethea, L., King, M. R. & McKeown, R. E. (2000). "Physical health consequences of physical and psychological intimate partner violence," *Archives of Family Medicine*, *9*, 451-457.

Courtois, C. A. (2004). "Complex trauma, complex reactions: Assessment and treatment," *Psychotherapy: Theory, Research, Practice, Training*, *41*, 412-425.

Dietz, P. M., Gazmararian, J. A., Goodwin, M. M., Bruce, F. C., Johnson, C. H. & Rochat, R. W. (1997). "Delayed entry into prenatal care: Effect of physical violence," *Obstetrics and Gynecology*, *90*, 221-224.

Dietz, P. M., Spitz, A. M., Anda, R. F., Williamson, D. F., McMahon, P. M., Santelli, J. S., Nordenberg, D. F., Felitti, V. J. & Kendrick, J. S. (1999). "Unintended pregnancy among adult women exposed to abuse or household dysfunction during their childhood," *Journal of the American Medical Association*, *282*, 1359-1364.

Dominguez, T. P., Dunkel-Schetter, C., Mancuso, R., Rini, C. M. & Hobel, C. (2005). "Stress in African American pregnancies: Testing the roles of various stress concepts in prediction of birth outcomes," *Annals of Behavioral Medicine*, *29*, 12-21.

Elenkov, I. J., Iezzoni, D. G., Daly, A., Harris, A. G. & Chrousos, G. P. (2005). "Cytokine dysregulation, inflammation and well-being," *NeuroimmunoModulation*, *12*, 255-269.

Engel, S. M., Berkowitz, G. S., Wolff, M. S. & Yehuda, R. (2005). "Psychological trauma associated with the World Trade Center attacks and its effect on pregnancy outcome," *Paediatric and Perinatal Epidemiology*, *19*, 334-341.

Eskanazi, B., Fenster, L. & Sidney, S. (1991). "A multivariate analysis of risk factors for preeclampsia," *Journal of the American Medical Association*, *266*, 237-241.

Farley, M., Golding, J. M. & Minkoff, J. R. (2002). "Is history of trauma associated with a reduced likelihood of cervical cancer screening?" *Journal of Family Practice*, *51*, 827-831.

Foa, E. B. & Rothbaum, B. O. (1998). *Treating the trauma of rape: Cognitive-behavioral therapy for PTSD*, New York, NY: Guilford Press.

Ford, J. D. & Russo, E. (2006). "Trauma-focused, present-centered, emotional self-regulation approach to integrated treatment for posttraumatic stress and addiction: Trauma adapative recovery group education and therapy (TARGET)" *American Journal of Psychotherapy*, *60*, 335-355.

Grimstad, H. & Schei, B. (1999). "Pregnancy and delivery for women with a history of child sexual abuse," *Child Abuse and Neglect*, *23*, 81-90.

Grote, N. K., Swartz, H. A. & Zuckoff, K. (2008). "Enhancing interpersonal psychotherapy for mothers and expectant mothers on low incomes: Adaptations and additions," *Journal of Contemporary Psychotherapy*, *38*, 23-33.

Grote, N. K., Zuckoff, A., Swartz, H., Bledsoe, S. E. & Geibel, S. (2007). "Engaging women who are depressed and economically disadvantaged in mental health treatment," *Social Work*, *52*, 295-308.

Healy, A. J., Malone, F. D., Sullivan, L. M., Porter, T. F., Luthy, D. A., Comstock, C. H., Saade, G., Berkowitz, R., Klugman. S., Dugloff, L., Craigo, S. D., Timor-Tritsch, I., Carr, S. R., Wolfe, H. M., Bianhi, D. W. D'Alton ME, 2006, "Early access to prenatal care: Implications for racial disparity in perinatal mortality," *Obstetrics and Gynecology*, *107*, 625-631.

Heath, N. M., Chesney, S. A. & Hobfoll, S. E. (2012). "The aftermath of traumatic stress on psychological and immunological functioning: Preliminary results from a pilot study of inner-city OB/GYN patients," Paper presented at the meeting of the Chicagoland Pelvic Floor Research Consortium, Chicago, IL.

Herman, J. L. (1992). *Trauma and recovery: The Aftermath of Violence – From Domestic Abuse to Political Terror*, New York, NY: Basic Books.

Kahn, J. A., Huang, B., Rosenthal, S. L., Tissot, A. M. & Burk, R. D. (2005). "Coercive sexual experiences and subsequent human papillomavirus and squamous intraepithelial lesions in adolescents and young adult women," *Journal of Adolescent Health*, *36*, 363-371.

Keane, T. M. & Barlow, D. H. (2004). "Posttraumatic stress disorder," In DH Barlow (Ed.), *Anxiety and Its Disorders: The Nature and Treatment of Anxiety and Panic* (Second Edition), 418-453), New York, NY: The Guilford Press.

Kendall-Tackett, K. A. & Giacomoni, S. (2007). *Intimate Partner Violence*, Kingston, NJ: Civic Research Institute.

Kessler, R. C., Sonnega, A., Bromet, E., Hughes, M. & Nelson, C. B. (1995). "Posttraumatic stress disorder in the National Comorbidity Survey," *Archives of General Psychiatry*, *52*, 1048-1060.

Koss, M. P., Koss, P. G. & Woodruff, W. J. (1991). "Deleterious effects of criminal victimization on women's health and medical utilization," *Archives of Internal Medicine*, *151*, 342-347.

Lopez, W. D., Konrath, S. H. & Seng, J. S. (2011). "Abuse-related post-traumatic stress, coping, and tobacco use in pregnancy," *Journal of Obstetric, Gynecologic, and Neonatal Nursing*, *40*, 422-431.

Mahapatro, M., Gupta, R. N., Gupta, V. & Kundu, A. S. (2012). "Interpersonal violence as risk factor for women's sexually transmitted infection and reproductive health consequences in India: A community based study," *Journal of Public Health*, *20*, 399-403.

McEwen, B. (2003). "Mood disorders and allostatic load," *Biological Psychiatry*, *54*, 200-207.

McFarlane, J., Parker, B., Soeken, K. & Bullock, L. (1992). "Assessing for abuse during pregnancy: Severity and frequency of injuries and associated entry into prenatal care," *Journal of the American Medical Association*, *267*, 3176-3178.

Melendez, R. M., Hoffman, S., Exner, T., Leu, C. S. & Ehrhardt, A. A. (2003). "Intimate partner violence and safer sex negotiation: Effects of a gender-specific intervention," *Archives of Sexual Behavior*, *32*, 499-511.

Moore, M. (1999). "Reproductive health and intimate partner violence," *Family Planning Perspectives*, *31*, 302-306, 312.

Najavits, L. M. (2002). *Seeking Safety: A Treatment Manual for PTSD and Substance Abuse*, New York, NY: Guilford Press.

Pedersen, A. H. & Cohen, B. E. (2010). "Identifying and overcoming barriers to cervical cancer screening in women with a history of sexual violence and posttraumatic stress disorder," *Journal of Women's Health*, *19*, 1239-1241.

Raj, A., Silverman, J. G. & Amaro, H. (2000). "The relationship between sexual abuse and sexual risk among high school students: Findings from the 1997 Massachusetts Youth Risk Behavior Survey," *Maternal and Child Health Journal*, *4*, 125-134.

Records, K. & Rice, M. J. (2009). "Lifetime physical and sexual abuse and the risk for depression symptoms in the first 8 months after birth," *Journal of Psychosomatic Obstetrics and Gynecology*, *31*, 181-190.

Resnick, H. S., Acierno, R. & Kilpatrick, D. G. (1997). "Health impact of interpersonal violence 2: Medical and mental health outcomes," *Behavioral Medicine*, *23*, 65-78.

Resnick, H. S., Kilpatrick, D. G., Dansky, B. S., Saunders, B. E. & Best, C. L. (1993). "Prevalence of civilian trauma and posttraumatic stress disorder in a representative national sample of women," *Journal of Clinical and Consulting Psychology*, *61*, 984-991.

Robins, C. J., Schmidt, H. & Linehan, M. M. (2004). "Dialectical Behavior Therapy: Synthesizing radical acceptance with skillful means," In SC Hayes, VM Follette, MM Linehan (Eds), *Mindfulness and Acceptance: Expanding the Cognitive-Behavioral Tradition*, 30-44, New York, NY: Guilford Press.

Roemer, L. (2001). "Measures for anxiety and related constructs," In MM Antony, SM Orsillo, L Roemer, (Eds), *AABT Clinical Assessment Series: Practitioner's Guide to Empirically Based Measures of Anxiety*, 49-83, New York, NY: Kluwer Academic/Plenum Publishers.

Rosenberg, T. J., Garvers, S., Chavkin, W. & Chiasson, M. A. (2003). "Prepregnancy weight and adverse perinatal outcomes in an ethnically diverse population," *Obstetrics and Gynecology*, *102*, 1022-1027.

Ruggiero, K. J., Ben, K. D., Scotti, J. R. & Rabalais, A. E. (2003). "Psychometric properties of the PTSD Checklist – Civilian Version," *Journal of Traumatic Stress*, *16*, 495-502.

Schroll, A., Tabor, A. & Kjaergaard, H. (2011). "Physical and sexual lifetime violence: Prevalence and influence on fear of childbirth before, during and after delivery," *Journal of Psychosomatic Obstetrics and Gynecology*, *32*, 19-26.

Schumm, J. A., Briggs-Phillips, M. & Hobfoll, S. E. (2006). "Cumulative interpersonal traumas and social support as risk and resiliency factors in predicting PTSD and depression among inner-city women," *Journal of Traumatic Stress*, *19*, 825-836.

Schumm, J. A., Stines, L. R., Hobfoll, S. E. & Jackson, A. P. (2005). "The double-barreled burden of child abuse and current stressful circumstances on adult women: The kindling effect of early traumatic experience," *Journal of Traumatic Stress*, *18*, 467-476.

Seng, J. S., Kohn-Wood, L. P., McPherson, M. D. & Sperlich, M. (2011). "Disparity in posttraumatic stress disorder diagnosis among African American pregnant women,"*Archives of Women's Mental Health*, *14*, 295-306.

Seng, J. S., Low, L. K., Sperlich, M., Ronis, D. L. & Liberzon, I. (2011). "Posttraumatic stress disorder, child abuse history, birthweight and gestational age: A prospective cohort study," *British Journal of Obstetrics and Gynecology*, *118*, 1329-1339.

Seng, J. S., Oakley, D. J., Sampselle, C. M., Killion, C., Graham-Bermann, S. & Liberzon, I. (2001). Post-traumatic stress disorder and pregnancy complications," *Obstetrics and Gynecology*, *97*, 17-22.

Seng, J. S., Rauch, S. A. M., Resnick, H., Reed, C. D., King, A., Low, L. K., McPherson, M., Muzik, M., Abelson, J. & Liberzon, I. (2010). "Exploring posttraumatic stress disorder symptom profile among pregnant women," *Journal of Psychosomatic Obstetrics and Gynecology*, *31*, 176-187.

Seng, J. S., Sparbel, K. J., Low, L. K. & Killion, C. (2002). "Abuse-related posttraumatic stress and desired maternity care practices: Women's perspectives," *Journal of Midwifery and Women's Health*, *47*, 360-370.

Seng, J. S., Sperlich, M. & Low, L. K. (2008). "Mental health, demographic, and risk behavior profiles of pregnant survivors of childhood and adult abuse,"*Journal of Midwifery and Women's Health*, *53*, 511-521.

Soet, J. E., Brack, G. A. & Dilorio, C. (2003). "Prevalence and predictors of women's experience of psychological trauma during childbirth," *Birth*, *30*, 36-46.

Spielberger, C. D., Gorsuch, R. L., Lushene, R., Vagg, P. R., Jacobs, G. A. (1983). *Manual for the State–Trait Anxiety Inventory (Form Y),* Palo Alto, CA: Mind Garden.

Stevens, N. R., Gerhart, J., Goldsmith, R. E., Heath, N. M., Chesney, S. A. & Hobfoll, S. E. (2013). "Emotion regulation difficulties, low social support, and interpersonal violence mediate the link between childhood abuse and posttraumatic stress symptoms," *Behavior Therapy*, *44*, 152-161.

Sutherland, C. A., Sullivan, C. M. & Bybee, D. I. (2001). "Effects of intimate partner violence versus poverty on women's health," *Violence Against Women*, *7*, 1122-1143.

Tjaden, P. & Thoennes, N. (1998). "Prevalence, incidence, and consequences of violence against women: The National Violence Against Women Survey," Retrieved from http://www.ncjrs.gov/pdffiles/172837.pdf

Van der Kolk, B. A., Pelcovitz, D., Roth, S., Mandel, F. S., McFarlane, A. & Herman, J. L. (1996). Dissociation, somatization, and affect dysregulation: The complexity of adaptation to trauma," *American Journal of Psychiatry*, *153*, 83-93.

Van der Kolk, B. A., Roth, S., Pelcovitz, D., Sunday, S. & Spinazzola, J. (2005). "Disorders of extreme stress: The empirical foundation of a complex adaptation to trauma," *Journal of Traumatic Stress*, *18*, 389-399.

Weathers, F. W., Litz, B. T., Huska, J. A. & Keane, T. M. (1994). *PTSD Checklist – Civilian Version,* Boston, MA: National Center for PTSD, Behavioral Science Division.

Weaver, T. L. (2009). "Impact of rape on female sexuality: Review of selected literature," *Clinical Obstetrics and Gynecology*, *52*, 702-711.

Weitlauf, J. C., Finney, J. W., Ruzek, J. I., Lee, T. T., Thrailkill, A., Jones, S. & Frayne, S. M. (2008). "Distress and pain during pelvic examinations: Effect of sexual violence," *Obstetrics and Gynecology*, *112*, 1343-1350.

Weitlauf, J. C., Frayne, S. M., Finney, J. W., Moos, R. H., Jones, S., Hu, K. & Spiegel, D. (2010). "Sexual violence, posttraumatic stress disorder, and the pelvic examination: How do beliefs about the safety, necessity, and utility of the examination influence patient experiences?" *Journal of Women's Health*, *19*, 1271-1280.

Wingood, G. M. & DiClemente, R. J. (1997). "The effects of an abusive primary partner on the condom use and sexual negotiation practices of African-American women," *American Journal of Public Health*, *87*, 1016-1018.

Xiong, X., Harville, E. W., Mattison, D. R., Elkind-Hirsch, K., Pridjian, G. & Buekens, P. (2008). "Exposure to Hurricane Katrina, post-traumatic stress disorder and birth outcomes," *American Journal of the Medical Sciences*, *336*, 111-115.

In: Assaults
Editor: Keith V. Bletzer
ISBN: 978-1-62808-051-3

Chapter 4

POST-ASSAULT SOCIAL SUPPORT: THE ROLE OF OTHERS IN HELPING SEXUAL ASSAULT VICTIMS RECOVER

Lisa A. Paul* and Sapir Sasson
Department of Psychology, Northern Illinois University, DeKalb, IL, US

ABSTRACT

Although assault victims can receive important support and assistance from others by disclosing their assault, victims report a range of barriers to disclosure (e.g., self-blame, perceived stigma). Further, those victims who do disclose might encounter a range of positive and negative reactions from others, of which the latter can have a deleterious impact on post-assault outcomes. These responses to disclosure vary for a number of reasons, including factors related to the victim (e.g., perceived coping ability), the assault (e.g., perpetrator type) and the disclosure recipient (e.g., informal versus formal recipient).

Unfortunately, little information is available regarding disclosure recipients, despite the critical role that they play in the disclosure experience. Further examining disclosure recipients and their experiences with sexual assault disclosure is important for better understanding this group, as well as how they can best help victims. To that end, this chapter reviews the literature on sexual assault disclosure, including the prevalence of disclosure and disclosure receipt, the people to whom assaults are disclosed (i.e., formal versus informal support sources) and the range of responses provided to victims, both positive and negative. Responses of disclosure recipients are examined within the relevant theoretical framework provided by Victimization Perspective Theory. Possible outcomes of, and barriers to, disclosure are discussed. Finally, implications are provided, including suggestions for ways to improve the disclosure process for both victims and recipients.

Keywords: Rape, sexual assault, disclosure, disclosure recipients, social support, Victimization Perspective Theory

* Corresponding author: Lisa A. Paul, Email: lpaul1@niu.edu.

INTRODUCTION

Sexual assault is an increasingly prevalent crime. The proportion of women who report an incident of unwanted sex in national studies is close to one-fifth. One national study found that 18% of U.S. women reported they were raped (i.e., legally defined as oral, anal or vaginal penetration) during their lifetime (Kilpatrick, Resnick, Ruggiero, Conoscenti & McCauley, 2007), and another study found that 22% of women reported an experience of sexual assault by threat or use of force during their lifetime (Elliott, Mok & Briere, 2004). As the research in this area has increased in recent decades, new facets of assault are a focus of interest; one of these is sexual assault disclosure. The disclosure context is an interesting one to examine, given its essential nature for connecting victims to resources and supportive services (Ahrens, Campbell, Ternier-Thames, Wasco & Sefl, 2007; Filipas & Ullman, 2001; Ullman, 1999; Ullman, Foynes & Tang, 2010). Most work in this area focuses on the experiences that victims have with disclosing their assaults to others, but little research examines the experiences of the recipients of these disclosures.

Further developing our knowledge of this group, particularly with reference to what is known about the experiences of victims, is critical for understanding how to optimize the disclosure experience for both victims and disclosure recipients. To that end, this review will examine the general research regarding sexual assault disclosure, including the frequency of disclosure and its receipt, information about disclosure recipients, and their reactions to disclosure. Possible outcomes of, and barriers to, victim disclosure and supportive responses to disclosure will also be discussed. Finally, the implications of this information will be provided, including suggestions for ways to improve the disclosure process for both victims and recipients. In the context of this review, sexual assault refers to both attempted and completed rape, as well as other unwanted sexual contact; the disclosure "recipient" is any individual whom the victim tells about the assault. Of note, although men can be victims of sexual assault and women may be perpetrators, female victims of male-perpetrated assaults are the focus of this review, given that the vast majority of the available research is conducted on this population.

Prevalence of Disclosure to Informal and Formal Disclosure Recipients

Sexual assault victims rarely disclose their assault to professionals. Statistics indicate that only 2 to 20 percent of victims disclose their assault to formal recipients, which includes police, doctors and mental health providers (Binder, 1981; Brickman & Briere, 1984; Fisher, Daigle, Cullen & Turner, 2003; George, Winfield & Blazer, 1992; Golding, Siegel, Sorenson, Burnam & Stein, 1989; Kilpatrick et al, 2007; Orchowski & Gidycz, 2012; Rennison, 2002; Russel, 1982; Tjaden & Thoennes, 2000; Ullman, 1996a; Wolitzky-Taylor, Resnick, McCauley, Amstadter, Kilpatrick & Ruggiero, 2011). Not surprisingly, sexual assault is one of the most underreported crimes in the United States (Allen, 2007). However, one-half to two-thirds of sexual assault victims disclose their assault to informal recipients, which includes friends, family and acquaintances (Ahrens & Aldana, 2012; Ahrens, Cabral & Abeling, 2009; Ahrens et al, 2007; Daane, 2005; Fisher et al, 2003; George et al, 1992;

Golding et al, 1989; Koss, Dinero, Siebel & Cox, 1988; Starzynski, Ullman, Filipas & Townsend, 2005; Ullman, 1996a; Ullman & Filipas, 2001a).

Rates of disclosure receipt corroborate these findings from the perspective of the recipients, with approximately one-third of study participants reporting they have received a sexual assault disclosure (Banyard, Moynihan, Walsh, Cohn & Ward, 2010; Dunn, Vail-Smith & Knight, 1999; Paul, Walsh, McCauley, Ruggiero, Resnick & Kilpatrick, 2013a; 2013b). Taken together, these findings highlight the vast number of individuals involved in the sexual assault disclosure process, either as victims or disclosure recipients. It appears that, although sexual assault victims do talk to others about their victimization, these conversations are usually with informal support providers and often exclude the formal reporting of their assaults.

IMPORTANCE OF DISCLOSURE RECIPIENTS

Possible Benefits of Disclosure

A victim's disclosure of sexual assault can help her obtain necessary medical care, receive emotional support and reduce her likelihood of negative post-assault psychological outcomes immediately after the assault, as well as in the long-term (e.g., Ahrens et al, 2007; Andrews, Brewin & Rose, 2003; Filipas & Ullman, 2001; Stewart et al, 1987; Ullman, 1996a, 1996b, 1999, 2010). To this end, research shows that victims often disclose when they believe that doing so will connect them to needed services, help them to feel better, or result in justice regarding themselves and the perpetrators of assault (Ahrens et al, 2007; Bachman, 1998; Feldman-Summers & Norris, 1984; Golding et al, 1989; Ullman & Filipas, 2001a). This assistance can come in a number of forms, including the receipt of needed medical care, emotional support and formal mental health care services, and the formal reporting of the assault to legal authorities.

Medical Care

Obtaining medical care after an assault can be of vital importance, especially if the victim was injured during the attack. Moreover, this assistance allows the victim to get tested for pregnancy, sexually transmitted infections, and other adverse outcomes that may follow a sexual assault (Campbell, Wasco, Ahrens, Sefl & Brown, 2001). Unfortunately, rates of post-rape medical care are low, with 26.2% of rape victims in a national sample reporting the receipt of such services after the assault (Resnick et al, 2000).

Emotional Support and Mental Health Care

Disclosure of a sexual assault can also have mental health implications for victims (Ullman, Foynes & Tang, 2010). Victims of sexual assault often experience anxiety, post-traumatic stress disorder (PTSD), depression, low self-esteem, and other adjustment difficulties (Resick, 1993). The provision of emotional support post-assault is quite important, given research showing that social support and negative reactions to disclosure predicted PTSD and depression symptoms among victims (Littleton, 2010).

Formal mental health care services are particularly important for reducing psychological distress following a sexual assault (Campbell et al, 1999). Importantly, disclosing to formal support sources such as mental health providers can help the victim obtain the support and knowledge needed to make informed decisions about obtaining medical care or pursuing a formal report of the assault to police (Wasco et al, 2004), as well as support during the legal process. Not only are mental health providers advocates for victims, but they are also neutral sources of information. Mental health providers have knowledge of, and access to, resources that informal support providers may not have. Unfortunately, a substantial proportion of victims in a national sample (40%) did not seek mental health services post-assault (Amstadter, McCauley, Ruggiero, Resnick & Kilpatrick, 2008), thus limiting access to these important resources.

Formal Reporting of Sexual Assault

A victim may choose to formally report the assault to the police, which can prevent the perpetrator from committing additional crimes if he is apprehended (Kilpatrick et al, 1992), although this deterrence is not guaranteed. Koss (2006) provides a comprehensive review of studies that details the dwindling rates of prosecution and conviction of rape cases. For example, DuMont and Parnis (2006) examined legal outcomes for reported rape cases in 31 international studies; while the global average rate of prosecuted cases was 28%, the two studies examining U.S. jurisdictions indicated a rate of 16%. Of rape cases that were prosecuted, only 12% of cases tried resulted in conviction. This pattern is not unique to cases in the United States; conviction rates for rape have declined steadily in every country over the past 30 years (Kelly, 2001).

Despite this low conviction rate, reporting to authorities can result in benefits to the victim, and is necessary in order to stop perpetrators and obtain justice; however, reporting rates are low (Allen, 2007) and reporting may result in negative consequences for victims. Many victims choose not to formally report their assault because of the emotional and social difficulties that may arise out of doing so; these include reliving the assault, having others find out about the assault, being blamed for the assault and going through a lengthy legal trial - one that may not result in a guilty verdict (e.g., Allen, 2007; Bachman, 1998; Felson & Pare, 2005; Patterson & Campbell, 2010; Patterson, Greeson & Campbell, 2009; Wolitzky-Taylor et al, 2011). Clearly, the decision to report to authorities is an important one that involves many factors, and the benefits of stopping the perpetrator can outweigh the costs for some victims.

Reactions to Disclosure and the Disclosure Experience

A variety of social reactions are documented in response to sexual assault disclosure. Broadly, Ullman (2000) organized the possible social responses that victims receive from others into seven categories, including both positive and negative reactions. These categories include: providing emotional support, offering tangible aid, blaming the victim, taking control of the victim's decisions, trying to distract the victim, treating the victim differently after the disclosure, and responding with egocentric reactions (e.g., getting so upset that the victim has to tend to the recipient). Researchers also describe indifferent or "cold" reactions toward victims in addition to these other types of negative responses (Ahrens et al, 2007).

Yet, these reactions to victims are not always so easily categorized. Some researchers suggest a need to distinguish between blatantly negative reactions toward victims and support attempts that are ineffective. These latter reactions include those in which the disclosure recipient is altruistically motivated, but his or her response is ultimately perceived negatively by the victim and is not helpful to her, for example, by having encouraged secrecy (see Herbert & Dunkel-Schetter, 1992; Ullman, 1999). Importantly, regardless of the type of response provided, victims are likely to view it negatively if they perceive that the recipient blames them, is condescending, or does not have the time to help them (Ahrens et al, 2009; Ullman, 2010). Alternately, some reactions that are typically thought of as negative may be perceived positively by victims. If the victim perceives that the reaction (e.g., attempted distraction) is motivated by care and concern, or is an effort to protect the victim from future harm, she is more likely to interpret it as a positive response, regardless of whether or not it is generally considered as such (Ahrens & Aldana, 2012; Ahrens et al, 2009).

Sexual assault victims report receiving high levels of positive and negative reactions; estimates vary from 74 to 97% receive at least one positive reaction and 80 to 98% receive at least one negative reaction (Campbell et al, 2001; Filipas & Ullman, 2001; Golding et al, 1989; Ullman 1996a). Of note, sexual assault victims tend to report more negative reactions than victims of other types of trauma (e.g., Davis & Brickman, 1996; Filipas & Ullman, 2001; Kahn, 1984). This type of response is likely due to the types of emotions engendered by sexual assault, including confusion, helplessness, fear of sexual assault, and victim blame (Davis & Brickman, 1996); however, these findings are not uniform (compare Davis, Taylor & Bench, 1995). Regardless of the type of reaction received, this literature underscores the importance of factors associated with social reactions, including both the reaction provided and its interpretation. In order to further assess the impact of reactions to disclosure on victims, it is important to examine the responses provided by, and experiences of, both informal and formal disclosure recipients.

Informal Disclosure Recipients and Responses to Disclosure

These aforementioned options cover a wide range of possible responses that can be formative in determining how victims respond to an assault emotionally, cognitively and behaviorally. Generally, victims report that informal disclosure recipients engage in more positive social reactions than formal recipients (Ahrens et al, 2007, 2009; Filipas & Ullman, 2001; Golding et al, 1989). Moreover, it is widely accepted that informal disclosure recipients can play a substantial role in meeting the emotional needs of victims (e.g., Ahrens et al, 2007; Andrews et al, 2003; Bard & Sangrey, 1979, 1980; Filipas & Ullman, 2001; Friedman et al, 1982; Ruback, Greenberg & Westcott, 1984; Ullman, 1996a, 1999, 2010). In fact, Green and colleagues (2005) found that social support can moderate the relation between victimization and distress, underscoring its effect on the well-being of crime victims. They speculated that social support may even mediate this relation by buffering against post-victimization distress, although this association was not formally tested. Regardless of the mechanism by which it buffers against distress, the role of emotional support provided by informal recipients is a notable and valuable resource for victims.

In addition to providing emotional support, informal disclosure recipients also influence the way that victims think about the sexual assault. For instance, informal recipients can help the victim to reframe the event (e.g., reiterate the severity of the assault). As described by Ruback and colleagues (1984, 2001), informal disclosure recipients can help victims to conceptualize and label what happened to them, particularly in an ambiguous situation that might be hard to understand. This assistance can involve providing corrective information (e.g., an assault perpetrated by an acquaintance or a romantic partner can still be considered a rape) and cue victims on subsequent actions to take (e.g., formally reporting the assault) given this revised understanding of the event.

In that regard, informal recipients can also influence the behaviors in which victims engage by connecting them to needed resources, such as medical and mental health care (e.g., Ahrens et al, 2007; Andrews et al, 2003; Filipas & Ullman, 2001; Ullman, 1996a; 1999; 2010). In many cases, informal support providers can also facilitate formal rape reporting by providing support throughout the reporting process (Kilpatrick et al, 2007; Patterson & Campbell, 2010). Recipients can help in a number of ways, including through categorization of the assault as a crime and help in overcoming concerns about reporting (e.g., stigma, perceived blame); recipients can also make the report themselves (Greenberg, Ruback & Westcott, 1982; Holmstrom & Burgess, 1979; Ruback et al, 1984; Ruback & Thompson, 2001). Encouragement of victims also appears to be an important role for informal disclosure recipients in the reporting process. Paul, Resnick and colleagues (2013c) found that, among respondents to a national survey, only 17% of rape victims consulted with someone else about reporting the assault, and about half of those who consulted with someone prior to reporting were subsequently encouraged to report the assault to police. These encouraged women were significantly more likely to formally report their assault (56%) than women who were discouraged from reporting (15%) or did not consult with someone else about reporting (9%). Taken together, informal disclosure recipients can have a notable impact on post-assault outcomes for victims. However, it is important to explore disclosure from the recipient's perspective in order to have a more thorough understanding of their experience.

Informal Disclosure Recipients and Disclosure Experiences

Although the experience of receiving an assault disclosure can be stressful, informal disclosure recipients report a number of positive emotions related to the experience, including feeling needed and feeling good about having helped the victim (e.g., Ahrens & Campbell, 2000; Banyard et al, 2010; Friedman et al, 1982). Some recipients also report a closer relationship with the victim after the disclosure (Ahrens & Campbell, 2000; Christiansen, Bak & Elklit, 2012). In fact, Ahrens and Campbell found that the majority of recipients reported positive experiences, in that they felt able to help and were happy to provide the support, and were not unduly distressed by the experience. In general, these participants also reported that they felt the victims were coping well with such a stressful event. Moreover, they reported their relationships with victims were not substantially negatively affected, and might have even improved. Of note, the recipients assessed in this study reported long-standing, close relationships to victims, which the authors noted as a possible source of bias in their results. Similarly, Christiansen and colleagues (2012) found similar widespread positive reactions among recipients nominated for study participation by the rape victims who disclosed to them, although they acknowledged that this sampling procedure would likely over-represent close victim-recipient relationships, as well. When viewed in isolation, these findings indicate that recipients are seemingly well prepared to deliver appropriate responses to victims in the post-assault period, can do so without experiencing significant upset or attenuation of their relationship with the victim, and reap positive outcomes as a result of their assistance.

Unfortunately, in addition to these well-adjusted and positive portrayals of the disclosure experience, Ahrens and Campbell (2000) observed two other general types of sexual assault disclosure reactions among their participants. The first of these was characterized by a relatively neutral response, in which recipients appeared generally unfazed by the disclosure experience. Although they reported feeling able to provide support to the victim and perceived that the victim was coping effectively, they did not note any changes in their relationship to the victim or any significant distress related to the disclosure. The authors pointed out that this pattern could accurately represent a balanced, neutral response to the disclosure, but might also signal emotional detachment from the experience, a response noted in other studies (e.g., Ahrens et al, 2007; Filipas & Ullman, 2001; Starzynski et al, 2005). Second, and more troubling, some recipients reported significant doubt about their ability to provide help, and experienced notable disclosure-related distress, including shock, anger, and vengeance. Some recipients also reported feelings of helplessness and guilt because they were not able to stop the assault from occurring. These responses were tied to subsequent recipient behaviors, ranging from avoidance of further discussion of the assault and/or the victim herself, to overprotectiveness and controlling behavior, to resentment and increased tension in the relationship with the victim (Ahrens & Campbell, 2000). Similar findings are reported with other samples of disclosure recipients, including friends, family members and romantic partners of sexual assault victims. A minority of participants reported other distressing reactions, including nightmares about the assault, fear of what others would think about the event, and the perception that he or she was alone in dealing with the victim's disclosure (e.g., Ahrens & Aldana, 2012; Christiansen et al, 2012; Daane, 2005).

These potential negative consequences for disclosure recipients might be referred to as secondary victimization, when recipients are indirectly affected by the victim's primary victimization (e.g., Condry, 2010; Daane, 2005; Friedman et al, 1982; Ruback & Thompson, 2001). This experience is relatively common, with 80% of support providers in a study by Friedman and colleagues (1982) reporting symptoms of secondary victimization. Extreme adverse reactions to disclosure, which include significant distress and impairment, can be classified as secondary traumatization (for a review, see Morrison, Quadara & Boyd, 2007). This reaction is also experienced by many, with approximately one-half of the 107 recipients nominated by rape victims reporting clinically significant (i.e., diagnostic or sub-clinical) symptoms of PTSD in a study by Christiansen and colleagues (2012). Symptoms of PTSD were significantly associated with time since the assault and the recipient's perceptions and behaviors (e.g., support provided, management of thoughts about being able to prevent the assault). Taken together, although many disclosure recipients have positive experiences with helping victims, a large proportion of recipients are at risk for disclosure-related distress; this experience can negatively impact their relationships with victims, which could consequently impair their ability to provide assistance.

Formal Disclosure Recipients and Responses to Disclosure

Despite the range of unique and important services that formal recipients can provide (e.g., medical and mental health care, legal services), victims are less likely to disclose to them (e.g., Ahrens & Aldana, 2012; Ahrens et al, 2009; Golding et al, 1989). Unfortunately, despite their significant potential role in post-assault outcomes, formal disclosure recipients are associated with higher rates of negative reactions to disclosure than informal recipients, particularly those individuals involved in the legal process such as police officers and lawyers

(Ahrens et al, 2007, 2009; Filipas & Ullman, 2001; Rich & Seffrin, 2012; Starzynski et al, 2005; Ullman, 1996a, 1996b). These negative reactions to disclosure can exacerbate post-assault problems for victims and prevent them from receiving other important services, further compounding these concerns (e.g., not pursuing medical care or not formally reporting if treated insensitively; Campbell et al, 2001; Ruback & Thompson, 2001).

However, these findings are mixed, and victims perceived some formal support sources to be helpful (cf., Burgess & Holmstrom, 1975; Golding et al, 1989). Counselors, in particular, appear to play an important and positive role in providing formal assistance. Ahrens and colleagues (2009) reported on interviews conducted with 103 sexual assault victims, and virtually all of the reactions provided by counselors were rated significantly more positively than those provided by other disclosure recipients. Victims reported that counselors provided the most emotional support, fairly high levels of tangible aid, and generally low levels of most types of negative reactions. Further, this relation held even when the reaction provided might traditionally be thought of as negative (e.g., encouraging the victim to move on, sharing about one's own victimization). Thus, in contrast to other sources of formal support, counselors (e.g., therapists, rape crisis workers, clergy) appear to play a unique and valuable role in helping victims post-assault.

Formal Disclosure Recipients and Experiences with Disclosure

What little research is available on examining the experience of formal disclosure recipients shows that some report positive experiences after having disclosed their assault. Specifically, a small body of research indicates that counselors report some positive aspects of their interactions with victims, including feeling privileged to help them work through their trauma (Iliffe & Steed, 2000). Such findings are not surprising, given the aforementioned research attesting to positive reactions from, and support provided by, these recipients.

However, disclosure receipt can cause distress for formal recipients; such an experience among professionals working with victims is often described as "compassion fatigue" (Figley, 1995). Ruback and Thompson (2001) provided an overview of some of the symptoms professionals might experience, including general emotional upset, physiological symptoms of anxiety (e.g., heart palpitations), detachment from professional and personal relationships, substance abuse, and the development of victim blaming attitudes. Those professionals who are likely to be exposed to a high volume of disclosures (e.g., emergency room doctors, rape crisis counselors) are more likely to develop an extreme reaction to the disclosure, including vicarious traumatization and related symptoms of PTSD (e.g., nightmares, hyper-vigilance for potential danger cues; see Condry, 2010; Morrison et al, 2007; Ruback & Thompson, 2001). Other risk factors for development of these problems among professionals include a personal history of trauma - particularly that which is unresolved - high empathy for the victims with whom one is working, and working with child victims (Dunkely & Whelan, 2006; Figley, 1995). Thus, although formal recipients can provide a number of valuable services to victims, their help can be experienced negatively by victims, and might cause the recipients notable distress. Counselors can be the exception to this experience, although they may still be vulnerable to developing compassion fatigue and vicarious traumatization. Of note, the literature regarding reactions to disclosure among informal and formal recipients is almost non-existent; this review is a summation of the available research, but further investigation is needed to better understand the experiences of these populations.

FACTORS AFFECTING DISCLOSURE AND REACTIONS TO DISCLOSURE

Assault Characteristics

Several factors can affect a sexual assault victim's decisions about disclosure and the manner with which recipients respond to her. One important set of variables is the characteristics of the sexual assault. These include, but are not limited to, whether the assault conforms to the script of a stereotypical rape, including the identity of the perpetrator (i.e., stranger or acquaintance), the use of force and resistance in the assault, and whether alcohol was consumed by either party prior to, or during, the assault.

Research in this area indicates that victims are more likely to disclose their assault to both informal and formal support providers when their assault conforms to the idea of a "stereotypical rape" (Ahrens, Stansell & Jennings, 2010; Allen, 2007; Feldman-Summers & Norris, 1984; Golding et al, 1989; Starzynski et al, 2005; Temkin & Krahe, 2008). Stereotypical rapes involve those characteristics that society most often associates with a "real rape," including a stranger perpetrator who surprises the victim, attacks her using force and/or a weapon, and is resisted by the victim (Burt & Albin, 1981; Estrich, 1987). Social norms like these can influence the labels that victims and recipients use to describe the assault, and thus affect perceptions of what happened (Ruback et al, 1984). Victims whose assaults include stereotypical characteristics are less likely to be viewed as precipitating the rape (Krahe, 1992). These assaults are disclosed more quickly to formal recipients compared to non-stereotypical assaults, which might not be disclosed for months or years, if at all (Ullman, 1996b). Of note, stereotypical rapes are the exception (Koss, Heise & Russo, 1994). Unfortunately, more common, non-stereotypical sexual assaults, such as those involving an acquaintance perpetrator or the presence of alcohol, may not be interpreted as serious acts of sexual violence and rape.

Perpetrator Type

The type of perpetrator - stranger versus acquaintance - is shown to influence the victim's disclosure behaviors. Ullman and Filipas (2001a) found that victims who were assaulted by an acquaintance were more likely to disclose their assault to informal support providers (42.4%) than victims who were assaulted by strangers (22%). Victims who were assaulted by a stranger, on the other hand, were more likely to disclose the assault to formal support providers (78%); disclosure rates to formal support providers by victims assaulted by an acquaintance were lower (57.6%). College students assaulted by a stranger were also more likely to formally report their assaults to campus police, but also disclosed to more informal recipients, than victims of acquaintance rape (Fisher et al, 2003). Assaults committed by a known perpetrator are also associated with a greater delay in disclosure than those perpetrated by a stranger (Stewart et al, 1987; Ullman, 1996b).

With respect to known perpetrators, the degree of acquaintance was negatively associated with disclosure in a sample of sexual assault victims, and the various authors speculated that an ongoing relationship with the perpetrator - either intimately, in the same social circles, or through some other manner - can affect willingness to disclose (Orchowski & Gidycz, 2012). Thus, it seems that the nature of the victim's relationship to the perpetrator might affect not only to whom she discloses, but also when she chooses to do so.

Use of Force and Resistance

The use of force and resistance during the assault has been shown to influence the victim's decision to disclose. Consistent with the pattern of increased disclosure rates following a "stereotypical rape," victims who were verbally threatened, held down, beaten, or threatened with a weapon were more likely to disclose their assault to both informal and formal disclosure recipients than victims whose perpetrators did not use force or a weapon (Starzynski et al, 2005). In conjunction with this phenomenon, Ullman and Filipas (2001a) found that women who were injured and/or perceived that their life was in danger during the attack were more likely to disclose to formal recipients; these results were replicated in later research (Fisher et al, 2003; Starzynski, Ullman, Townsend, Long & Long, 2007). Non-injured women and those who did not believe their life was in danger, on the other hand, were more likely to tell informal, rather than formal, recipients (Ullman & Filipas, 2001a), although more severe assaults are associated overall with greater disclosure to informal recipients (Fisher et al, 2003).

With respect to victim behavior, women who reported lower rates of physical resistance toward the perpetrator were more likely to delay disclosure and treatment-seeking for months or even years (Stewart et al, 1987). Starzynski and colleagues (2005) found that physical resistance, a characteristic typical of stereotypical assaults, was associated with higher rates of disclosure; the majority (58%) of victims surveyed who actively resisted the perpetrator disclosed to informal recipients, and 62% disclosed to both informal and formal recipients. These results are consistent with an earlier study by Golding and colleagues (1989), which showed that victims who resisted their assault verbally or physically were more likely to disclose their assault, especially to informal recipients. However, these authors also found that disclosure to formal recipients was significantly higher when the victim physically resisted the assault than when she verbally resisted or did not resist at all, whereas Starzynski and colleagues found no association between victim resistance and type of disclosure recipient.

Alcohol

Consumption of alcohol can also influence disclosure decisions. It is possible that victims will be less likely to disclose their assault if they were drinking prior to, or during, the assault. Disclosure patterns could be influenced by a number of related factors, including victim concerns related to feeling guilty about drinking, being worried that alcohol consumption can lead to victim-blaming reactions from disclosure recipients and as memory impairment for the assault due to alcohol's effect on consciousness. Research shows that victims are less likely to disclose their assault if they were engaged in underage drinking (Ruback, Menard, Outlaw & Shaffer, 1999). Results are mixed regarding the effect of victim intoxication on disclosure to formal disclosure recipients. Starzynski and colleagues (2007) found no effect of the victim's use of intoxicants on disclosure to mental health professionals, while Ullman & Filipas (2001a) found that women who experienced alcohol-related sexual assaults were more likely to disclose to mental health professionals (59.2%) than women whose assaults did not involve alcohol (45.7%). These conflicting results and the lack of research on the effects of victim alcohol consumption on disclosure recipient reactions underscore the need for additional research in this area.

With respect to both types of recipients, Ullman and Filipas (2001a) did not find differences in the type of disclosure recipient (i.e., formal and informal combined versus informal recipients only) between victims of alcohol-related (i.e., were under the influence of alcohol at the time of assault) and non-alcohol-related assaults. However, those women who experienced an alcohol-related assault were less likely to disclose to recipients other than mental health professionals (40.8%) compared to women whose assaults did not involve alcohol (54.3%). Importantly, rates of disclosure to mental health professionals did not differ between groups. However, other research shows that both victim and perpetrator use of alcohol were significantly positively associated with informal disclosure among college sexual assault victims (Fisher et al, 2003; Orchowski & Gidycz, 2012). The difference between these findings are likely attributable to the different populations (i.e., heterogeneous victim samples versus college student samples), the assault context (i.e., victim intoxication versus victim and perpetrator alcohol use) and the type of disclosure recipients assessed (i.e., informal and formal recipients combined versus informal recipients only). Interestingly, although victim consumption of alcohol did not affect the timing of sexual assault disclosure, perpetrator consumption of alcohol was associated with significantly faster disclosure (Ullman, 1996b), possibly due to women feeling less responsible for the assault, and perceiving that others will also find them less responsible, and thus be more supportive (Fisher et al, 2003; Ullman, 1996b).

With respect to disclosure receipt, Paul, Walsh and colleagues' (2013b) analysis of data from a national survey, using non-mutually exclusive categories, revealed that respondents who reported receiving a disclosure were more likely to have received disclosure of a forcible rape (92.8%) than a rape that involved drugs or alcohol (39.2%). These findings are attributable to the greater prevalence of forcible rape in the sample, but indicate that rape incidents that involve drugs and alcohol are reported to informal recipients by a substantial number of victims. Finally, although victims might experience drug- and alcohol-facilitated rapes (i.e., the perpetrator assaults the victim after giving her alcohol or drugs without her knowledge) and incapacitated rapes (i.e., the victim voluntarily consumes alcohol or drugs but is too intoxicated or high to consent), research on these rape tactics is scarce and further research is needed.

Perceptions of Sexual Assault by Victims and Recipients

In addition to the actual circumstances of the sexual assault, the manner with which victims and disclosure recipients think about sexual assault, its victims, and its perpetrators can also affect disclosure-related behaviors. These perceptions include both victim-related beliefs, such as self-blame and rape acknowledgement, and recipient-related beliefs, such as rape myth acceptance (RMA).

Self-blame

Self-blame following a sexual assault may influence disclosure decisions (Starzynski et al, 2005, 2007; Ullman, 1999). Self-blame can instigate fears of being blamed or stigmatized by others, which might understandably affect a victim's decision to disclose her assault. Ahrens (2006) found that threat of sexual assault stigma was a pervasive factor that discouraged victims from disclosing their assaults. This perceived threat of stigma included "fears of being blamed, doubted, and treated insensitively" (p. 269). Not surprisingly, feelings of self-blame, guilt and embarrassment are implicated in decisions to not disclose the assault (Finkelson & Oswalt, 1995; McGregor, Wiebe, Marion & Livingstone, 2000; Starzynski et al, 2005).

Self-blame can also influence to whom the victim discloses. Research shows that women who endorsed greater behavioral self-blame (i.e., attributing the assault to their behaviors) were more likely to only disclose to informal disclosure recipients, compared to women who only disclosed to formal recipients (Starzynski et al, 2007) or informal and formal recipients combined; self-blame (i.e., attributing the assault to their character flaws) was not significantly associated with disclosure recipient type (Starzynski et al, 2005). It is postulated that victims who blame themselves do not feel that they deserve to receive help from formal recipients, or believe that formal disclosure recipients will also blame them for the assault (Patterson, Greeson & Campbell, 2009). Taken together with the greater rate of negative reactions reported from formal disclosure recipients, it is not surprising that victims are less likely to disclose to formal recipients when they blame themselves for the assault.

Rape Acknowledgement

The victim's perception of what happened, and the way that she categorizes the incident (e.g., "rape," "crime," "misunderstanding") can affect disclosure-related decisions. These perceptions can be particularly important for victims who might be unsure about how best to conceptualize what occurred. This confusion is likely to happen after an unexpected and stressful event, like an assault, and particularly in ambiguous situations (Ruback et al, 1984), like acquaintance or intimate partner assaults. When victims do not acknowledge the assault as a rape, they may believe that they should not disclose because there is no incident of interest to discuss (Pitts & Schwartz, 1993; Ullman & Filipas, 2001a). In other words, rather than labeling the experience as a rape, sexual assault victims may give the experience a benign label (Littleton, Axsom, Breitkopf & Berenson, 2006) that can affect their subsequent disclosure and help-seeking behaviors. Research attests to the widespread prevalence of this type of perception among victims. Koss (1989) found that 70% of women who endorsed having experienced forced, unwanted sex did not believe that they had been raped. Similar studies have found similar results with unacknowledgment or outright minimization of the rape (Bondurant, 2001; Fisher et al, 2003, Frazier & Seales, 1997; Kahn, Mathie & Torgler, 1994; Koss, Figueredo, Bell, Tharan & Tromp, 1996).

One of the reasons that rape victims might not acknowledge their experience as rape is that what they experienced does not match their rape script; that is, what they think a rape entails. Research findings indicate that the rape scripts of unacknowledged victims are generally consistent with stereotypical rape, in that these scripts typically involve a stranger perpetrator (Kahn et al, 1994), notable use of force by the perpetrator and use of resistance by the victim (Bondurant, 2001; Kahn et al, 1994). In contrast to this cognitive construct, the actual rapes of unacknowledged victims often involve acquaintance perpetrators (Frazier & Seales, 1997; Kahn, Jackson, Kully, Badger & Halvorsen, 2003; Koss, 1985) who do not use high levels of force (Bondurant, 2001; Botta & Pingree, 1997; Kahn et al, 1994; 2003; Koss, 1985; Layman, Gidycz & Lynn, 1996), and situations in which victims do not report using significant resistance against the perpetrator (Bondurant, 2001; Koss, 1985; Layman et al, 1996). This discrepancy highlights the effect of the victim's perceptions of rape and her categorization of her own sexual assault experience. Previous research supports the notion that victims who acknowledge their assault as a rape are more likely to disclose their assaults (Ahrens et al, 2010; Botta & Pingree, 1997; Layman et al, 1996; Littleton et al, 2006), underscoring the importance of perceptions in post-assault behaviors.

Rape Myth Acceptance

Disclosure recipient beliefs about sexual assault and victim perceptions of the beliefs of others are other important factors that affect disclosure-related behaviors. Rape myth acceptance (RMA), refers to an individual's level of agreement with false stereotyped beliefs about rape, and its victims and perpetrators (e.g., a woman who is dressed provocatively is asking to be assaulted, inviting a man into one's home or apartment after a date is an invitation for sex; Burt, 1980; Gerger, Kley, Bohner & Siebler, 2007). Thus, individuals who report strong endorsement of these beliefs are likely to have stereotypical, negative attitudes towards sexual assault victims. Research demonstrates a significant relation between high levels of RMA and negative attitudes and behaviors towards victims, including perceptions of blame and the nature of the assault (e.g., perception of it as sexual assault versus rape; Burt & Albin, 1981; Koppelaar, Lange & van de Velde, 1997), as well as an increased likelihood of engaging in sexually aggressive behavior (Hamilton & Yee, 1990) and actual perpetration of sexual aggression among men (Earle, 1996; Koss, Leonard, Beezley & Oros, 1985).

Regardless of the actual beliefs that potential recipients may hold, victims might be unlikely to disclose if they feel that others hold victim-blaming beliefs, and/or that they might be blamed or stigmatized (Paul, Gray, Elhai & Davis, 2009). Although Paul and colleagues found that victims who thought their peers endorsed high levels of RMA disclosed their assault to more individuals, they postulated that this effect could be due to receiving negative reactions during disclosure, which would have subsequently increased the estimated peer RMA of victims. Further clarifying this relation, Heath and colleagues (2011) found that one-third of victims reported that they were worried about the extent of the RMA of others and subsequent victim blaming, which consequently affected decisions to not disclose their assault. Taken together, it is clear that rape-related attitudinal variables can influence both victims and recipients, even if these beliefs are not accurate reflections of reality.

Factors that Affect Disclosure and Recipient Reactions

Finally, there are socio-demographic and individual characteristics about the victim and recipient that influence disclosure-related behaviors. These factors can influence whether or not the victim discloses to a given person, as well as that recipient's reactions.

Victim-related Variables

Several socio-demographic variables are significantly associated with disclosure behaviors among sexual assault victims. With respect to race, Black women were significantly more likely to formally report their assault to police than victims of other races within samples of college victims (Bachman, 1998; Fisher et al, 2003). However, racial minorities were less likely to disclose to other types of recipients (e.g., other campus authorities, informal recipients) than White victims, although these differences were not significant (Fisher et al, 2003). Further, Ullman and Filipas (2001a) found that ethnic minority women in a mixed college and community sample were more than two times as likely to disclose their assaults to informal and formal support sources combined, versus to informal sources alone. Thus, although it seems that race can play a role in disclosure-related behaviors, this relation is not yet clear and is in need of further study. With respect to other socio-demographic characteristics, it appears that motherhood may affect the likelihood of victim disclosure. Ullman & Filipas (2001a), for example, found that 72.5% of women with children were more likely to tell formal recipients, compared to only 57.6% of women without children, whereas only 27.5% of the women with children disclosed to informal recipients, compared to 42.4% of women without children.

Victim-related variables can also affect social perceptions of and reactions to the victim. Ruback and colleagues (1984) reviewed the literature and identified victim-related variables that influence the interpretations of sexual assault. Among these, victims who had a prior history of rape, had a previous relationship with the perpetrator, and were of moderate age (i.e., 20 to 50 years old) were judged more harshly and held more accountable for the assault than women without these personal characteristics. Recently, Krahe's (1992) summary of sexual assault vignette studies showed that victims were judged less harshly if they conformed to the standard of "ideal" victim, in that they were considered respectable, had high status and behaved consistent with the more stereotypical gender roles.

In addition to these socio-demographic characteristics, research shows that victims who are viewed as expressing high levels of distress and engaging in poor coping are perceived more negatively than other victims (for a brief review, see Herbert & Dunkel-Schetter, 1992). Unfortunately, victims might be perceived negatively due to factors outside of their control (e.g., age, societal mores), and those victims who appear notably distressed or are perceived as coping poorly may be at even greater risk for negative reactions from recipients. Recipients might feel that they are helpless to affect positive change among distressed victims, thus exacerbating their own negative emotional responses, likely negatively impacting the help they provide, and consequently generating problems in their relationships with victims (Silver, Wortman & Crofton, 1990).

Recipient-related Variables

Despite limited work in this area, research has identified a number of recipient-related variables that can impact the disclosure receipt experience. Some variables are associated with an increase in the likelihood of receiving a rape disclosure. Among these, personal sexual assault history was significantly associated with disclosure receipt in samples of women in college and community-residing populations (Paul et al, 2013a; 2013b). Although this cross-sectional research could not speak to the reasons for an increased rate of disclosure, viable possibilities include the victim seeking out the recipient because she is aware of the recipient's assault history, reciprocal sharing in a conversation that involves a disclosure, or shared high-risk behaviors such as frequent binge drinking (Paul et al, 2013a; 2013b). Paul and colleagues (2013a) found that employment was also significantly associated with disclosure receipt in a national sample of college students. Although it is possible that employment is a marker of stability, and victims are more likely to disclose to those whom they feel can support them, it is also possible that this variable is a proxy for another construct, such as age.

Some recipient-related variables are associated with changes in reactions to disclosure. Among college students, personal sexual assault history was significantly associated with increased perceived severity of the immediate impact of the assault on the victim, decreased perception of the victim's responsibility for the assault, and more positive, and fewer negative, changes in the victim-recipient relationship (Ahrens & Campbell, 2000).

Gender also affects responses to disclosure. Men are often associated with negative responses to disclosure. More specifically, Ahrens and Campbell (2000), and Banyard and colleagues (2010), found that male undergraduate recipients of a sexual assault disclosure endorsed significantly more blame of, and less empathy for, the victim, as well as more negative and fewer positive changes in their relationship with the victim. Undergraduate men reported more confusion about how to best help the victim and greater perceived ineffectiveness of their help. Greater negative responses from men were also reported among adults who received disclosures of violent crime, including rape (Daane, 2005; Davis & Brickman, 1996), although these findings have not been confirmed by other researchers (cf. Christiansen et al, 2012; Krahe, 1992). Differences in attitudes towards rape might explain some discrepant responses from men and women, as research demonstrates that men tend to hold more negative attitudes towards both women and rape victims than those held by women (for a review, see Daane, 2005). Further, the differences in which female victims and male recipients respond emotionally to sexual assault (e.g., fear and guilt versus anger and hostility) can contribute to communication issues and persistent problems in the victim-recipient relationship (Miller, Williams & Bernstein, 1982). Of note, women are shown to report more distress related to the disclosure experience (Banyard et al, 2010), including an increase in one's own fear of victimization (Coates, Wortman & Abbey, 1979; Davis et al, 1995), which may affect their own coping and subsequent responses to victims.

The relationship between the victim and the recipient can also have an important influence on reactions to disclosure. With respect to the nature of the relationship, partners and family members are often associated with more negative reactions towards sexual assault victims, although this research is mixed (for reviews, see Davis & Brickman, 1996; Daane, 2005). Regardless of those findings, the possibility for an increase in negative reactions may be due to the distressing emotions reported by partners and family members, such as inadequacy, guilt, helplessness, anger, blame (Ahrens & Campbell, 2000; Burge, 1983; Cwik, 1996; Daane, 2005; Davis & Brickman, 1996; Holmstrom & Burgess, 1979; Silverman, 1978; Smith, 2005; White & Rollins, 1981).

Length of time in an interpersonal relationship prior to the assault was associated with a report of positive changes in the relationship post-disclosure by the recipients (Ahrens & Campbell, 2000). Although close relationships may, at times, be beneficial for victims and recipients alike (Ahrens & Campell, 2000), this same quality can also heighten the problems that later are experienced following disclosure. For example, the impact of rape on the victim might alter the routine and typical manner of coping within a family or romantic partnership, resulting in disrupted stability and problems in relationships with those with whom the victim interacts on a regular basis and relies on for support (Burge, 1983; Cwik, 1996; Daane, 2005). In sum, although this research is still new, a number of individual difference characteristics of both victims and recipients are identified that can affect disclosure-related behaviors. Continued study of these, and other, victim-based and recipient-related factors is important in better understanding the disclosure experience.

Theoretical Framework to Understand Negative Disclosure Experiences

Taken together, a number of factors, ranging from socio-demographic variables and events in one's personal history, to personal attitudes and behaviors and social mores, can affect the behaviors in which both sexual assault victims and disclosure recipients engage. Although victims report some positive responses to disclosure (e.g., Campbell et al, 2001; Filipas & Ullman, 2001; Golding et al, 1989; Ullman, 1996a), and the majority of recipients have positive experiences with the disclosure experience (e.g., Ahrens & Campbell, 2000; Banyard et al, 2010; Friedman et al, 1982; Iliffe & Steed, 2000), some problems remain. The persistence of negative reactions to disclosure (e.g., Ahrens & Aldana, 2012; Ahrens & Campbell, 2000; Banyard et al, 2010; Friedman et al, 1982) and the substantial distress reported by a notable minority of disclosure recipients (e.g., Ahrens & Aldana, 2012; Ahrens & Campbell, 2000; Daane, 2005; Smith, 2005) underscores the need for improving the disclosure experience. The bulk of available research is focused on victim distress and improving post-assault outcomes, but little work has assessed the distress experienced by disclosure recipients. Thus, it is important to better understand the experience of this group to determine how to improve post-disclosure outcomes for both parties. To that end, a theoretical framework for better understanding negative responses to disclosure is presented.

Victimization Perspective Theory

An effective framework for understanding negative interactions toward the victim of a stressful life event (e.g., cancer diagnosis, sexual assault) and support providers, including disclosure recipients, is articulated through Victimization Perspective Theory (Dunkel-Schetter & Wortman, 1981; Herbert & Dunkel-Schetter, 1992; Silver et al, 1990; Wortman & Dunkel-Schetter, 1979). This theoretical framework explains how people might want to provide assistance to victims of stressful events but they might have difficulty doing so due to their own distress related to receiving the disclosure of the event (Herbert & Dunkel-Schetter, 1992; Silver et al, 1990). Disclosure-related distress is understandable, given that it is upsetting to hear about another person experiencing a stressful event. Although it is not comparable to personally experiencing the event, the receipt of a disclosure is made more upsetting because a recipient must first tend to the victim's needs prior to addressing their own (Daane, 2005). Compounding this distress, recipients may feel unable to clearly and honestly express their own negative emotions to victims; they might even feel the need to portray opposite emotions, such as optimism or normalcy, to the victim, leading to further personal distress due to this inconsistency with their actual experience (Daane, 2005; Silver et al, 1990).

How disclosure recipients perceive the help they provide, including how the victim responds, is an important component of this theory. Per Victimization Perspective Theory, recipients may experience additional problems if they feel helpless in the face of the disclosure, whether they doubt their own ability to help, feel that the victim is not coping well with the event on her own, or feel that she is not responding well to the help provided to her (Herbert & Dunkel-Schetter, 1992; Silver et al, 1990). Per the aforementioned research, responses to victims can be ineffective, or even harmful, either because they are overt negative reactions (e.g., blame), or because they are well intentioned but ineffective attempts to help (e.g., vowing revenge on the perpetrator, encouraging avoidance of the assault; Ahrens et al, 2007; Filipas & Ullman, 2001; Starzynski et al, 2005; Ullman, 1996c, 2000). If the response provided by the disclosure recipient is not effective, it might not only lead to distress on the part of the victim, but also result in difficulties in the victim-recipient relationship (Silver et al, 1990).

Perceived ineffectiveness of one's help can exacerbate the stress experienced by the recipient, which, in severe cases, can result in PTSD (Riggs & Kilpatrick, 1990). According to Victimization Perspective Theory, disclosure recipients who evidence a distressed style of response are likely to have more difficulties in managing their own emotions, as well as in responding supportively to victims. Ahrens and Campbell (2000) initially applied Victimization Perspective Theory to recipients of sexual assault disclosure. As noted above, they identified a subgroup of participants that reported feeling unprepared to cope with the disclosure and endorsed notable distress related to the experience. They found that not knowing how to best help the victim, and subsequently feeling helpless in the face of the disclosure, was associated with negative changes in the recipient's relationship with the victim. Taken together, these conflicts can create a difficult situation with which the recipient must cope, possibly leading to a range of negative responses to the victim, including visible discomfort and avoidance of her presence. Of note, the authors cautioned that this theory was not an accurate description of the disclosure experience for the majority of recipients in their study. Their victim-recipient relationships were notably long-standing and close, which might have enhanced the recipient's perception of his or her ability to provide help and correctly interpret feedback about whether or not the provided help is working - critical components of Victimization Perspective Theory.

Adding to these problems are other victim-related perceptions that can influence views of victims and their ability to provide help to them (Coates et al, 1979; Dunkel-Schetter & Wortman, 1981; Herbert & Dunkel-Schetter, 1992; Silver et al, 1990). First, perceptions of the victim by disclosure recipients can be negatively influenced if they have beliefs about how they should be able to respond (i.e., provision of effective support), but their feelings of helplessness prevent them from responding in this way. Second, victims may directly engender negative reactions and derogation from others if it seems that they are not making efforts on their own to cope with the stressful event, and thus are fully dependent on others for assistance. These factors are understandably related to potential problems already set forth in Victimization Perspective Theory, thus providing further understanding for why recipients might respond negatively to, and be unable to effectively assist, victims.

Improving the Disclosure Experience

Despite the potential benefits of disclosure, it is understandable that some victims do not tell others about their assaults, given the aforementioned potential barriers to, and possible negative consequences of, this act. These consequences include negative responses - both intentional and unintentional - from disclosure recipients. Both parties may experience distress due to the assault disclosure, as well as the manner in which the disclosure process unfolds. Given the potential problems that can arise for both victims and recipients, it is important to determine the best ways to encourage victims to engage in disclosure in order to receive needed support, while also increasing the likelihood that such efforts will be met with positive and helpful responses. Suggestions for interventions that could be implemented with both groups, as well as further research that is greatly needed in this area, are provided.

Implications for Victims

Positive responses from disclosure recipients are never guaranteed, particularly given that responses are subject to interpretation by the individual victim. However, there appear to be some ways to increase the likelihood that victims will receive a desired and helpful response. Among these, the victim's direct communication of her need for support is important. Such statements alert the victim's support network that she needs assistance, as well as tell them what they can do to best help her, thus increasing the likelihood that she will receive desired and effective support (Kaniasty & Norris, 1992).

After examining the effects of different needs presentations among patients with cancer, Silver and colleagues (1990) recommended that victims present a balanced portrayal of coping. They stated that victims are more likely to receive effective support when they exhibit enough distress to indicate they need assistance, but not so much that it is overwhelming to recipients. Further, victims were encouraged to make known the steps that they are personally taking to cope with the stressful event. According to Victimization Perspective Theory, this type of presentation is preferred because it would best demonstrate to recipients that (a) the victim is in need of help; (b) efforts at help are likely to be well received; and (c) the recipient is not the sole source of support, which decreases the perceived burden on the recipient for the provision of assistance.

This approach is likely beneficial for those victims for whom this portrayal is consistent with their actual experiences. Problems that may arise per Victimization Perspective Theory are minimized and victims are able to express their own feelings in this situation, thus increasing validation of their own experience. However, this perspective gives some victims a challenging, and unfair, task. Some victims might not have a reaction consonant with this approach and find that they are unable to display and regulate their experience in this way. In fact, victims who are highly distressed and in great need of assistance might be the least likely to get help due to the negative reactions that their emotional presentation may engender in recipients (Coates et al, 1979; Ruback et al, 1984; Silver et al, 1990), consistent with Victimization Perspective Theory. Alternately, those victims who are not experiencing distress at the time and evidence a more positive portrayal of coping are at risk of being perceived as not needing assistance now, or at any time in the future, decreasing their likelihood of receiving any assistance, even if the victim should later become distressed (Silver et al, 1990).

Thus, it is important to explore ways that victims can be empowered to seek out assistance in a manner that is authentic with their actual experiences. In order to help victims best acknowledge and present their emotional experience, whatever it might be, it is important to guide them to supportive others who will be able to respond positively to them. Given the importance of social support in the well-being of crime victims, evaluating the support networks victims have, working to bolster them, and facilitating connections to supportive others may help to decrease victimization-related distress (Green & Pomeroy,

2007; Kaniasty & Norris, 1992). Friedman and colleagues (1982) found empirical proof for these recommendations, as crime victims who had poor social networks within their neighborhoods and small support networks overall were less likely to have their post-victimization needs met than victims with better developed social connections. Of note, given the relatively stronger influence of perceived versus received social support on buffering against post-crime distress (Kaniasty & Norris, 1992), helping victims to focus on evaluating their support networks and enhance them, if necessary, is likely to be of great use.

Counselors can be particularly helpful in this regard, as they are noted for their positive responses to victims (Ahrens et al, 2009) and are trained to address the outcomes of assaults and other upsetting events. Thus, they can directly provide victims with emotional support, which is particularly valuable for those victims who are experiencing significant distress that might seem overwhelming to other formal or informal disclosure recipients. Counselors can also help victims evaluate their own support networks and determine the individuals in it who are most likely to respond positively and supportively.

Additionally, helping victims to learn to acknowledge and modulate their emotional responses is likely to be of use, regardless of the distress level experienced. Techniques that help victims to tolerate, and cope with, upsetting emotions can help them to manage some of their distress on their own, thus improving their own emotional regulation skills and making requests for help from others more effective, per Victimization Perspective Theory. In studies of crime victims, emotion-focused coping was more effective than problem- or avoidance-focused coping (Green et al, 2005; Green & Pomeroy, 2007), and instruction in this and other techniques, such as distress tolerance skills (Linehan, 1993), is likely to be of use. Disclosure recipients can be particularly helpful in reinforcing these techniques among victims, given the significant association between social support and emotion-focused coping (Green & Pomeroy, 2007).

Of note, none of these options suggest the burden is on victims to present themselves in a way that makes recipients more likely to respond effectively to them, or that they must cope with their distress on their own. Instead, they are provided as a means through which victims might be able to better cope with assaults, regardless of the help that is - or is not - provided to them. Importantly, it is also valuable to educate victims about the range of possible positive and negative reactions to disclosure that they receive, so that they are prepared for what they may encounter and are better able to cope with responses that are provided to them (Ahrens & Campbell, 2000). Not only could this approach help to buffer against potential negative responses to disclosure, but it may also assist in further empowering victims in their coping efforts.

Implications for Disclosure Recipients

The research presented here shows that post-assault outcomes among victims can be significantly affected by the manner in which others respond to them (e.g., Bard & Sangrey, 1979, 1980; Cwik, 1996; Riggs & Kilpatrick, 1990; Ruback & Thompson, 2001). Unfortunately, per Victimization Perspective Theory and the empirical research reviewed, learning about an assault experienced by another can be a very stressful event that can be difficult to manage and one that results in negative outcomes. The internal experience of this event can result in problematic responses to disclosure. This problem is exacerbated if recipients feel that they cannot honestly express their own distress, and if recipients feel as if they are unable to help the victim, or that their help is not working. Research bears out these postulations, in that increased distress among support providers is associated with greater unsupportive behaviors towards crime victims (Ahrens & Campbell, 2000; Davis et al, 1995; Riggs & Kilpatrick, 1990).

In 1996, Cwik argued that "other victims" (i.e., disclosure recipients and support providers, such as the victim's family members and romantic partner) are neglected in post-sexual assault intervention efforts. Unfortunately, this situation remains the same today, and efforts to help these individuals manage their own distress, while providing assistance to victims, are sorely needed. The value of support for this population is emphasized in the literature, as providing appropriate assistance to those who receive a disclosure not only directly benefits them, but also better prepares them to support other victims and improves their post-assault outcomes (Christiansen et al, 2012; Cwik, 1996; Daane, 2005; Morrison et al. 2012; Paul et al, 2013a; Silverman, 1978; Smith, 2005; Ullman, 1999, 2010).

After their review of the effect that others can have on victims of crime, Ruback and colleagues (1984) made the important point that it is likely more effective to intervene with the public from the perspective that they can be sources of assistance in their role as disclosure recipients and not recipients of that assistance as victims. They recommended instructing others in how to accurately and supportively respond to victims in order to improve post-crime outcomes, including education about the possible impact that support provision can have on victims. In addition to this argument for providing intervention to the broader group of potential disclosure recipients, it is also possible, but unfortunate, that people who participate in such programming as potential disclosure recipients might already have been victimized, or might be victimized in the future. Thus, such efforts can provide this group with needed information regardless of their victimization status, hopefully minimizing the distress experienced in their roles as both a victim and disclosure recipient.

There are a number of possible targets for intervention with potential disclosure recipients. Broadly, Bard and Sangrey (1979, 1980) emphasized that crime victims do not respond in a formulaic, predictable manner. Instead, each victim will respond differently, even to similar situations, underscoring the importance of individual responses to victimization and post-assault needs. Kaniasty and Norris (1992) echoed this finding by explaining that matching the victim's needs to the support from which she would most benefit is likely to result in the best outcomes for the victim. Although this individual tailoring of response is important, there are some general themes that are likely to emerge in these helping attempts that could benefit the broader populations of recipients and victims.

Informal Disclosure Recipients

Researchers have provided suggestions for helping specific close others (e.g., family members) cope with the sexual assault disclosure and support experience, and these techniques are likely valuable targets of future intervention for all potential disclosure recipients. First, improving the understanding of sexual assault and the victimization experience among potential recipients is critical (e.g., Burge, 1983; Daane, 2005; Dunn et al, 1999; Silverman, 1978). This education can cover a number of topics, and certainly needs to include factual information about assault. Not only would the inclusion of such topics provide corrective information to potential recipients about sexual assault, its prevalence and its characteristics, but it would also help to combat and counter rape myths and rape-supportive beliefs. Targeting these negative attitudes is important, as they were determined to be a significant predictor of sexually aggressive behavior in a review of the literature (Earle, 1996).

Additionally, providing education about different types of assaults (e.g., acquaintance rape, drug- and alcohol-facilitated rape) can help in correcting misperceptions about the prevalence of types of assaults and clarifying any ambiguity about them. As Ruback and colleagues (1984) noted that the influence of others on the categorization of events is stronger in ambiguous situations, it is hoped that this corrective information can help in appropriate labeling of the assault experience by victims and disclosure recipients, which can facilitate seeking needed services (e.g., reporting the assault, seeking medical care).

Providing potential recipients with information about tangible aid is also valuable. Recipients could use this information to refer victims to needed resources (e.g., counseling, medical care, formal reporting), thus connecting victims to other important forms of care (Dunn et al, 1999). Such information is particularly important because this type of assistance was shown to significantly buffer against later distress for victims of violent crime, relative to victims of property crime and non-victims (Kaniasty & Norris, 1992). Facilitation of this connection through informal support providers is also valuable because many victims do not seek out formal support services (Amstadter et al, 2008). Such steps can help to alleviate some of the helping burden that recipients may perceive, a situation that can lead to negative responses from recipients, per Victimization Perspective Theory.

Information about formally reporting the assault is of importance, given the role that informal recipients can play in encouraging reporting (Feldman-Summers & Norris, 1984; Kilpatrick et al, 2007; Patterson & Campbell, 2010; Paul et al, 2013c; Ruback et al, 1984). Informing recipients about formal reporting procedures is helpful, as this information can help potential recipients to understand the process, particularly as it is related to the victim's case, and facilitate her participation in, and cooperation with, the legal system (Riggs & Kilpatrick, 1990). Finally, potential recipients should also be reminded that rape does not necessarily result in irreparable harm, and that victims can recover despite the trauma of the event. This information can help to reassure both victims and recipients about the effects of this crime (White & Rollins, 1981), as well as prevent both parties from feeling that recovery is impossible, a situation that would exacerbate the problems articulated in Victimization Perspective Theory.

Second, instruction in and strengthening of coping skills are worthwhile targets for intervention among disclosure recipients, as is building up their support networks (Burge, 1983; Daane, 2005; Silverman, 1978). Such information could be provided in a number of formats, ranging from general psycho-education (e.g., instruction in behavioral activation principles and diaphragmatic breathing techniques) to individual counseling sessions. This latter option is especially important for those recipients who are experiencing significant disclosure-related distress and would benefit from more formal individual assistance (Riggs & Kilpatrick, 1990). Couples or family therapy can be appropriate for victims and their significant others in order to facilitate the recovery process and support of the victim (Cwik, 1996; Silverman, 1978).

Finally, for recipients who are close to victims, it is beneficial to foster open communication within the relationship (Burge, 1983; Cwik, 1996; Silverman, 1978). Facilitating open communication helps victims to communicate their needs and perceptions of help provided to them, as well as aid recipients in expressing appropriately their own reactions to the disclosure, thus circumventing some of the problems predicted by Victimization Perspective Theory. Additionally, providing victims with an opportunity to discuss their assault openly can help to buffer against distress, given findings that seeking to distract victims and/or encourage them to move on past the assault are associated with greater PTSD symptoms (Ullman & Filipas, 2001b).

For recipients who are notably distressed by the disclosure, it is important to first resolve any negative emotional responses to the assault in order to provide more constructive assistance (Holmstrom & Burgess, 1979). Thus, initial efforts to improve coping skills are particularly important. Consistent with the suggestion above, providing corrective information about one's risk for victimization is also important in this regard, as some recipients report discomfort in talking to victims about the crime that occurred because they feel more at risk for victimization themselves (Friedman et al, 1982), and the perception of increased risk might lead to greater negative reactions towards victims (Coates et al, 1979).

More broadly, recipients can benefit from instruction in empathic listening. A survey of college sexual assault disclosure recipients and non-recipients revealed that many participants identified that important supportive responses to victims included listening to them and being empathic (Paul & Sasson, in preparation), and such training would better prepare recipients to respond in this manner. Given that some recipients report concerns about not knowing what to say to victims to best help them (Dunn et al, 1999; Emm & McKenry, 1988), instruction in empathic listening can give them a technique to use that does not require specific statements, but instead, just being supportive of, and open with, the victim.

As all potential recipients would benefit from intervention with these components, such intervention efforts are applicable to everyone, given that anyone could receive an assault disclosure (Ruback & Thompson, 2001). Information and skills taught (e.g., coping, empathic listening) have broad applications and are not restricted to assault disclosures. Because men are associated with more negative reactions toward victims (e.g., Ahrens & Campbell, 2000; Banyard et al, 2010; Davis & Brickman, 1996) and women are associated with increased rates of distress related to the disclosure and helping experience (e.g., Banyard et al, 2010; Davis et al, 1995), it seems that intervention would benefit both genders.

The limited research assessing disclosure recipient interest in such interventions is promising. Kilpatrick and colleagues (2007) found that respondents to a national survey of women endorsed public education about sexual assault, particularly acquaintance rape, as a means to lead to greater encouragement of, and engagement in, the formal reporting process. Respondents also recommended expanded services (e.g., counseling, medical care) for victims and their families. Paul and Sasson (in preparation) found that qualitative data from surveys of recipients and non-recipients echoed this interest. The requested intervention targets were consistent with those noted above, including factual information about sexual assault, contact information for local resources, and emotional support for the recipients themselves. Finally, Christiansen and colleagues (2012) reported that the majority of recipients surveyed in their study indicated interest in services to help them post-disclosure. The greatest level of interest was for information about how to best help the victim, followed by personal counseling services and receiving support from other recipients. Clearly, there is interest in, and likely benefits from, intervention with the public regarding sexual assault and its disclosure. Importantly, regardless of the nature of the intervention, it must be empirically evaluated following dissemination in order to determine whether or not it is helping both recipients and victims (Ullman, 1999).

Formal Disclosure Recipients

It is important to identify ways to best assist formal support providers and to help them learn how to minimize the negative reactions to victims with which they are associated (e.g., Ahrens et al, 2007, 2009; Filipas & Ullman, 2001; Starzynski et al, 2005), particularly as these reactions might result in secondary victimization of the victim (Ullman, 1999). Intervention is likely to be of significant assistance to this group given the degree of distress that these individuals may experience (Daane, 2005; Morrison et al, 2007), thus highlighting the importance of helping this population learn how to cope effectively with their own reactions.

Although these efforts are likely to benefit formal disclosure recipients, there are additional considerations in working with these providers. Preparation for the possible receipt of a disclosure and related assistance can be particularly useful for non-mental health professionals. Not only are counselors already associated with more positive reactions to sexual assault disclosure than other formal disclosure recipients (Ahrens et al, 2009), but these individuals are in a field that readily recognizes the impact of working with victims, as opposed to other professionals (e.g., lawyers, police officers) who work in an environment that less readily recognizes the potential stress of this experience (Daane, 2005; Morrison et al, 2007). In addition to the aforementioned suggestions, broader recommendations in the workplace include providing peer support and supervision, alterations to the work environment (e.g., caseload), and encouragement of appropriate coping skills (e.g., using self-care behaviors, maintaining clear boundaries). However, these efforts have not been rigorously evaluated and findings regarding their effectiveness are mixed (e.g., Dunkley & Whelan, 2006; Morrison et al, 2007).

Training for police officers, to whom a victim must disclose in order to formally report the assault, is particularly important. Positive responses from police officers can increase trust among victims, thus increasing participation in, and cooperation with, police and legal proceedings (Ruback & Thompson, 2001). Research shows that a history of sexual assault training is associated with significant decrements in rape-supportive attitudes, and more positive views of victims, among police officers (Ask, 2010; Rich & Seffrin, 2012), as well as the use of more supportive behaviors when interviewing sexual assault victims (Rich & Seffrin, 2012). Important factors to target in helping the police to work more effectively with, and support, victims include educating police about possible emotional presentations among victims (e.g., highly distressed, seemingly numb) and memory for the assault (e.g., incomplete), how to develop rapport, and how to help victims determine further steps to take (e.g., contacting family or friends for help, seeking physical or mental health assistance; see National Sheriff's Association, 2008). One suggestion in this regard is helping officers learn how to gather critical, but sensitive, assault-related information when interviewing the victim (e.g., the victim's behavior during the assault, why the victim was with the perpetrator) in a minimally distressing manner (Campbell, 2005; National Sheriff's Association, 2008). Finally, targeting corrective information about what behaviors constitute sexual assault and rape is of particular use, given that certain assault characteristics (i.e., prior interaction between the perpetrator and victim, a lack of mental health history of the perpetrator, assault location at the victim's or perpetrator's home) were associated with more doubt of rape accounts among police officers (Krahe, 1992).

CONCLUSION

It is evident that the literature on disclosure recipients is sparse. Thus, significant research is needed to better understand the experience of this population, as well as how they can best help victims. Further research is needed assessing sexual assault more broadly, and research focusing on different assault characteristics (e.g., perpetrator type, use of force and resistance, presence of alcohol) and rape tactics (e.g., drug- and alcohol-facilitated rape, incapacitated rape) is greatly needed. Focusing on discrepancies between stereotypical sexual assaults and actual assault characteristics is crucially important, given the influence that victim and recipient perceptions of the assault can have on post-assault outcomes.

Additionally, different groups of disclosure recipients should be surveyed. As reviewed, the limited research available has centered on college students, family members, the male partners of female victims, counselors and police officers. Not only must these populations be studied in more depth, but so must other groups of potential recipients to bolster the external validity of the research. For instance, although Ahrens and Campbell (2000) provided important information about informal sexual assault disclosure recipients, the generalizability of their findings is limited to long-term, close relationships among college-aged individuals. Additional information about groups who are more likely to receive a disclosure – such as family and friends, resident advisors, nurses and first responders – is very important. Addressing the disclosure-related experiences of sexual assault victims who receive a disclosure from someone else is particularly valuable, given the elevated rate of disclosure receipt in this population (Paul et al, 2013a; 2013b), as well as the experience of triggered personal memories of sexual victimization reported by some recipients (Dunn et al, 1999) that might lead to additional distress.

Although research has assessed sexual assault victims to determine their experience and the type of assistance they desire (e.g., Andrews et al, 2003; Filipas & Ullman, 2001; Ullman, 1996a), recipients have not received comparable attention. Findings from the only known studies in this area indicate that this group would like to receive assistance in learning how to best help victims, including receiving corrective information about sexual assault, as well as resources to which they can refer victims. Recipients also note concern about how others may respond to sexual assault, and thus, emphasize the need to combat misperceptions about sexual assault and provide factual information about it and resources for getting help (Kilpatrick et al, 2007; Paul & Sasson, in preparation). Thus, further research is needed to determine what information and resources potential recipients would like to have in order to best help themselves and victims.

Finally, assessment of Victimization Perspective Theory and its various components is important. Better characterization of the experiences of disclosure recipients will help to explain the problems that can arise for this group in the provision of support, and specific attention should be focused on determining sources of frustration and negative reactions. Among these topics, assessing how recipients perceive different victim need presentations is of interest. Despite the encouragement of a balanced portrayal of coping (Silver et al, 1990), further information is needed to assess the best ways that victims can communicate, and recipients can interpret, the victim's desire for help, in order to improve the match between the recipient's efforts at support and the victim's needs. Not only would this information improve the probability that victims will receive the help that they desire, it would help to provide recipients with more direct suggestions for how they can help, thus circumventing some of the problems proposed in Victimization Perspective Theory.

The utility of intervening with recipients in order to improve the disclosure experience is clear. Ability to determine the best ways to intervene with this population is currently limited, owing to the lack of extant information about this group and its needs. In addition to exploring the aforementioned targets for research, couching such findings within Victimization Perspective Theory or other relevant theories is important in helping to guide such efforts within a specific and informative framework. It is hoped that, by continuing to develop this area of the field, it will be possible to determine the means through which to best prepare and support sexual assault disclosure recipients, and ultimately, improve disclosure-related outcomes for both the victims of sexual assault and disclosure recipients.

REFERENCES

Ahrens, C. E. (2006). "Being silenced: The impact of negative social reactions on the disclosure of rape," *American Journal of Community Psychology*, *38*, 263-274.

Ahrens, C. E. & Aldana, E. (2012). "The ties that bind: Understanding the impact of sexual assault disclosure on survivors' relationships with friends, family, and partners," *Journal of Trauma and Dissociation*, *13*, 226-243.

Ahrens, C. E., Cabral, G. & Abeling, S. (2009). "Healing or hurtful: Sexual assault survivors' interpretations of social reactions from support providers," *Psychology of Women Quarterly*, *33*, 81-94.

Ahrens, C. E. & Campbell, R. (2000). "Assisting rape victims as they recover from rape: The impact on friends," *Journal of Interpersonal Violence*, *15*, 959-986.

Ahrens, C. E., Campbell, R., Ternier-Thames, N. K., Wasco, S. M. & Sefl, T. (2007). "Deciding whom to tell: Expectations and outcomes of rape survivors' first disclosures," *Psychology of Women Quarterly*, *31*, 38-49.

Ahrens, C. E., Stansell, J. & Jennings, A. (2010). "To tell or not to tell: The impact of disclosure on sexual assault survivors' recovery," *Violence and Victims*, *25*, 631-648.

Allen, D. W. (2007). "The reporting and underreporting of rape," *Southern Economic Journal*, *73*, 623-641.

Andrews, B., Brewin, C. R. & Rose, S. (2003). "Gender, social support and PTSD in victims of violent crime," *Journal of Traumatic Stress*, *16*, 421-427.

Amstadter, A. B., McCauley, J. L., Ruggiero, K. J., Resnick, H. S. & Kilpatrick, D. G. (2008). "Service utilization and help seeking in a national sample of female rape victims," *Psychiatric Services*, *59*, 1450-1457.

Ask, K. (2010). "A survey of police officers' and prosecutors' beliefs about crime victim behaviors," *Journal of Interpersonal Violence*, *25*, 1132-1149.

Bachman, R. (1998). "The factors related to rape reporting behavior and arrest: New evidence from the National Crime Victimization Survey," *Criminal Justice and Behavior*, *25*, 8-29.

Banyard, V. L., Moynihan, M. M., Walsh, W. A., Cohn, E. S. & Ward, S. (2010). "Friends of Survivors: The community impact of unwanted sexual experiences," *Journal of Interpersonal Violence*, *25*, 242-256.

Bard, M. & Sangrey, D. (1979). *The Crime Victim's Book*, New York, NY: Basic Books.

Bard, M. & Sangrey, D. (1980). "Things fall apart: Victims in crisis" (Special Issue), *Evaluation and Change*, 28-35.

Binder, R. L. (1981). "Why women don't report sexual assault," *Journal of Clinical Psychiatry*, *42*, 437-438.

Bondurant, B. (2001). "University women's acknowledgment of rape: Individual, situational, and social factors," *Violence Against Women*, *7*, 294-314.

Botta, R. A. & Pingree, S. (1997). "Interpersonal communication and rape: Women acknowledge their assaults," *Journal of Health Communication*, *2*, 197-212.

Brickman, J. & Briere, J. (1984). "Incidence of rape and sexual assault in an urban Canadian population," *International Journal of Women's Studies*, *7*, 195-206.

Burge, S. (1983). "Rape: Individual and family reactions," In C. Figley & H. McCubbin (Eds.), *Stress and the Family* (pp. 103-119). New York, NY: Brunner-Mazel.

Burgess, A. W. & Holmstrom, L. L. (1975). "Rape: The victim and the criminal justice system," *Victimology: A New Focus*, *3*, 101-110.

Burt, M. R. & Albin, R. S. (1981). "Rape myths, rape definitions, and probability of conviction," *Journal of Applied Social Psychology*, *11*, 212-230.

Campbell, R. (2005). "What really happened? A validations study of rape survivors' help-seeking experiences with the legal and medical systems," *Violence and Victims*, *20*, 55-68.

Campbell, R., Sefl, T., Barnes, H. E., Ahrens, C. E., Wasco, S. M. & Zaragoza-Diesfield, Y. (1999). "Community services for rape survivors: Enhancing psychological wellbeing or increasing trauma," *Journal of Consulting and Clinical Psychology*, *67*, 847-858.

Campbell, R., Wasco, S. M., Ahrens, C. E., Sefl, T. & Barnes, H. E. (2001). "Preventing the 'second rape': Rape survivors' experiences with community service providers," *Journal of Interpersonal Violence*, *16*, 1239-1259.

Christiansen, D., Bak, R. & Elklit, A. (2012). "Secondary victims of rape," *Violence and Victims*, *27*, 246-262.

Coates, D., Wortman, C. B. & Abbey, A. (1979). "Reactions to victims," In I. H. Frieze, D. Bar-Tel, & J. S. Carroll (Eds.), *New Approaches to Social Problems* (pp. 21-52). San Francisco, CA: Jossey-Bass.

Condry, R. (2010). "Secondary victims and secondary victimization," In S. G. Shoham, P. Knepper, & M. Kett (Eds.), *International Handbook of Victimology* (pp. 219-249). Boca Raton, FL: CRC Press.

Cwik, M. S. (1996). "The many effects of rape: The victim, her family, and suggestions for family therapy," *Family Therapy*, *23*, 95-116.

Daane, D. M. (2005). "The ripple effect: Secondary sexual assault survivors," In F.P. Reddington & B. W. Kreisel (Eds.), *Sexual Assault: The Victims, the Perpetrators, and the Criminal Justice System* (pp. 113-131). Durham, NC: Carolina Academic Press.

Davis, R. C. & Brickman, E. (1996). "Supportive and unsupportive aspects of the behavior of others toward victims of sexual and nonsexual assault," *Journal of Interpersonal Violence*, *11*, 250-262.

Davis, R., Taylor, B. & Bench, S. (1995). "Impact of sexual and nonsexual assault on secondary victims," *Violence and Victims*, *10*, 73-84.

DuMont, J. & Parnis, D. (2006). "The uses and impacts of medico-legal evidence in sexual assault cases: A global review," Unpublished document prepared for the Gender Health Unit, World Health Organization, Geneva, Switzerland.

Dunkel-Schetter, C. & Wortman, C. B. (1981). "Dilemmas of social support: Parallels between victimization and aging," In S. B. Kiesler, J. N. Morgan, & V. K. Oppenheimer (Eds.), *Aging: Social Change* (pp. 349-381). New York, NY: Academic Press.

Dunkley, J. & Whelan, T. A. (2006). "Vicarious traumatisation: Current status and future directions," *British Journal of Guidance and Counseling*, *34*, 107-116.

Dunn, P. C., Vail-Smith, K. & Knight, S. M. (1999). "What date/acquaintance rape victims tell others: A study of college student recipients of disclosure," *Journal of American College Health*, *47*, 213-219.

Earle, J. P. (1996). "Acquaintance rape workshops: Their effectiveness in changing the attitudes of first year college men," *NASPA Journal*, *34*, 2-18.

Elliott, D. M., Mok, D. S. & Briere, J. (2004). "Adult sexual assault: Prevalence, symptompatology, and sex differences in the general population," *Journal of Traumatic Stress*, *17*, 203-211.

Emm, D. & McKenry, P. C. (1988). "Coping with victimization: The impact of rape on female survivors, male significant others, and parents," *Contemporary Family Therapy*, *10*, 272-279.

Estrich, S. (1987). *Real Rape*, Cambridge, MA: Harvard University Press.

Feldman-Summers, S. & Norris, J. (1984). "Differences between rape victims who report and those who do not report to a public agency," *Journal of Applied Social Psychology*, *14*, 562-573.

Felson, R. B. & Pare, P. P. (2005). "The reporting of domestic violence and sexual assault by non-strangers to the police," *Journal of Marriage and Family*, *67*, 597-610.

Figley, C. R. (1995). *Compassion Fatigue: Coping with Secondary Traumatic Stress Disorder in Those who Treat the Traumatized*, London, England: Brunner-Routledge.

Filipas, H. H. & Ullman, S. E. (2001). "Social reactions to sexual assault victims from various support sources," *Violence and Victims*, *16*, 673-692.

Finkelson, L. & Oswalt, R. (1995). "College date rape: Incidence and reporting," *Psychological Reports*, *77*, 526.

Fisher, B. S., Daigle, L. E., Cullen, F. T. & Turner, M. G. (2003). "Reporting sexual victimization to the police and others: Results from a national-level study of college women," *Criminal Justice and Behavior*, *30*, 6-38.

Frazier, P. A. & Seales, L. M. (1997). "Acquaintance rape is real rape," In M. D. Schwartz (Ed.), *Researching Sexual Violence against Women: Methodological and Personal Perspectives* (pp. 54-64). Thousand Oaks, CA: Sage.

Friedman, K., Bischoff, H., Davis, R. & Person, A. (1982). *Victims and Helpers: Reactions to Crime*, NIJ Publication No. 79-NI-AX-0059), Rockville, MD: National Institute of Justice.

George, L. K., Winfield, I. & Blazer, D. G. (1992). "Sociocultural factors in sexual assault: Comparison of two representative samples of women," *Journal of Social Issues*, *48*, 105-125.

Gerger, H., Kley, H., Bohner, G. & Siebler, F. (2007). "The acceptance of modern myths about sexual aggression scale: Development and validation in German and English," *Aggressive Behavior*, *33*, 422-440.

Golding, J. M., Siegel, J. M., Sorenson, S. B., Burnam, M. A. & Stein, J. A. (1989). "Social support sources following sexual assault," *Journal of Community Psychology*, *17*, 92-107.

Green, D. L., Streeter, C., Pomeroy, E. (2005). "A multivariate model of the stress and coping process for victims of crime," *Stress, Trauma, and Crisis: An International Journal*, *8*, 61-73.

Green, D. L. & Pomeroy, E. C. (2007). "Crime victims: What is the role of social support?" *Journal of Aggression, Maltreatment and Trauma*, *15*, 97-113.

Greenberg, M. S., Ruback, R. B. & Westcott, D. R. (1982). "Decision making by crime victims: A multi-method approach," *Law and Society Review*, *17*, 47-84.

Hamilton, M. & Yee, J. (1990). "Rape knowledge and propensity to rape," *Journal of Research in Personality*, *24*, 111-122.

Heath, N. M., Lynch, S. M., Fritch, A. M., McArthur, L. N. & Smith, S. L. (2011). "Silent survivors: Rape myth acceptance in incarcerated women's narratives of disclosure and reporting of rape," *Psychology of Women Quarterly*, *35*, 596-610.

Herbert, T. L. & Dunkel-Schetter, C. (1992). "Negative social reactions to victims: An overview of responses and their determinants," In L. Montada, S. H. Filipp, & M. J. Lerner (Eds.), *Life Crises and Experiences of Loss in Adulthood* (pp. 497-518). Hillsdale, NJ: Lawrence Erlbaum.

Holmstrom, L. L. & Burgess, A. W. (1979). "The husband's and boyfriend's initial reactions," *The Family Coordinator*, *28*, 321-330.

Iliffe, G. & Steed, L. G. (2000). "Exploring the counselor's experience of working with perpetrators and survivors of domestic violence," *Journal of Interpersonal Violence*, *15*, 393-412.

Kahn, A. S. (1984). *Victims of Crime and Violence: Final Report of the APA Task Force on the Victims of Crime and Violence*, Washington, DC: American Psychological Association.

Kahn, A. S., Jackson, J., Kully, C., Badger, K. & Halvorsen, J. (2003). "Calling it rape: Differences in experiences of women who do or do not label their sexual assault as rape," *Psychology of Women Quarterly*, *27*, 233-242.

Kahn, A. S., Mathie, V. A. & Torgler, C. (1994). "Rape scripts and rape acknowledgment," *Psychology of Women Quarterly*, *18*, 53-66.

Kaniasty, K. & Norris, F. H. (1992). "Social support and victims of crime: Matching event, support, and outcome," *American Journal of Community Psychology*, *20*, 211-241.

Kelly, L. (2001). *Routes to (In)justice: A Research Review on the Reporting, Investigation and Prosecution of Rape Cases*, United Kingdom: University of North London, Child and Woman Abuse Studies Unit.

Kilpatrick, D. G., Edmunds, C. N. & Seymour, A. K. (1992). *Rape in America: A Report to the Nation*, Arlington, VA: National Victim Center and Medical University of South Carolina.

Kilpatrick, D. G., Resnick, H. S., Ruggiero, K. J., Conoscenti, L. M. & McCauley, J. (2007). *Drug-facilitated, Incapacitated, and Forcible Rape: A National Study*, U.S. Department of Justice, National Institute of Justice Publication No. NCJ 219181 (Washington, DC).

Koppelaar, L., Lange, A. & Van de Velde, J. (1997). "The influence of positive and negative victim credibility on the assessment of rape victims: An experimental study of expectancy confirmation bias," *International Review of Victimology*, *5*, 61-85.

Koss, M. P. (1985). "The hidden rape victim: Personality, attitudinal, and situational characteristics," *Psychology of Women Quarterly*, *9*, 193-212.

Koss, M. P. (1989). "Hidden rape: Sexual aggression and victimization in a national sample of students in higher education," In M. A. Pirog-Good & J. E. Stets (Eds.), *Violence in Dating Relationships: Emerging Social Issues* (pp. 145-184). New York, NY: Praeger.

Koss, M. P. (2006). "Restoring rape survivors: Justice, advocacy, and a call to action," *Annals of the New York Academy of Sciences*, *40*, 1-30.

Koss, M. P., Dinero, T. E., Seibel, C. A. & Cox, S. L. (1988). "Stranger and acquaintance rape: Are there differences in victim experience?" *Psychology of Women Quarterly*, *12*, 1-24.

Koss, M. P., Figueredo, A. J., Bell, I., Tharan, M. & Tromp, S. (1996). "Traumatic memory characteristics: A cross-validated meditational model of response to rape among employed women," *Journal of Abnormal Psychology*, *105*, 421-432.

Koss, M. P., Leonard, K. E., Beezley, D. A. & Oros, C. J. (1985). "Nonstranger sexual aggression: A discriminant analysis of the psychological characteristics of undetected offenders," *Sex Roles*, *12*, 981-992.

Koss, M. P., Heise, L. & Russo, N. F. (1994). "The global health burden of rape," *Psychology of Women Quarterly*, *18*, 509-537.

Krahe, B. (1992). "Coping with rape: A social psychological perspective," In L. Montada, S. Filipp, & M. J. Lerner (Eds.), *Life Crises and Experience of Loss in Adulthood* (pp. 477-496). Hillsdale, NJ: Erlbaum.

Layman, M. J., Gidycz, C. A. & Lynn, S. J. (1996). "Unacknowledged versus acknowledged rape victims: Situational factors and posttraumatic stress," *Journal of Abnormal Psychology*, *105*, 124-131.

Linehan, M. M. (1993). *Skills Training Manual for Treating Borderline Personality Disorder*, New York, NY: Guildford Press.

Littleton, H. L. (2010). "The impact of social support and negative disclosure reactions to sexual assault victims: A cross-sectional and longitudinal investigation," *Journal of Trauma and Dissociation*, *11*, 210-227.

Littleton, H. L., Axsom, D., Breitkopf, C. R. & Berenson, A. (2006). "Rape acknowledgement and post-assault experiences: How acknowledgment status relates to disclosure, coping, worldview, and reactions received from others," *Violence and Victims*, *21*, 761-778.

McGregor, M. J., Wiebe, E., Marison, S. A. & Livingstone, C. (2000). "Why don't more women report sexual assault to the police?" *Canadian Medical Association Journal*, *162*, 659- 660.

Miller, W. R., Williams, A. M. & Bernstein, M. H. (1982). "The effects of rape on marital adjustment," *The American Journal of Family Therapy*, *10*, 51-58.

Morrison, Z., Quadara, A. & Boyd, C. (2007). "'Ripple effects' of sexual assault," *ACSSA Issues*, *7*, 1-31.

National Sheriff's Association, (2008). *First Response to Victims of Crime: A Guidebook for Law Enforcement Officers*, U.S. Department of Justice, Publication No. NCJ 217272, Rockville, MD: OVC Resource Center.

Orchowski, L. M. & Gidycz, C. A. (2012). "To whom do college women confide following a sexual assault? A prospective study of sexual assault disclosure and social reactions," *Violence Against Women*, *18*, 264-288.

Patterson, D. & Campbell, R. (2010). "Why rape survivors participate in the criminal justice System," *Journal of Community Psychology*, *38*, 191-205.

Patterson, D., Greeson, M. & Campbell, R. (2009). "Understanding rape survivors' decisions not to seek help from formal social systems," *Health and Social Work*, *34*, 127-136.

Paul, L. A., Gray, M. J., Elhai, J. D. & Davis, J. D. (2009). "Perceptions of peer rape myth acceptance and disclosure among college sexual assault survivors," *Psychological Trauma: Theory, Research, Practice, and Policy*, *1*, 231-241.

Paul, L. A., Resnick, H. S., Zinzow, H. B., McCauley, J. L. & Kilpatrick, D. G. (2013c). "Reporting sexual assault: The role of consultation with, and encouragement by, others," Manuscript submitted for publication.

Paul, L. A. & Sasson, S. (In preparation). "Intervention with sexual assault disclosure recipients: Stated needs and promising directions."

Paul, L. A., Walsh, K., McCauley, J. L., Ruggiero, K. J., Resnick, H. S. & Kilpatrick, D. G. (2013a). "College women's experiences with rape disclosure: A national study," Manuscript accepted for publication, *Violence Against Women*.

Paul, L. A., Walsh, K., McCauley, J. L., Ruggiero, K. J., Resnick, H. S. & Kilpatrick, D. G. (2013b). "Community residing women's experiences with rape disclosure: A national study," Manuscript accepted for publication, *Journal of Community Psychology*.

Pitts, V. L. & Schwartz, M. D. (1993). "Promoting self-blame in hidden rape cases," *Humanity and Society*, *17*, 383-398.

Rennison, C. M. (2002). *Rape and Sexual Assault: Reporting to Police and Medical Attention, 1992-2000*, Retrieved from Bureau of Justice Statistics website > http://bjs.ojp.usdoj.gov/content/pub/pdf/rsarp00.pdf

Resick, P. A. (1993). "The psychological impact of rape," *Journal of Interpersonal Violence*, *8*, 223-255.

Resnick, H. S., Holmes, M. M., Kilpatrick, D. G., Clum, G., Acierno, R., Best, C. L. & Saunders, B. E. (2000). "Predictors of post-rape medical care in a national sample of women," *American Journal of Preventive Medicine*, *19*, 214-219.

Rich, K. & Seffrin, P. (2012). "Police interviews of sexual assault reporters: Do attitudes matter?" *Violence and Victims*, *27*, 263-279.

Riggs, D. S. & Kilpatrick, D. G. (1990). "Families and friends: Indirect victimization by crime," In A. J. Lurigio, W. G. Skogan, & R. C. Davis (Eds.), *Victims of Crime: Problems, Policies and Programs* (pp. 120-138). Newbury Park, CA: Sage Publications.

Ruback, R. B., Greenberg, M. S. & Westcott, D. R. (1984). "Social influence and crime victim decision-making," *Journal of Social Issues*, *40*, 51-76.

Ruback, R. B., Menard, K. S., Outlaw, M. C. & Shaffer, J. N. (1999). "Normative advice to campus crime victims: Effects of gender, age, and alcohol," *Violence and Victims*, *14*, 381-396.

Ruback, R. B. & Thompson, M. P. (2001). *Social and Psychological Consequences of Violent Victimization*, Thousand Oaks, CA: Sage.

Russel, D. E. H. (1982). "The prevalence and incidence of forcible rape and attempted rape of females," *Victimology: An International Journal*, *7*, 81-93.

Silver, R. C., Wortman, C. B. & Crofton, C. (1990). "The role of coping in support provision: The self-presentational dilemma of victims of life crises," In B. R. Sarason, I. G. Sarason, & G.R. Pierce (Eds.), *Social Support: An Interactional View* (pp. 397-426). Oxford, England: John Wiley and Sons.

Silverman, D. C. (1978). "Sharing the crisis of rape: Counseling the mates and families of victims," *American Journal of Orthopsychiatry*, *48*, 166-173.

Smith, M. E. (2005). "Female sexual assault: The impact on the male significant other," *Issues in Mental Health Nursing*, *26*, 149-167.

Starzynski, L. L., Ullman, S. E., Filipas, H. H. & Townsend, S. M. (2005). "Correlates of women's sexual assault disclosure to informal and formal support sources," *Violence and Victims*, *20*, 417-432.

Starzynski, L. L., Ullman, S. E., Townsend, S. M., Long, L. M. & Long, S. M. (2007). "What factors predict women's disclosure of sexual assault to mental health professionals?" *Journal of Community Psychology*, *35*, 619-638.

Stewart, B. D., Hughes, C., Frank, E., Anderson, B., Kendall, K. & West, D. (1987). "The aftermath of rape: Profiles of immediate and delayed treatment seekers," *The Journal of Nervous and Mental Disease*, *175*, 90-94.

Temkin, J. & Krahe, B. (2008). *Sexual Assault and the Justice Gap: A Question of Attitude*, Portland, OR: Hart Publishing.

Tjaden, P. & Thoennes, N. (2000). *Full Report of the Prevalence, Incidence, and Consequences of Violence against women: Findings from the National Violence Against Women Survey*, National Institute of Justice Report No. NCJ 181867, Washington, DC: US Department of Justice.

Ullman, S. E. (1996a). "Do social reactions to sexual assault victims vary by support provider?" *Violence and Victims*, *11*, 143-156.

Ullman, S. E. (1996b). "Correlates and consequences of adult sexual assault disclosure," *Journal of Interpersonal Violence*, *11*, 143-156.

Ullman, S. E. (1996c). "Social reactions, coping strategies and self-blame attributions in adjustment to sexual assault," *Psychology of Women Quarterly*, *20*, 505-526.

Ullman, S. E. (1999). "Social support and recovery from sexual assault: A review," *Aggression and Violent Behavior*, *4*, 343-358.

Ullman, S. E. (2000). "Psychometric characteristics of the Social Reactions Questionnaire: A measure of reactions to sexual assault victims," *Psychology of Women Quarterly*, *24*, 257-271.

Ullman, S. E. (2010). *Talking about Sexual Assault: Society's Response to Survivors*, Washington, DC: American Psychological Association.

Ullman, S. E. & Filipas, H. H. (2001a). "Correlates of formal and informal support seeking in sexual assault victims," *Journal of Interpersonal Violence*, *16*, 1028-1047.

Ullman, S. E. & Filipas, H. H. (2001b). "Predictors of posttraumatic stress disorder symptom severity and social reactions in sexual assault victims," *Journal of Traumatic Stress*, *14*, 369-389.

Ullman, S. E., Foynes, M. M. & Tang, S. S. (2010). "Benefits and barriers to disclosing sexual trauma: A contextual approach," *Journal of Trauma and Dissociation*, *11*, 127-133.

Wasco, S. M., Campbell, R., Howard, A., Mason, G. E., Staggs, S. L., Shewe, P. A. & Riger, S. (2004). "A statewide evaluation of services provided to rape survivors," *Journal of Interpersonal Violence*, *19*, 252-263.

White, P. N. & Rollins, J. C. (1981). "Rape: A family crisis," *Family Relations*, *30*, 103-109.

Wolitzky-Taylor, K. B., Resnick, H. S., McCauley, J. L., Amstadter, A. B., Kilpatrick, D. G. & Ruggiero, K. J. (2011). "Is reporting of rape on the rise? A comparison of women with reported versus unreported rape experiences in the National Women's Study-Replication," *Journal of Interpersonal Violence*, *26*, 807-832.

Wortman, C. B. & Dunkel-Schetter, C. (1979). "Interpersonal relationships and cancer: A theoretical analysis," *Journal of Social Issues*, *35*, 120-155.

In: Assaults
Editor: Keith V. Bletzer

ISBN: 978-1-62808-051-3

Chapter 5

Interventions to Reduce College Women's Risk for Sexual Assault

Amy S. Untied[1,*] and Lindsay M. Orchowski[2]

[1]Department of Psychology, Xavier University, Cincinnati, OH USA
[2]Department of Psychiatry and Human Behavior, The Alpert Medical School of Brown University, Providence, RI US

Abstract

United States federal law mandates all colleges and universities that receive federal funding to implement some type of violence prevention program. Despite this initiative, women on college campuses continue to experience sexual victimization at alarmingly high rates. The high rates of sexual victimization and the range of psychological after-effects associated with sexual violence underscore the importance of developing effective programs to reduce women's risk for sexual violence. As such, this chapter reviews the rationale, content, structure, theoretical underpinnings, and efficacy of sexual assault risk reduction programs for women in college. Recommendations for developing and administrating risk reduction programs are also delineated.

Introduction

Rates of sexual victimization among women are alarmingly high (Gross, Winslet, Roberts & Gohm, 2006; Testa, VanZile-Tamsen, Livingston & Koss, 2004). Women are more likely than men to experience sexual victimization (Koss, Goodman, Browne, Fitzgerald, Keita & Russo, 1994), and the vast majority of assaults are perpetrated by men against women (Tjaden & Thoennes, 1998; Truman & Rand, 2009). Approximately 15 to 25 percent of women and one to 14 percent of men experience rape at some time in their life (for reviews see Gross et al, 2006; Peterson, Voller, Polusny & Murdoch, 2011). Rape is defined as anal, oral or vaginal penetration or "intercourse," obtained through physical force, threat of

* Corresponding author: Email: salinga@xavier.edu.

physical force, verbal coercion or situations in which the individual is unable to consent due to age, intoxication or mental state (Koss, 1992). The prevalence of sexual victimization for both men and women increases when including not only unwanted sexual intercourse obtained through force or the threat of force, but also counting other experiences of sexual victimization (a broader term) such as unwanted acts like harassment, lewd behavior in public, sexual acts obtained through verbal or emotional pressure, indecent bodily exposure and unwanted bodily contact or "inappropriate touching" (Choudhary, Gunzler, Tu & Bossarte, 2012).

There is a strong connection between sexual victimization and a wide range of health effects, including increased physician visits and health care costs (Koss, Woodruff & Koss, 1991; Leserman, 2005), depression (Najdowski & Ullman, 2011), post-traumatic stress disorder (Steenkamp, Dickstein, Salters-Pedneault, Hofmann & Litz, 2012), alcohol use (Resnick et al, 2012) and gynecological/obstetric problems (see related chapter, this volume). The high rates of sexual victimization and range of associated health consequences underscore the importance of developing effective programs to reduce women's risk for sexual assault (for reviews see Gidycz, Orchowski & Edwards, 2011; Gidycz, Rich & Marioni, 2002; Orchowski, Gidycz & Murphy, 2010; Yeater & O'Donohue, 1999).

The term *sexual assault risk reduction program* refers to courses, workshops or interventions designed to reduce women's risk for victimization and to increase women's awareness and knowledge of risk factors for sexual assault (Orchowski et al, 2010). Programs for women are often referred to as sexual assault "risk reduction" as opposed to "prevention" programs in order to emphasize that only those individuals who perpetrate violence can truly prevent its occurrence (Gidycz et al, 2011). The majority of interventions and awareness campaigns developed with the aim of reducing women's risk for sexual victimization have been implemented on college campuses. In fact, U.S. federal law mandates that all colleges and universities that receive federal funding implement some type of violence prevention program (National Association of Student Personnel Administrators, 1994). Women in college are sexually victimized at a rate higher than women in the community and not enrolled in college (Sorenson, Stein, Seigel, Golding & Burnam, 1987). In fact, over a three-month period during the fall, winter and spring months, 15% of college women will experience some form of sexual victimization (Gidycz, Orchowski, King & Rich, 2008).

The content and approach of sexual assault risk reduction programs vary. Some common goals include: a) increasing awareness of sexual assault (i.e., awareness-based programs); b) teaching skills to reduce risk for sexual assault (i.e., skills-based or self-defense programs); and c) engaging women to intervene when they witness risky social/dating situations among their peers in the community (i.e., bystander intervention programs). Although programs are sometimes administered to a mixed-sex audience (e.g., Coker et al, 2011), experts in the field suggest that programs are best administered within a single-sex format (Gidycz et al, 2010; Orchowski et al, 2011) in order to lessen defensiveness among participants (Gidycz, Loh & Rich, 2003) and reduce the risk that women's protective strategies are shared with potential male perpetrators of violence (Gidycz et al, 2002). It should be noted, however, owing to a small number of sexual assaults that are perpetrated by women against women (Oliver, 2007), administering risk reduction programs to single-sex groups does not eliminate the possibility that women's protective strategies are shared with a potential (female) perpetrator. Further, administering programs to single-sex groups of women (in the absence of programming provided to men) might be seen inadvertently as victim-blaming in that it communicates the message that men have no a role in preventing sexual violence (Gidycz et al, 2011). As a result, the "dual-pronged" approaches which concurrently offer programs adapted to separate groups of men and women are becoming more common on college campuses (see Gidycz, Orchowski & Berkowitz, 2011; Gidycz; Orchowski, Probst, Edwards, Murphy & Tansil, in press).

THEORIES OF ATTITUDE AND BEHAVIOR CHANGE

Sexual assault risk reduction programs are informed by several theories of attitude and behavior change. Two theories – Elaboration Likelihood Model (ELM) and Social Learning Theory (SLT) – have been commonly incorporated within risk reduction literature and are described in detail below.

Elaboration Likelihood Model

According to the Elaboration Likelihood Model (ELM), attitudes change via peripheral and central route processing (Petty & Cacioppo, 1986; Petty, Cacioppo & Goldman, 1981). Peripheral route processing occurs when individuals do not find a message to be personally relevant, resulting in enhanced attention to peripheral cues, such as the attractiveness of the presenter, perceived degree of expert knowledge, and/or the perceived trustworthiness of the presenter. In other words, when engaging in peripheral route processing, the listener attends to the characteristics of the person presenting the information (or venue) instead of attending to the message itself. Peripheral route processing is problematic because attitude change via this route is considered transitory and unlikely to result in a lasting change. Central route processing, on the other hand, is likely to occur when the listener has a high level of personal involvement with the information and is motivated to hear what is presented. Central route processing includes reflective evaluation of the message and engagement in issue-relevant thinking. Thus, this route of cognitive processing is likely to result in more stable attitude change and it increases the salience of program content and activities for participants.

Informed by the ELM, some sexual assault risk reduction programs aim to increase program saliency by providing women with *local* statistics on the prevalence of assaults (e.g., Gidycz, Rich, Orchowski, King & Miller, 2006; Orchowski, Gidycz & Raffle, 2008). Drawing on the ELM, other programs have aimed to maximize intervention effectiveness by personalizing the program content (Gray, Lesser, Quinn & Bounds, 1990). The impact of programming has also been assessed by examining whether program participants engage in more central or peripheral route processing while participating.. For example, Heppner and colleagues (1995) evaluated a one-hour rape prevention program for college women and men. Data revealed that women demonstrated more central route attitude change and males attended more to the peripheral cues of the speaker. Over a 2-month follow-up, the change reported by the women was greater and longer lasting whereas the change reported by males was less substantial and more transient. Following the ELM, these data may indicate that since the program was administered in a mixed-sex format, it is feasible that men did not find the content personally relevant.

Social Learning Theory

Social Learning Theory (SLT) is a psychological theory of learning that assumes an individual's behavior is determined by modeling, reinforcement contingencies (e.g., positive effects, reinforcement, sanctions or punishments), cognitive appraisals, and an ability to engage in behavior change (see Bandura, 1969, 1977). Informed by SLT, risk reduction programs incorporate videos displaying potentially risky situations, model assertive responses to risk and demonstrate how to garner peer support for engaging in self-protective behavior (Gidycz et al, 2006; Marx, Calhoun, Wilson & Meyerson, 2001). Consistent with this theory, some researchers have developed risk reduction programs that include modeling of self-defense strategies and participant engagement in an active practice of self-protective skills (Gidycz et al, 2006; Orchowski et al, 2008). Programs based on SLT can benefit participants through sustained behavior change.

Risk reduction programs draw from various conceptual models constructed from factors that most influence women's risk for sexual assault. Based on SLT, two of these conceptual models – "Assess-Acknowledge-Act"and "Optimistic Bias" – are outlined below.

Asess, Acknolwedge and Act

Models based on SLT acknowledge that even when women are aware of situational risk factors for sexual victimization, the decision to respond assertively to a potential threat is complicated by an array of social and cognitive variables (Norris, Nurius & Dimeff, 1996; Norris, Nurius & Graham, 1999; Nurius, 2000; Nurius & Norris, 1995). For example, responding assertively in an uncomfortable dating situation might have undesirable social consequences, such as rejection or embarrassment, if the potential threat is ungrounded (Nurius, 2000). The Assess, Acknowledge and Act ("AAA") model described by Rozee and Koss (2001) suggests that to effectively decrease risk for sexual assault, women must <u>a</u>ppraise their environment for risks, <u>a</u>cknowledge when risks are present, and <u>a</u>ct assertively in response to threats. The decision to act protectively induces a cost/benefit appraisal, and women may fail to engage in self-protective behaviors in threatening situations if personal beliefs and the perception of potential drawbacks to act assertively outweigh the perceived benefits (Norris et al, 1996; Nurius, 2000). Ascription to cultural dating norms also makes it difficult to attend to the subtle and often ambiguous cues that a date is potentially threatening (Norris et al, 1999; Nurius, 2000). When socializing, women are apt to be involved in cognitive processing schemes that emphasize "entertainment" and/or "friendship" rather than a vigilant mode of self-protection, and risk cues may be normalized and therefore ignored (Nurius, 2000; Nurius & Norris, 1995). Drawing from this model, risk reduction programs stress the subtlety of risk cues and reiterate the importance of trusting one's intuition even in seemingly familiar situations.

The AAA model based on socio-cognitive theory serves as the framework for several risk reduction programs, including the Ohio University Sexual Assault Risk Reduction Program (Gidycz et al, 2006; Gidycz et al, in press; Orchowski et al, 2008). Senn and colleagues (2011) also employed the AAA model in concert with emancipatory sexuality education, which encourages women's exploration of their sexual values and desires. After participating in the emancipatory sexuality education sexual assault risk reduction program, women were better able to identify risk when presented with hypothetical situations of acquaintance sexual assault (Senn et al, 2011).

Optimistic Bias

The belief that one is personally less likely than his or her same-age peers to experience a negative consequence is called "optimistic bias" and it occurs in both men and women across all age and educational levels (Dibonaventura, 2009; Klein & Helwig-Larsen, 2002; Levi, 2009; Park et al, 2009; Plastow, 2007). Unrealistic optimism implies that individuals believe they have a lower chance of experiencing negative events in comparison to peers, and that they have a higher change of experiencing positive events in comparison to peers (Gold & Brown, 2009). Further, individuals tend to experience higher rates of unrealistic optimism for negative events than positive events (Gold & Brown, 2009).

In the context of sexual assault, the concepts of optimistic bias and unrealistic optimism form the foundation of the commonly held belief that sexual assault "couldn't happen to me." College women tend to report that their chances for experiencing an assault are lower than other women (Hickman & Muehlenhard, 1997; Yeater, Viken, Hoyt & Dolan, 2009) and they tend to believe that they are better able to effectively handle potentially dangerous situations than other individuals (Parks, Miller, Collins & Zetes-Zanatta, 1998). However, studies suggest that women are only partially accurate in assessing their personal risk in dating situations (Cue, George & Norris, 1996).

Following the model of Optimistic Bias, risk reduction programs seek to increase women's awareness that all women can experience sexual violence with the aim that this knowledge increases women's ability to acknowledge risky situations when they occur, and react quickly and assertively in response. Although it is necessary to urge women to acknowledge their risk for sexual assault, it is important to avoid instilling such fear in participants that their self-efficacy is lowered and their capacities for assertive responding are diminished. Since individuals tend to show a reduction in their optimistic bias when they compare themselves to someone who is similar and closer to themselves in physical appearance and presented in greater detail (Helweg-Larsen & Shepperd, 2001), risk reduction programs have also attempted to depict survivors who are similar to program participants in a variety of ways in order to debunk the myth that sexual assault "couldn't happen to me" (Gidycz et al, 2006).

CONTENT AND EFFICACY OF INTERVENTIONS

The content of sexual assault risk reduction programs includes presenting statistics regarding the prevalence of rape, information about situational risk factors for sexual assault and descriptions of perpetrator characteristics as well as personal stories from survivors of sexual assault. Programs may also include a discussion of rape myths, education about the role of alcohol in sexual assaults, assertiveness or self-defense training, information about how to respond to unwanted sexual advances and resources for survivors of sexual assault. The content of risk reduction programs and forms of media implemented can vary. Programs can also differ in length, although single-session programs are most common.

Awareness-Based Programs

The goal of awareness-based sexual assault risk reduction programs is to increase knowledge and awareness regarding the pervasiveness of sexual assault. Awareness-based programs include public speakers, who talk about personal experiences of assault, as well as presentations of prevalence data and definitions. Awareness programs can vary in length and are commonly one or two hours in duration. Colleges and universities often implement awareness campaigns through campus posters, fliers and brochures.

Although the content of some programs may focus solely on raising awareness about sexual assault, other programs include awareness-building and skills-based program content. The integration of awareness-building and skills-based components within risk reduction interventions makes it difficult to directly determine the unique utility of each. As a result, the empirical evaluation of awareness programs is limited. Furthermore, efficacy of utilizing poster campaigns as a strategy to reduce violence has yet to be evaluated and although awareness-building talks provided by public speakers have been evaluated, there is a lack of evidence to support their efficacy (Gidycz et al, 2011). Programs that solely aim to increase participant awareness of sexual assault have been criticized for failing to provide participants with an opportunity to learn and practice key skills that may be helpful in responding to threatening dating situations (Gidycz et al, 2011). Given the pervasiveness of sexual assault experiences, and the limited efficacy of existing awareness-based campaigns, it is likely that awareness-based programs are best utilized in concert with more intensive, skills-based programs.

Skills-Based Programs

Skills-based sexual assault risk reduction programs focus on providing women with skills and knowledge of sexual assault to reduce risk. One of the earliest programs, the Women Against Rape Program (1980), focuses on assertive behaviors while utilizing a form of confrontation training and self-defense as well as a discussion of the politics of rape to stress the overall program goal of self-empowerment. Other skills-based programs include modules on communication skills (Rothman & Silverman, 2007). Presently, the most extensive development of a skills-based sexual assault risk reduction program has been conducted within the Laboratory for the Study and Prevention of Sexual Assault at Ohio University under the direction of Dr. Christine Gidycz.

The Ohio University Sexual Assault Risk Reduction Program (SARR) is a skills-based intervention that has been developed and tested over the course of the past 25 years (Breitenbecher & Gidycz, 1998; Gidycz et al, 2001; Gidycz et al, 2006; Gidycz et al, in press; Hanson & Gidycz, 1993; Marx, Calhoun, Wilson & Meyerson, 2001; Orchowski et al, 2008). The program begins with a discussion of general information on violence against women and women participants are reminded that perpetrators are responsible for acts of violence. Societal factors that foster and support sexual violence are discussed, and the definition and prevalence of rape and sexual assault are provided. A video entitled, "I Thought it Would Never Happen to Me" (Gidycz, 2000) is shown in which sexual assault survivors discuss their experiences. Following the video, participants discuss their reactions to the tape. The characteristics of perpetrators and situations that increase risk for sexual assault are delineated, and the process of recovery following an assault is discussed. The program continues with a facilitated discussion of strategies to employ when confronted with potentially threatening dating situations. The role of alcohol as a risk factor for sexual victimization is discussed. A video is shown entitled "Keep Your Options Open: Alternative Solutions for Stressful Social Situations" (Gidycz, 2000) that models various risk reduction techniques.

The Ohio University SARR Program was originally three hours in length and it aimed to reduce college women's risk for sexual victimization through the application of theoretical models of behavior and attitude change within an interactive, didactic and multi-media protocol. Evaluation of the program found that it was effective in decreasing sexual assaults among women without a history of sexual victimization (Hanson & Gidycz, 1993). Since the program was not effective for women with a history of sexual victimization, it was next modified to include information specifically relevant to the survivors of sexual victimization. However, this revision was found to be ineffective for women with and without a history of sexual assault (Breitenbecher & Gidycz, 1998). Next, the program was again revised to improve personal relevancy of the information to program participants (Gidycz et al, 2001). Evaluation of the third iteration of the program found no significant differences in preventing sexual victimization at the 2-month follow-up. However, participants who were victimized during a 2-month follow-up period were less likely to be re-victimized during 6-month follow-up than women who did not participate in the risk reduction program (Gidycz et al, 2001).

Another revision of the program was evaluated among women with a history of sexual assault (Marx et al, 2001). Sixty-six women with a history of sexual victimization were randomly assigned to one of two conditions: a prevention intervention group or a no-treatment control group. The intervention group attended two 2-hour sessions. In the first session, participants were presented with definitions and statistics, as well as information about offender characteristics, situational and personal risk factors and danger signals from men. Participants then viewed a videotaped depiction of a date rape encounter and participated in a dialogue about risk factors and possible protective behaviors. At the second session, participants were provided with additional information and practice activities on assertiveness, communication skills, problem-solving skills, and recognition of and responses to risk. Although the intervention and control groups did not significantly differ in levels of risk recognition, the program was effective in reducing the occurrence of rape re-victimization.

Through a grant from the Ohio Department of Health, the program was modified again to draw on a combination of the Health Belief Model, ELM and SLT and expanded to seven hours in length (Gidycz et al, 2006). Specific objectives of this iteration of the program included the addition of a feminist self-defense class and enhancement of the cognitive elaboration of program protocol as well as a booster session for review of the program material. While findings suggest that the enhanced program was not effective in decreasing women's chances of being sexually assaulted over the 3-month or the 6-month follow-up period, the program increased participants' use of self-protective dating behaviors and decreased blame among survivors of sexual assault (Gidycz et al, 2006).

In another iteration of the program (Orchowski et al, 2008), the intervention length at seven hours and use of a feminist self-defense workshop and booster session was maintained, yet the program was revised to address psychological barriers to assertive responding in risky dating situations. Evaluation in comparison to an alternative health intervention indicated that the program was effective in increasing women's use of self-protective behaviors, assertive sexual communication and self-efficacy in resisting threatening situations over a 4-month follow-up period. Over the 2-month follow-up period, three times as many rapes were reported by individuals in the control condition than by the individuals who had participated in the risk reduction program.

Self-Defense

Strategies such as hitting (forceful physical strategies), running from a potential attacker (non-forceful physical strategies) or screaming (forceful verbal strategies) are among the most common self-defense tactics taught to decrease the likelihood of completed rape (Ullman & Knight, 1992). Notably, the effectiveness of implementing self-protective acts to avoid rape completion is maintained even when offenders are under the influence of alcohol or other drugs or when multiple attackers are involved (Kleck & Tark, 2005). Consistent with the research, most women believe that self-defense strategies will be helpful when they encounter a risky situation. Furby, Fischhoff and Morgan (1989), for example, reported that respondents anticipated a 40% reduction in their risk for sexual assault by engaging in a combination of fourteen self-defense strategies.

Self-defense training programs focus on changing women's preparedness to respond effectively when confronted with a threatening situation (Schoting, Fairbrother & Koch, 2004). Self-defense includes not only the actual ability to physically engage a potential assault perpetrator, but also the capacity to communicate assertively and believe in one's ability to respond effectively in threatening dating situations. Therefore, risk reduction programs that include a self-defense component focus on increasing both verbal assertiveness skills as well as physical self-defense tactics (e.g., Gidycz et al, 2006; Orchowski et al, 2008). Currently, it is not possible to parcel out the specific impact of self-defense training in reducing rates of sexual victimization as programs that include a self-defense component also engage participants in other activities designed to decrease their risk. Nonetheless, risk reduction programs that include a self-defense component have been found to result in increased use of self-protective behaviors and decreased self-blame after victimization experiences (Gidycz et al, 2006). In another program that included self-defense training, women evidenced increased engagement in self-protective behaviors as well as increased self-efficacy to resist attacks and use assertive sexual communication (Orchowski et al, 2008).

Bystander Interventions

Bystander interventions aim to educate students about potentially threatening situations, while providing instruction about ways to intervene when witnessing potentially risky behaviors/interactions (Banyard, Moynihan & Crossman, 2009; Banyard, Moynihan & Plante, 2007; Banyard, Plante & Moynihan 2004; Banyard, Plante & Moynihan, 2005; DeKeseredy, Schwartz & Alvi, 2000). All the members of a community are called to aid in shifting the campus norms that support violence against women. Bystander inventions refrain from identifying women as victims and men as perpetrators, and instead assume that both women and men can be witnesses to violence (Banyard et al, 2005). Although bystander interventions have been administered to college men more often than to college women (see

Berkowitz, 2003; Foubert, 2000; Foubert & Marriott, 1997), several bystander intervention programs have been developed and administered to men and women in mixed-sex as well as dual-pronged formats.

Bystander interventions draw from social psychological research regarding helping behavior. For example, having confidence in one's skills suggests that individuals will be more likely to intervene when presented with a potentially risky situation (Goldman & Harlow, 1993). Within interpersonal situations there is often a diffusion of responsibility that occurs, resulting in individuals becoming less likely to respond when placed in a situation with other people due to the assumption that someone else with intervene (Checkroun & Brauer, 2002). Individuals are more likely to act when they witness someone else modeling proactive behaviors (Rushton & Campbell, 1977).

The Green Dot intervention program, as one example, aims to increase active bystander behaviors, defined as behaviors implemented by students to reduce violence (Coker et al, 2011). Two sessions are administered to a mixed-sex audience. Phase One involves a 50-minute motivational speech to students, school leaders, faculty and administration designed to increase awareness of the problem on college campuses, motivate prevention involvement, present bystander interventions as a manageable activity and link students to campus resources. Phase Two is comprised of an intervention program entitled Students Educating and Empowering to Develop Safety (SEEDS) which provides students with skills to be proactive bystanders to prevent violence. In addition, a systematic method is used to identify Peer Opinion Leaders (POLs) who have influence in a specific community. Based on modeling principles, utilization of POLs has been found effective with other prevention programs and assumes that new behaviors are more likely to be accepted if they are modeled by influential peers. Data suggests that those students who participated in the Green Dot bystander intervention training evidenced improved engagement in more bystander behaviors when compared to untrained students. Moreover, the students who were trained displayed lower acceptance of rape myths and reported observing more self-reported active bystander behaviors than students who were not trained. Interestingly, compared with those who received no intervention, students who heard the Green Dot speech reported significantly more active bystander behaviors and more observed bystander behaviors. Further, those who participated in the bystander training reported more active bystander behaviors than those who only participated in the speech. Taken together, such data suggest that combining the program phases appears to facilitate positive changes in both attitude and behavior (Coker et al, 2011). Other bystander intervention programs have evidenced similarly encouraging results (Foubert, Langhinrichsen-Rohling, Brasfield & Hill, 2010).

A bystander intervention program has also sustained development at the University of New Hampshire. Banyard and colleagues (2007) explored the utility of a program which introduced basic prevalence data along with causes and consequences of sexual violence. The role and responsibility of individuals who may observe potentially threatening situations was also addressed. College students participated in either a single session or three-session version of the program. Following a dual-pronged approach, men and women completed the intervention in single-sex groups. Data indicated that both male and female participants evidenced a reduction in rape myth acceptance and an increase in attitudes regarding bystander efficacy and self-reported bystander behavior occurring over a 2-month follow-up. Moreover, most program effects continued to exist at the longer 4-month and 12-month follow-ups. Results from this study were similar to findings reported by Banyard and colleagues (2004) in earlier research, in which undergraduate men and women participated in a one-session or three-session version of the program administered to a single-sex audience. Data indicated that individuals in each treatment condition (those attending one or three sessions) evidenced improvements in measures of attitude, knowledge and behaviors over a 2-month follow-up.

Recommendations

It is clear that further development and evaluation of sexual assault risk reduction programs is warranted. Recommendations for campus administrators seeking to implement sexual assault risk reduction programs are delineated below.

Evaluation of Intervention Efficacy

Of the colleges and universities that implement some form of sexual assault risk reduction programming, few evaluate the effectiveness of the program in promoting attitude and/or behavior change (McCall, 1993). Studies frequently fail to examine to what extent the program decreases the incidence of sexual assault (Yeater & O'Donohue, 1999). Owing to the lack of evaluation, it is often unclear if existing interventions are effective in combatting sexual violence (Gidycz et al, 2002). To ensure that colleges and universities are implementing programs that benefit students and decrease rates of violence, it is vital that programming efforts sustain an evaluation component using longitudinal pre/post research designs that employ a control/experimental comparison. Studies must seek to assess whether a program reduces victimization across an adequate interim through a comprehensive array of measures of attitudinal and behavioral change. Behaviorally-based assessments that may be less subject to demand characteristics and self-report biases can be particularly informative. Additional research on the impact of gender and/or training level of facilitators along with perceived level of credibility is also warranted (Paul & Gray, 2011). Meta-analyses provide valuable data (Anderson, 2005; Bachar & Koss, 2001). Thus, more meta-analyses are needed. Research on sexual assault prevention programming on college campuses must be an ongoing process, whereby the programs are developed according to theories of attitude and behavior change, adapted to meet the needs of the target population, evaluated, and then revised according to outcome data and participant feedback.

Web-Based Programs

Consistent with current trends in our society often mirrored in campus campaigns for new college students, there is an increasing interest in evaluating web-based sexual assault risk reduction and prevention programs. If found to be effective, web-based programs could be a cost-effective strategy for reaching large audiences with minimal staffing requirements. Given the importance of providing women with the necessary skills to avoid and/or resist potential attackers, it is vital that web-based sexual assault risk reduction programs do more than simply raise awareness regarding sexual assault.

Evaluation through Comparison

Comparison of treatment groups to a non-treatment control group has long been considered problematic in the field of treatment outcome research. Yet, studies that evaluate sexual assault risk reduction programs often fail to implement an equivalent intervention among control participants (that has been shown to not produce the change expected through the treatment condition) while holding consistent other factors and outcomes. Further, participants in the treatment condition (risk reduction program group) might maintain greater investment in program participation than control group members who simply complete questionnaires that collect background information. As such, results of previous studies may be biased by dissimilar comparison between groups. It is therefore necessary for the field of sexual assault intervention research to improve on the validity of standard treatment/no-treatment research design, and look toward evaluating program efficacy using summative evaluation, and comparisons to attention-matched and dose-matched control groups or other risk reduction programs with promising efficacy.

Beyond Single-Session Interventions

Across many evaluative studies, attitude and behavior changes evidenced over short-term follow-up often return to pre-test levels at long-term follow-up (Heppner et al, 1995). In light of data that indicate single-session programs are generally less effective than multiple-session interventions (Anderson & Whiston, 2005), where learning is enhanced by interim reflection before return to additional sessions, it is possible that single-session efforts (one point in time) to reduce risk for sexual assault might not be strong enough to counter the longstanding cultural beliefs and gender inequalities that serve to condone, promulgate and support sexual violence. Given that rates of sexual violence have yet to decline, despite decades of past efforts to raise awareness of violence against women, more intensive sexual assault risk reduction efforts are clearly warranted. Programs that directly engage participants in an active practice of skills and multi-session interventions may be more effective in enhancing women's safety (Paul & Gray, 2011; Vladutiu, Martin & Macy, 2011).

Targeting the Audience

Several researchers contend that sexual assault prevention should be aimed at women who display evidence of situational and behavioral factors that place them at increased risk for assault (Fisher, Daigle & Cullen, 2008), such as women with a history of victimization (Vladitiu et al, 2011). A history of victimization is consistently established as the strongest predictor of future victimization within college populations (Gidycz, Coble, Latham & Layman, 1993; Gidycz et al, 2001). Still in need of improvement, programs have been shown to be less effective for individuals who have a history of sexual assault victimization compared to individuals without this history (Hanson & Gidycz, 1993). Broadly, whenever administering a risk reduction program, it is important to keep it mind that survivors are likely to be in the audience, and that some women will possibly experience victimization if not re-victimization at some point after the intervention. It is therefore important for program content to avoid any inclination that increases the blame for past and/or subsequent assault.

Disclosure

Women who have experienced sexual victimization often go through "secondary victimization," when they are the ones blamed or stigmatized for the incident (Ahrens, 2006). Alarmingly, 25 to 75 percent of women who disclose their experience of sexual victimization receive negative social reactions (Ahrens, 2006). Negative social reactions to disclosure are linked to an array of psychological consequences, including post-traumatic stress disorder and self-blame (Ullman, Townsend, Filipas & Starzynski, 2007). College women are more likely to disclose experiences of sexual victimization to informal support providers, such as family or friends, rather than formal providers, such as the police or staff at a rape crisis center (Orchowski & Gidycz, 2012). Furthermore, women are generally unlikely to seek counseling immediately following an experience of sexual victimization (Frazier, Rosenberger & Moore, 2000). These findings underscore the importance of educating college students on how to effectively respond to sexual assault survivors who choose to disclose their experiences (see related chapter, this volume). Students in leadership positions, such as residential advisors, would benefit especially well from training on how to respond to sexual assault disclosure.

Alcohol as a Risk Factor

Alcohol use is consistently associated with experiences of sexual victimization, severity of victimization, and completed rape (Abbey, Ross, McDuffie & McAuslan, 1996; Koss, Gidycz & Wisniewski, 1987; Ullman, Karabatsos & Koss, 1999). Alarmingly, despite alcohol's known effects on physical coordination and problem-solving, women continue to believe that alcohol will not impair their cognitive abilities when it comes to perceiving risk in dating situations (Cue et al, 1996). When drinking, women are less likely to use physical resistance or verbal assertiveness in response to sexual aggression (Norris et al, 1996). Alcohol consumption increases women's proximity to perpetrators and likelihood of being targeted for an attack (Parks & Zetes-Zanatta, 1999). Further, alcohol may be used as a tactic to lessen a potential victim's inhibition and thus increase the aggressor's chances of obtaining sex. Kanin (1985) found that 76% of rapists, compared to 23% of men without a history of sexual aggression, reported attempting to intoxicate a woman with alcohol in order to have sex with her. These findings highlight the importance of discussing alcohol's role as a risk factor for sexual assault in the context of risk reduction programming. Problematically, sexual assault risk reduction programs have yet to include evidence-based alcohol interventions.

Conclusion

Interventions designed to reduce women's risk for sexual victimization are continuing to evolve and, through evaluative research, important efforts are made to improve those currently in use. Campus administrators are presented with the challenge of assessing the current state of programs in this area, while considering the feasibility of each intervention in relation to cost and the potential for effectiveness with their student population. Given the prevalence of sexual victimization on college campuses and the after-effects of assault, it is important that researchers and advocates continue to search for strategies to reduce rates of campus-based violence. Although only a change in the inclinations and behavior of perpetrators of sexual violence can truly prevent its occurrence, colleges and universities can work to foster a supportive climate that refuses to tolerate sexual assault and provides all women with opportunities to gain pertinent knowledge and relevant skills to avoid victimization by "fighting back."

REFERENCES

Abbey, A., Ross, L. T., McDuffie, D. & McAuslan, P. (1996). "Alcohol and dating risk factors for sexual assault among college women," *Psychology of Women Quarterly, 20*, 147–169.

Ahrens, C. E. (2006). "Being silenced: The impact of negative social reactions on the disclosure of rape," *American Journal of Community Psychology, 38*, 263-274.

Anderson, L. A. & Whiston, S. C. (2005). "Sexual assault education programs: A meta-analytic examination of their effectiveness," *Psychology of Women Quarterly, 29*, 374-288.

Bandura, A. (1969). "*Principles of Behavior Modification,*" New York, NY: Holt, Rinehart and Winston.

Bandura, A. (1977). "*Social Learning Theory,*" New York, NY: General Learning Press.

Banyard, V. L., Moynihan, M. M. & Crossman, M. T. (2009). "Reducing sexual violence on campus: The role of student leaders as empowered bystanders," *Journal of College Student Development, 50*, 446-457.

Banyard, V. L., Moynihan, M. M. & Plante, E. G. (2007). "Sexual violence prevention through bystander education: An experimental evaluation," *Journal of Community Psychology, 35*, 463-481.

Banyard, V. L., Plante, E. G. & Moynihan, M. M. (2004). "Bystander education: Bringing a broader community perspective to sexual violence prevention," *Journal of Community Psychology, 32*, 61-79.

Banyard, V. L., Plante, E. G. & Moynihan, M. M. (2005). "*Rape prevention through bystander education: Final report to NIJ for grant 2002-WG-BX-0009*" [electronic report] www.ncjrs.gov/pdffiles1/nij/grants/208701.pdf.

Berkowitz, A. D. (2003). "Applications of social norms theory to other health and social justice issues," In W Perkins (Ed.), *The Social Norms Approach to Preventing School and College Age Substance Abuse: A Handbook for Educators, Counselors, and Clinicians*, 259–279, San Francisco, CA: Jossey-Bass.

Breitenbecher, K. H. (2000). "Sexual assault on college campuses: Is an ounce of prevention enough," *Applied and Preventative Psychology, 9*, 23-52.

Breitenbecher, K. H. & Gidycz, C. A. (1998). "An empirical evaluation of a program designed to reduce the risk of multiple sexual victimization," *Journal of Interpersonal Violence, 13*, 472-488.

Checkroun, P. & Brauer, M. (2002). "The bystander effect and social control behavior: The effect of the presence of others on people's reactions to norm violations," *European Journal of Social Psychology, 32*, 853–867.

Choudhary, E., Gunzler, D., Tu, X. & Bossarte, R. M. (2012). "Epidemiological characteristics of male sexual assault in a criminological database," *Journal Of Interpersonal Violence*, *27*, 523-546.

Coker, A. L., Cook-Craig, P. G., Williams, C. M., Fisher, B. S., Clear, E. R., Garcia, L. S. & Hegge, L. M. (2011). "Evaluation of Green Dot: An active bystander intervention to reduce sexual violence on college campuses," *Violence Against Women*, *17*, 777-796.

Cue, K. L., George, W. H. & Norris, J. (1996). "Women's appraisals of sexual-assault risk in dating situations," *Psychology of Women Quarterly*, *20*, 487-504.

DeKeseredy, W. S., Schwartz, M. D. & Alvi, S. (2000). "The role of profeminist men in dealing with women on the Canadian college campus," *Violence Against Women*, *6*, 918–935.

Dibonaventura, M. (2009). "*Optimistically biased colon cancer risks: Motivational causes and consequences,"* Dissertations and Theses: A and I, AAT 3319424.

Fisher, B. S., Daigle, L. E. & Cullen, F. T. (2008). "Rape against women: What can research offer to guide the development of prevention programs and risk reduction interventions," *Journal of Contemporary Criminal Justice*, *24*, 163-177.

Foubert, J. D. (2000). "The longitudinal effects of a rape-prevention program on fraternity men's attitudes, behavioral intent, and behavior," *Journal of American College Health*, *48*, 158–163.

Foubert, J. D., Langhinrichsen-Rohling, J., Brasfield, H. & Hill, B. (2010). "Effects of a rape awareness program on college women: Increasing bystander efficacy and willingness to intervene," *Journal Of Community Psychology*, *38*, 813-827.

Foubert, J. D. & Marriott, K. A. (1997). "Effects of a sexual assault peer education program on men's beliefs in rape myths," *Sex Roles*, *36*, 259-268.

Frazier, P., Rosenberger, S. & Moore, N. (2000). "Correlates of service utilization among sexual assault survivors," Poster presented at annual meeting of the American Psychological Association, Washington DC.

Furby, L., Fischhoff, B. & Morgan, M. (1989). "Judged effectiveness of common rape prevention and self-defense strategies," *Journal of Interpersonal Violence*, *4*, 44-64.

Gidycz, C. A. Producer and Director, (2000). "*Keep Your Options Open: Alternative Solutions for Stressful Social Situations*" [Film], Available from Christine A. Gidycz, Department of Psychology, Ohio University, Athens, OH 45701.

Gidycz, C. A., Coble, C. N., Latham, L. & Layman, M. J. (1993). "Sexual assault experience in adulthood and prior victimization experiences: A prospective analysis," *Psychology of Women Quarterly*, *17*, 151-168.

Gidycz, C. A., Loh, C. & Rich, C. L. (2003). "Theories and approaches to preventing sexual crime," In H Kury and J Obergfell-Fuchs (Eds.), *Crime Prevention: New Approaches*, 187–219, Mainz, Germany: Weisser Ring.

Gidycz, C. A., Lynn, S. J., Rich, C. L., Marioni, N. L., Loh, C. & Blackwell, L. M. et al, (2001). "The evaluation of a sexual assault risk reduction program: A multi-site investigation," *Journal of Consulting and Clinical Psychology*, *69*, 1073-1078.

Gidycz, C. A., Orchowski, L. M. & Berkowitz, A. D. (2011). "Preventing sexual aggression among college men: An evaluation of a social norms and bystander intervention program," *Violence Against Women*, *17*, 720-742.

Gidycz, C. A., Orchowski, L. M. & Edwards, K. (2011). "Standards of primary prevention of sexual assault," In M Koss and J White (Eds.), *Violence against Women and Children,*

Volume 2, Navigating Solutions, 159-179, Washington, DC: American Psychological Association.

Gidycz, C. A., Orchowski, L. M., King, C. R. & Rich, C. L. (2008). "Sexual victimization and health-risk behaviors: A prospective analysis of college women," *Journal of Interpersonal Violence*, *23*, 744-763.

Gidycz, C. A., Orchowski, L. M., Probst, D., Edwards, K., Murphy, M. & Tansil, E. in press, "Concurrent administration of sexual assault prevention and risk reduction programming for college students: Outcomes for women," *Violence Against Women.*

Gidycz, C. A., Rich, C. L. & Marioni, N. L. (2002). "Interventions to prevent rape and sexual assault," In J Petrak and B Hedge (Eds.), *The Trauma of Adult Sexual Assault: Treatment, Prevention, and Policy*, 235-260, New York, NY: John Wiley and Sons.

Gidycz, C. A., Rich, C. L., Orchowski, L., King, C. & Miller, A. (2006). "The evaluation of a sexual assault self-defense and risk-reduction program for college women: A prospective study," *Psychology of Women Quarterly*, *30*, 173-186.

Gold, R. S. & Brown, G. (2009). "Explaining the effect of event valence on unrealistic optimism," *Psychology, Health and Medicine*, *14*, 262-272.

Goldman, J. A. & Harlow, L. L. (1993). "Self-perception variables that mediate AIDS-preventive behavior in college students," *Health Psychology*, *12*, 489-498.

Gonzales, A. R., Schofield, R. B. & Schmitt, G. R. (2005). "Sexual assault on campus: What colleges and universities are doing about it," *National Criminal Justice Reference Service* [electronic report] > http://www.ncjrs. gov/pdffiles1/nij/205521.pdf

Gray, M. D., Lesser, D., Quinn, E. E. & Bounds, C. (1990). "The effectiveness of personalizing acquaintance rape prevention: Programs on perceptions of vulnerability and on reducing risk-taking behavior," *Journal of College Student Development*, *31*, 217-220.

Gross, A., Winslett, A., Roberts, M. & Gohm, C. (2006). "An examination of sexual violence against college women," *Violence Against Women*, *12*, 288−300.

Hanson, K. A. & Gidycz, C. A. (1993). "An evaluation of a sexual assault prevention program," *Journal of Consulting and Clinical Psychology*, *61*, 1046-1052.

Helweg-Larsen, M. & Shepperd, A. (2001). "Do moderators of the optimistic bias affect personal or target risk estimates? A review of the literature," *Personality and Social Psychology Review*, *5*, 74-95.

Heppner, M. J., Good, G. E., Hillenbrand-Gunn, T. L., Hawkins, A. K., Hacquard, L. L. & Nichols, R. K. et al, (1995). "Examining sex differences in altering attitudes about rape: A test of the Elaboration Likelihood Model," *Journal of Counseling and Development*, *73*, 640-647.

Heppner, M. J., Humphrey, C. F., Hillenbrand-Gunn, T. L. & Debord, K. A. (1995). "The differential effects of rape prevention programming on attitudes, behavior and knowledge," *Journal of Counseling Psychology*, *42*, 508-518.

Hickman, S. E. & Muehlenhard, L. (1997). "College women's fears and precautionary behaviors relating to acquaintance rape and stranger rape," *Psychology of Women Quarterly*, *21*, 527-547.

Himelein, M. J. (1999). "Acquaintance rape prevention with high-risk women: Identification and inoculation," *Journal of College Student Development*, *40*, 93-96.

Kanin, E. J. (1984). "Date rape: Unofficial criminals and victims." *Victimology*, *9*, 95.

Koss, M. P. (1992). "The underdetection of rape. A critical assessment of incidence data," *Journal of Social Issues*, *48*, 61-76.

Klein, C. T. & Helweg-Larsen, M. (2002). "Perceived control and the optimistic bias: A meta-analytic review," *Psychology and Health*, *17*, 437-446.

Koss, M. P., Gidycz, C. A. & Wisniewski, N. (1987). "The scope of rape: Incidence and prevalence of sexual aggression and victimization in a national sample of higher education students," *Journal of Consulting and Clinical Psychology*, *55*, 162-170.

Koss, M., Goodman, L., Browne, A., Fitzgerald, L., Keita, G. P. & Russo, N. F. (1994). "*No Safe Haven: Male Violence against Women at Home, at Work, and in the Community,*" Washington DC: American Psychological Association.

Koss, M. P., Woodruff, W. J. & Koss, P. G. (1991). "Criminal victimization among primary care medical patients: Prevalence, incidence, and physician usage," *Behavioral Sciences and the Law*, *9*, 85-96.

Leserman, J. (2005). "Sexual abuse history: Prevalence, health effects, mediators, and psychological treatment," *Psychosomatic Medicine*, *67*, 906-915.

Levi, M. (2009). "*The role of affect and personal experience on risk perception involving a motor vehicle accident*," Dissertations and Theses: A and I, AAT 3356957.

Marx, B. P., Calhoun, K. S., Wilson, A. & Meyerson, L. A. (2001). "Sexual revictimization prevention: An outcome evaluation," *Journal of Consulting and Clinical Psychology*, *69*, 25-32.

McCall, G. J. (1993). "Risk factors and sexual assault prevention," *Journal of Interpersonal Violence*, *8*, 277-295.

Najdowski, C. J. & Ullman, S. E. (2011). "The effects of revictimization on coping and depression in female sexual assault victims," *Journal of Traumatic Stress*, *24*, 218-221.

National Association of Student Personnel Administrators, (1994). "*Complying with the final regulations: The Student Right to Know and Campus Security Act*," Washington, DC: National Association of Student Personnel Administrators.

Norris, J., Nurius, P. S. & Dimeff, L. A. (1996). "Through her eyes: Factors affecting women's perception of and resistance to acquaintance sexual aggression threat," *Psychology of Women Quarterly*, *20*, 123-145.

Norris, J., Nurius, P. A. & Graham, T. L. (1999). "When a date changes from fun to dangerous: Factors affecting women's ability to distinguish," *Violence Against Women*, *5*, 230-250.

Nurius, P. S. (2000). "Risk perception for acquaintance sexual aggression: A social-cognitive perspective," *Aggression and Violent Behavior*, *5*, 63-78.

Nurius, P. S. & Norris, J. (1995). "A cognitive ecological model of women's responses to male sexual coercion in dating," *Journal of Psychology and Human Sexuality*, *8*, 117-139.

Oliver, B. E. (2007). "Preventing female-perpetrated sexual abuse," *Trauma, Violence and Abuse*, *8*, 19-32.

Orchowski, L. M. & Gidycz, C. A. (2012). "To whom do college women confide following sexual assault? A prospective study of predictors of sexual assault disclosure and social reactions," *Violence Against Women*, *18*, 264-288.

Orchowski, L. M., Gidycz, C. A. & Murphy, M. (2010). "Preventing campus based sexual violence," In K. Kaufman (Ed.), *Preventing Sexual Violence: A Practitioners' Sourcebook*, pp. 413-446, Holyoke, MA: NEARI Press.

Orchowski, L. M., Gidycz, C. A. & Raffle, H. (2008). "Evaluation of a sexual assault risk reduction and self-defense program: A prospective analysis of a revised protocol," *Psychology of Women Quarterly*, *32*, 204-218.

Park, K., Chang, S. J., Kim, H. C., Park, E. C., Lee, E. S. & Namc, C. M. (2009). "Big gap between risk perception for breast cancer and risk factors: Nationwide survey in Korea," *Patient Education and Counseling*, *76*, 113-119.

Parks, K. A., Miller, B. A., Collins, R. L. & Zetes-Zanatta, L. (1998). "Women's descriptions of drinking in bars: Reasons and risks," *Sex Roles*, *38*, 701-771.

Parks, K. A. & Zetes-Zanatta, L. M. (1999). "Women's bar-related victimization: Refining and testing a conceptual model," *Aggressive Behavior*, *25*, 349-364.

Paul, L. A. & Gray, M. J. (2011). "Sexual assault programming on college campuses: Using social psychological belief and behavior change principles to improve outcomes," *Trauma, Violence and Abuse*, *12*, 99-109.

Peterson, Z. D., Voller, E. K., Polusny, M. A. & Murdoch, M. (2011). "Prevalence and consequences of adult sexual assault of men: Review of empirical findings and state of the literature," *Clinical Psychology Review*, *31*, 1-24.

Petty, R. E. & Cacioppo, J. T. (1986). "Communication and persuasion: Central and peripheral routes to attitude change," New York, NY: Springer-Verlag.

Petty, R. E., Cacioppo, J. T. & Goldman, R. (1981). "Personal involvement as a determinant of argument-based persuasion," *Journal of Personality and Social Psychology*, *41*, 847-855.

Plastow, R. L. (2007). "*Lifestyle and chronic illness: Variables affecting risk perception,*" Dissertations and Theses: A and I, AAT NR17141.

Resnick, H. S., Walsh, K., McCauley, J. L., Schumacher, J. A., Kilpatrick, D. G. & Acierno, R. E. (2012). "Assault related substance use as a predictor of substance use over time within a sample of recent victims of sexual assault," *Addictive Behaviors*, *37*, 914-921.

Rothman, E. & Silverman, J. (2007). "The effect of a college sexual assault prevention program on first-year students' victimization rates," *Journal of American College Health*, *55*, 283-290.

Rushton, J. P. & Campbell, A. C. (1977). "Modeling, vicarious reinforcement, and extraversion on blood donating in adults: Immediate and long term effects," *European Journal of Social Psychology*, *7*, 297-306.

Senn, C. Y., Gee, S. S. & Thake, J. (2011). "Emancipatory sexuality education and sexual assault resistance: Does the former enhance the latter," *Psychology of Women Quarterly*, *35*, 72-91.

Sochting, I., Fairbrother, N. & Koch, W. J. (2004). "Sexual assault of women: prevention efforts and risk factors," *Violence Against Women*, *10*, 73-93.

Sorenson, S. B., Stein, J. A., Seigel, J. M., Golding, J. M. & Burnam, M. A. (1987). "The prevalence of adult sexual assault," *American Journal of Epidemiology*, *126*, 1154-1164.

Steenkamp, M. M., Dickstein, B. D., Salters-Pedneault, K., Hofmann, S. G. & Litz, B. T. (2012). "Trajectories of PTSD symptoms following sexual assault: Is resilience the modal outcome," *Journal of Traumatic Stress*, *25*, 469-474.

Testa, M., VanZile-Tamsen, C., Livingston, J. A. & Koss, M. P. (2004). "Assessing women's experiences of sexual aggression using the Sexual Experiences Survey: Evidence for validity and implications for research," *Psychology of Women Quarterly*, *28*, 256–265.

Tjaden, P. & Thoennes, N. (1998). *"Prevalence, Incidence, and Consequences of Violence against Women: Findings from the National Violence Against Women Survey. Research in Brief,"* Washington, DC: *U.S. Department of Justice.*

Truman, J. L. & Rand, M. R. (2009). *"Criminal victimization in the United States, 2009: National crime victimization survey"* Washington, DC: *US Department of Justice, Bureau of Justice Statistics.*

Ullman, S., Karabatsos, G. & Koss, M. P. (1999). "Alcohol and sexual assault in a national sample of college women," *Journal of Interpersonal Violence*, *14*, 603-625.

Ullman, S. E. & Knight, R. A. (1992). "Fighting back: Women's resistance to rape," *Journal of Interpersonal Violence*, *7*, 31-43.

Ullman, S. E., Townsend, S. M., Filipas, H. H. & Starzynski, L. L. (2007). "Structural models of the relations of assault severity, social support, avoidance coping, self-blame, and PTSD among sexual assault survivors," *Psychology of Women Quarterly*, *31*, 23-37.

Vladutiu, C. J., Martin, S. L. & Macy, R. J. (2011). "College- or university-based sexual assault prevention programs: A review of program outcomes, characteristics, and recommendations," *Trauma, Violence and Abuse*, *12*, 67-86.

Women Against Rape, (1980). "A rape prevention program in an urban area: Community action strategies to stop rape," *Signs*, *5*, 238-241.

Yeater, E. A. & O'Donohue, W. (1999). "Sexual assault prevention programs: Current issues, future directions, and the potential efficacy of interventions with women," *Clinical Psychology Review*, *19*, 739-771.

Yeater, E. A.,Viken, R. J., Hoyt, T. & Dolan, J. L. (2009). "Self-other perspective and sexual attitudes affect estimates of sexual risk," *Sex Roles*, *61*, 110-119.

In: Assaults
Editor: Keith V. Bletzer

ISBN: 978-1-62808-051-3

Chapter 6

THEATRE OF THE OPPRESSED AND SEXUAL ASSAULT PREVENTION

M. Candace Christensen*
Idaho State University, Pocatello, ID, US

ABSTRACT

Using theatre of the oppressed techniques as the basis for sexual assault prevention interventions is becoming increasingly popular. Interventions that use *theatre of the oppressed* aspire to change values and norms that perpetuate the acceptability of sexual assault and teach bystanders how to intervene in situations where sexual violence might occur. This chapter provides an overview of theatre of the oppressed theory and practice, review of scholarship investigating critical pedagogy prevention interventions, and personal stories from theatre of the oppressed practitioners about their experiences using theatre for social change techniques to prevent sexual violence. The goal of this chapter is to provide practitioners and researchers with a general understanding of theatre of the oppressed theory, practice, and research that target sexual violence prevention.

Keywords: Sexual assault, prevention, theatre of the oppressed, critical pedagogy, social change, feminist research

INTRODUCTION

"Cover the space, use every bit of the room, move your bodies, and fill the space" Shireen bids the audience of college students to leave their chairs and become engaged on stage in a presentation aimed at preventing sexual assault in a college student community. "Now, walk very, very slow…" Shireen is playing the Joker for this performance, a facilitator of an interactive drama presentation, who involves audience members in devising new outcomes to dramatic scenarios that depict situations in which sexual violence can occur.

* Corresponding author: Email: mccgalway@gmail.com.

"Freeze! Walk with your heads!" Shireen continues to involve the audience in theatrical warm-up games to prepare them to use their critical thinking skills and body movement to interact with the prevention intervention.

Shireen is a member of revolUtion, a group of college students committed to using theatre of the oppressed techniques to educate college students at the University of Utah about sexual violence prevention. The group was established by seven students that met once a week for eight months to devise a series of dramatic scenarios to portray common situations that illustrate the attitudes and behaviors that perpetuate sexual violence. These college students spent several weeks developing improvisational theatre skills before crafting the scenarios. Developing the improvisation skills provided the students with the flexibility, imagination, and confidence to develop authentic scenes, with which college students could relate. Students collaboratively determined the story each scene would tell and what the learning objectives should be for audience members.

The first scenario takes place at an end-of-the-semester party: a house full of college students, meeting new people, drinking alcohol, and celebrating. Andi is excited to attend the party because Jake is the host and she has a crush on Jake. Andi goes to the party with several friends and once she is there she is encouraged to have one or two drinks and talk to Jake. Andi musters up courage, starts a conversation with Jake, and eventually he convinces her to go up to his room. After spending time with Andi in his room Jake coerces her into having sex.

The second scenario takes place the following morning at Andi's house with her two housemates. The two housemates probe Andi for details about her night with Jake and Andi becomes sad and confused, "I think I might have been raped." One housemate minimizes Andi's interaction with Jake "I'm sure it's just a misunderstanding. Jake is a good guy; he's not a rapist. I'm sure you just had too much to drink." The other housemate catastrophizes the situation: "Andi, we need to call the police right now! You need to see a doctor. I hope you haven't showered. Where are your clothes? We need them for evidence!" Neither housemate considers Andi's feelings before responding to her initial statement. Andi's personal power is diminished each time her housemates tell her what to do, rather than asking what she would prefer to do.

The final scenario takes place several months later and shows Andi on a first date with someone new. Andi seems to be having a great time on the date until her date invites her up to his place for a drink. Andi freezes, unsure how to respond to a benign invitation, which reminds her of how Jake asked her up to his room. Andi's date is confused and offended by her response to his invitation and he ends up calling it an early night, which this leaves Andi feeling alone, guilty, and misunderstood.

The revolution team performs these three scenarios for college audiences. Shireen, as the Joker, asks pointed questions after each scenario is performed: "What did you see in this scene? What is happening? What does the main character want in this scene?" After thoroughly discussing each scenario, the Joker [facilitator] informs the audience that the scenarios will be played again, and this time, the audience has the option to stop the action of the play, jump on stage, and intervene to prevent the violence from occurring. As the scenes are replayed, audience members are shy about jumping on stage, but luckily there is always one brave audience member that steps onstage and prevents the sexual assault from occurring. This audience member paves the way for other students to come up on stage and continue creating solutions to the problematic situations. After an audience member acts out a solution, the Joker asks "What did our volunteer do differently from the original action of the play? Did it work? Are there other possibilities?" Audience members are invited on stage to perform solutions to the problematic scenarios, until the audience is satisfied with the array of potential solutions that one could use to prevent aspects of rape culture from infiltrating the story.

OVERVIEW OF THE PROBLEM

Sexual violence is a devastating social problem that impacts women, girls, boys, and men from all socio-economic classes, races, ages, and parts of the world. The World Health Organization (WHO) defines sexual assault as "any sexual act, attempt to obtain a sexual act, unwanted sexual comments or advances, or acts to traffic, or otherwise directed, against a person's sexuality using coercion, by any person regardless of their relationship to the victim, in any setting, including but not limited to home and work" (2002, p. 149). Sexual violence is a spectrum of behaviors that range from mild non-contact forms that include making unwanted sexual comments and indecent exposure, to the most harmful form which is forcible rape. The terms sexual violence, sexual assault, and rape are often used interchangeably. The U.S. Department of Justice similarly defines *sexual violence* as a cluster of specific crimes that include sexual assault and range from sexual harassment to rape (2009).

In the United States one in five women will be sexually assaulted or experience an attempted assault in her lifetime (Black et al, 2011; Tjaden & Thoennes, 2006). Black and associates (2011) conducted the National Intimate Partner and Sexual Violence Survey (NISVS) and found that 1.3 million women in the U.S. were raped in 2009. The investigators found that almost 80% of the survivors had been raped by a perpetrator before the age of 25 (Black et al, 2011). Although women are the primary targets for rape, men and boys are victimized as well. An estimated 1.6 million men have been raped by a perpetrator at some point in their lifetime, and over 25 million men have experienced some form of sexual violence other than rape (Black et al, 2011).

WHO (2010) describes the impact of sexual violence as a complex trauma that shocks all aspects of a survivor's health (see other chapters, this volume). Physical consequences include injuries to the genitals and other body surfaces, sexually transmitted infections or diseases, and unintended pregnancy (CDC, 2008; WHO, 2010). Psychological effects can result in post-traumatic stress, which is often associated with symptoms of depression, anxiety or adjustment concerns (CDC, 2008; WHO, 2010). Social traumas frequently experienced by the survivor include victim blaming and stigmatization by peers, family, partner, or community members (CDC, 2008; WHO, 2010).

Reporting Sexual Violence

Survivors of sexual assault face many obstacles, when reporting incidents to authorities (National Sexual Violence Reporting Center, 2012). Survivors experience a range of traumatic emotional and physical responses to the assault, which become a barrier to reporting (Archambault & Lonsway, 2006). Survivors are concerned about how reporting the incident will impact their family and friends. Survivors fear that the family system will be disrupted, particularly if the perpetrator is a family member (Campbell & Raja, 1999). Many survivors worry that authorities will not believe them or they will be blamed for the incident, and are they often are pressured by others to not report (National Sexual Violence Reporting Center, 2012). An estimated 63% of incidents of sexual violence are never reported to authorities (Rennison, 2002). The number of false reports in contrast is very low. Lisak and associates (2010) investigated 136 reports of sexual violence over a ten-year period and found that only eight reports were coded as "false."

Acquaintance Rape by Acquiescence

Women agree to have sex because they are coerced, manipulated or threatened into having sex (Tjaden & Thoennes, 2006; Yeater & O'Donohue, 1999; Young, 2009). The majority of sexual assaults are committed by persons known to the survivor (NCVC, 2008). This finding challenges the myth of "stranger rape." Approximately 90 percent of rape survivors know the perpetrator. Basile (1999) created the concept of "rape by acquiescence" after hearing reports of women being coerced into sex through various means of manipulation by the perpetrator using authority, threats of physical and psychological violence, pressure, and begging. "In fact, the more intimate the relationship the more likely it is for a rape to be completed" (Karjane, Fisher & Cullen, 2005, p. 10).

Men and boys are also victims of sexual violence. The National Institute of Justice Special Report found that 111,298 men in the U.S. were raped in 2006; 16.6% of the victims were 18-24 years old at the time of the assault (Christensen, in press; Tjaden & Thoennes, 2006). Many researchers have observed that male survivors also experience severe psychological and social trauma, which can include guilt, anger, depression, self-blame, lack of sexual desire, posttraumatic stress symptoms, and suicidality (Briere & Elliot, 2003; Dube, Anda, Whitfield et al, 2005; Lisak & Luster, 1994; Widom, 1999) all of which parallel the symptoms reported by female survivors. Male rape survivors face victim-blaming from peers, family and the larger community (Dube, Anda, Whitfield et al, 2005; Lisak & Luster, 1994). Recent scholarship thus shatters the myth that most male rape occurs in prison (Lipscomb et al, 1992). Widom and Morris (1997) investigated documented incidents of male sexual abuse, the survivors were asked to identify whether or not they had been abused. Only 16.6% of the men interviewed identified their experience as sexual abuse; and as a result child protection service agencies did not become involved with reported incidents.

Theoretical Frameworks

Theatre of the oppressed practitioners use critical pedagogy theory and theatre for social change theory, because these frameworks are the basis for the practice of theatre of the oppressed and core tenets are compatible with the goals of sexual assault prevention programs. These theories encourage individuals and communities to identify problems and create solutions, rather than have outside experts authorize or define issues and sanctify solutions. The purpose of these theories and practices is to show that using theatre of the oppressed to address sexual violence cultivates intrinsic motivation to explore a given concern, and is essential for advancing critical reflection that leads to taking action that will lead to social justice (Christensen, in press; Christensen, 2013).

Critical pedagogy and theatre of the oppressed theories are compatible with the models used to design sexual assault prevention programs. Many sexual assault prevention programs utilize feminist theory and social learning (Anderson & Whitson, 2005; Carmondy, 2006; Casey, 2009). Sexual assault prevention programs that utilize feminist theory explore how gender construction and socialization can perpetuate or prevent sexual violence (Anderson & Whitson, 2005). Programs that utilize social learning theory emphasize the concept of *modeling*, which is a core element of theatre of the oppressed (Robbins, Chatterjee & Canda, 2006; Rohd, 1998). Modeling engages intervention participants in an educational experience by having them watch their peers perform and/or "model" behavior in seeking to impact the audience through the on-stage performance and motivate them to practice the desired behavior (Robbins et al, 2006).

Critical Pedagogy theory encourages teachers and students to critique and analyze how we can build educational institutions, policies, and practices to achieve social change (McGettigan, 1999). Paolo Friere first proposed Critical Pedagogy theory with his book *Pedagogy of the Oppressed* (1970), which he wrote to illustrate a new method of teaching and learning he developed from his experiences teaching literacy to farm-workers in Brazil during the 1950's and 1960's (Dimitriadis & Kamberelis, 2006; Paulo Friere Institute UCLA, 2011). Friere argued that the goal of education is to bring communities together for dialogue, facilitate an understanding of a community's social reality, and encourage community members to critically reflect upon that reality. Through critical reflection, the community should be inspired to take action to transform community problems into solutions, a process Friere called "Praxis" (1970).

There are several key concepts from the *Pedagogy of the Oppressed* that need to be explained. One concept is "Limited Situations," which are situations where tangible social forces prevent people from living the life they want to live. Friere spent time with oppressed communities to help them visualize solutions to social problems. He would ask communities to generate words that describe this new life. These words hold strong emotional content for the community, which means that defining these words has the capacity to confront the social reality the community currently experiences. Words used as a starting point for teaching literacy were known as "Generative Words." Another concept is how educators can raise consciousness in students, termed "*Conscientization*" which is Portuguese for "critical consciousness," which means achieving a complex, nuanced understanding of the world and socio-political forces that shape one's daily experience. These practices culminate in Praxis, which is born from critical reflection turned into action in an effort to change the oppressive situations. Praxis is the process by which a concept or skill is practiced and embodied. When educators facilitate a "Dialogue" between students with the goal of creating *conscientization*, they hope that students will eventually use *conscientization* to engage in Praxis. Dialogue with people who have shared oppressive experiences and struggles is a necessary component of creating solidarity, which is essential to liberation and transformation (Dimitriadis & Kamberelis, 2006; Friere, 1970).

Theatre for Social Change

Augusto Boal worked as a teacher for Paolo Friere and was inspired by Friere's theories for creating change within communities. In response to Friere's work, Boal wrote *Theatre of the Oppressed* in 1973 as the theatrical response to *Pedagogy of the Oppressed.* Boal remarks: "Theatre is a form of knowledge; it should and can also be a means of transforming society. Theatre can help us build our future, rather than just waiting for it" (1992, p. xxxi). Boal continually refined and developed the philosophy and practice of using theatre as a tool for social change through writing, practicing with communities, and mentoring novice practitioners (Babbage, 2004).

Boal wanted to make theatre a tangible, workable art form aimed at ameliorating oppressive forces so the masses could live meaningful, unhampered lives (Babbage, 2004; Boal, 1985). His mission was to transform the passive audience member into an active performer on stage and, ultimately, in the community where she/he lives. Boal asserted that we are all actors wearing masks and performing to scripts that oppressive systems have written for us. Techniques for theatre of the oppressed utilize the precepts of Freire's *Pedagogy of the Oppressed.* A practitioner engages the community in dialogue to reveal oppressive situations that are limiting. Dialogue raises the community's awareness on how these situations could be changed. Finally everyone is inspired to rehearse the changes to these situations by stepping on stage and acting-out dialogue and behavior that demonstrate realistic solutions to real problems (Babbage, 2004; Boal, 1985).

Michael Rohd, a protégé of Augusto Boal, synthesized theatre of the oppressed techniques and applied them to tangible skills that could be used with a variety of populations in a variety of settings (1998). Rohd devised the manual *Theatre for Community, Conflict, and Dialogue* (1998), which utilizes exercises from Boal, Viola Spolin, and Anthony Jackson. The manual provides theatre of the oppressed practitioners with tools to develop a community-centered, interactive performance troupe. The troupe is prepared to enter a community, facilitate dialogue and train members how to use theatre of the oppressed techniques and collaboratively develop solutions to problems identified by the community (Rohd, 1998).

Sexual Assault Prevention

Critical Pedagogy Theory and Theatre of the Oppressed Theory have been utilized as the basis for sexual violence programs all over the world (International Theatre of the Oppressed Organization, 2012). Many universities in the United States, Canada, South America, United Kingdom, and Australia have developed programs that utilize theatre of the oppressed theory and practice as the basis for sexual assault prevention programs. The University of Utah, University of Texas at Austin, University of Oregon in Eugene, California State University at Long Beach, and University of North Carolina in Chapel Hill are a few sites that put these theories into practice. Many grassroots community organizations utilize these tools as well. Aarohan, a theatre group in Nepal has been in existence since 1982 and is known for utilizing theatre of the oppressed techniques to work with caste discrimination, violence against women, corruption, and disability. Dahlia Sabbour in Cairo, Egypt, utilizes theatre of the oppressed to work with adolescents to raise awareness on issues that impact women and girls.

Many theatre companies in the United States and Canada utilize theatre of the oppressed techniques to address a multitude of social issues. All Nations Theatre Society in Calgary, Center for Applied Theatre in Wisconsin, Citizens Dialogues in Washington State, and GTC Dramatic Dialogues in Chicago are a few of the many grassroots organizations that employ these theories and techniques (International Theatre of the Oppressed Organization, 2012).

Epstein and Langenbahn (1999) wrote *The Criminal Justice and Community Response to Rape*, which documents key reforms made by sexual violence prevention task forces in the United States to address sexual violence. The authors conducted a review of sexual violence prevention interventions and asserted that "theatrical presentations can simultaneously educate and entertain, adapting concerns to the interests, vocabularies and attention spans of their audiences" (Epstein & Langenbahn, 1994, p. 80). Since 1994, many scholars have conducted studies which illustrate that theatre-based interventions provide more effective learning than didactic methods (De los Rios Castillo & Sanchez-Sosa, 2002; Grey, Boland, Davidson & Tamborlane, 2000; Margalit, Glick & Benbassat, 2004). Researchers Millhausen, McBride, and Jun claim, "It is proposed that the interactive format results in a deeper level of processing and more attitude change than a lecture or structured presentation" (2006, p. 318).

Scholars have been debating for forty years about how to better define and effectively prevent sexual violence (Kimmel, 2002; Yodanis, 2004). Scholars agree that the causes of sexual violence are complex and as a result require multi-faceted prevention strategies (World Health Organization, 2012; Center for Disease Control, 2010). The most successful approach to ameliorating a social problem is to engage several different prevention strategies that stimulate the target population to grow, change, and take action within their communities (World Health Organization, 2012; Centers for Disease Control and Prevention, 2010). Theatre of the Oppressed engages people on many different levels: it forces the community members to critically reflect on the root cause of social problems, develop community-centered solutions, and practice the solution for other community members to obtain feedback.

Theatre-based prevention interventions have been increasingly utilized and evaluated as an effective tool for preventing sexual violence. Scholars began investigating the impact that theatre-based interventions were having with college student populations in the 1990's (Frazier, Valitson, & Candell, 1994; Lanier et al, 1998). Initial findings revealed that these interventions have the potential to significantly impact attitudes and behaviors that perpetuate sexual violence.

Frazier and associates (1994) evaluated an interactive, improvisational theatre rape prevention program, targeting members of fraternities and sororities. They used a quasi-experimental design with a treatment group and comparison group. They measured the impact of the intervention with designated scales that included an Attitudes toward Sexual Behavior scale (Bechhofer, 1990), Gender Role Beliefs (Burt, 1980), and Attitudes toward Dating Behaviors (Frazier et al, 1994). Quantitative results showed that the treatment group had significantly lower scores than the control group, immediately following the intervention; however, follow-up scores showed an equalization effect with no significant difference between the groups. These findings demonstrate that utilizing theatre of the oppressed techniques to prevent sexual violence shows promise as a prevention tool. Further research is needed to identify how to create a lasting change with target populations.

In the past twelve years the number of studies has increased substantially of interventions that were used in theatre of the oppressed aimed at sexual assault prevention. There is growing interest in quantitative studies that investigate the impact theatre-based prevention interventions have on variables associated with sexual violence perpetration (Black et al, 2000; Millhausen et al, 2006; Rodriguez et al, 2006). Researchers have measured how these interventions impact beliefs and behaviors associated with perpetuating the acceptability of sexual violence. Variables associated with beliefs and behaviors include the acceptance of rape myths, concepts of traditional gender roles/stereotypes, ability to empathize with and comfort survivors, and beliefs about sexual behaviors. Qualitative research exploring theatre of the oppressed techniques has had a recent emergence in sexual violence prevention literature (Brigell, 2010; Christensen, 2013; Pomeroy et al, 2011). Qualitative research provides a contextual, descriptive, nuanced illustration of how study participants experience theatre of the oppressed, sexual assault prevention programs.

Black and associates (2000) produced a theatre-based sexual assault prevention intervention aimed at college students. They measured participant responses with the Revised Rape Myths Acceptance Scale (Newman & Colon, 1994) by having participants in experimental/control groups complete the measure before and after the intervention (pre/post design). The post-test mean scores for the intervention participants were significantly lower than the pretest scores at p=.007 value, and there was a significant difference between the intervention group scores and control group scores. A calculation of effect sizes show that while there was a difference between two sets of scores, the difference was medium (Mean = .57). These findings underscore the continuing need for future research. Practitioners and activists that support theatre of the oppressed as a prevention intervention are utilizing an evidence-based prevention tool. It is essential that we explore which aspects of the intervention are effective and how these variables can be used to create lasting change with the target populations.

Rodriguez and associates (2006) developed a troupe called InterACT that utilized theatre of the oppressed to change attitudes and behaviors that perpetuate sexual violence. They conducted a quasi-experimental study that tested the impact of an interactive, theatrical performance aimed at sexual violence prevention with college students. They established a treatment group, control group and comparison group. The treatment group experienced the theatrical intervention; the comparison group listened to a didactic lecture on sexual violence prevention; the control group watched a movie on an unrelated topic. The researchers designed a quantitative measure that evaluated how attitudes associated with sexual assault prevention change after experiencing the InterACT performance. Variables on the instrument were perspective taking, emotional contagion, empathic concern, and comforting. The completed post-test measures revealed significant differences between all three groups, where the intervention/treatment group obtained the highest scores. The researchers did not conduct a follow-up *data capture*. Nonetheless, their findings illustrate that utilizing theatre of the oppressed to prevent sexual violence is evolving and becoming a more precise, refined prevention tool.

Brigell (2010) explored the impact of a participatory theatre program developed at the Escuela Equinoccio of Centro Bartolome de las Casas (CBC) located in San Salvador, El Salvador. The intervention was developed as a community program aimed at preventing gender-based violence among men, women, and adolescents. Intervention developers utilized theatre of the oppressed to create an interactive workshop aimed at deconstructing masculine gender socialization. Brigell conducted in-depth interviews with workshop participants and staff who developed the program. The author found that utilizing theatre of the oppressed techniques to raise awareness about gender-based violence is more effective than didactic or lecture style teaching, because theatre-based techniques provide study participants with real life situations where such violence occurs and skills to use in those situations. Another finding is that participating in workshops has changed how everyone involved with the project interacts with family, friends, and the larger community. Individuals expressed an increased awareness of attitudes and behaviors that perpetuate gender-based violence and taking action when confronted by problematic attitudes and behaviors.

Pomeroy and associates (2011) conducted a pilot study with a mixed methods design, comparing differences between peer education presentations where one was theater-focused and one was traditional, and a comparison group. The researchers conducted six focus groups two months prior and two months after implementing the intervention to explore attitudes about intimate partner violence (IPV) with social work students in an introductory social work course. Their findings indicated that both peer education presentations increased the students' knowledge and promoted healthier attitudes about IPV. However, students that participated in the theater presentation expressed a greater sense of self-efficacy and ability to integrate inter-disciplinary concepts regarding IPV than students that experienced only the traditional peer education presentation.

Finally, I conducted a qualitative evaluation of a theatre-based sexual assault prevention program that targeted college students (Christensen, 2013). With assistance from the University of Utah Women's Resource Center, I recruited seven college students to develop the intervention utilizing theatre of the oppressed techniques. This group of students performed the intervention for five different college classes. I conducted focus groups with the students of the class eliciting information about how they experienced the intervention. Through careful data analysis I found the intervention encouraged study participants to acquire an ethic of care for their community/peers, deconstruct social norms, and appreciate the need for co-constructing knowledge. In the focus groups, students discussed how the intervention inspired them to think deeply about language and behaviour they or their peers use and how this critical reflection inspired them to subvert social norms that perpetuate sexual violence. The students also said the intervention encouraged them to take responsibility for one another and take action in situations in which a peer might perpetrate sexual violence. Study members stated that they appreciated how the intervention encouraged them to collaboratively construct solutions to the problem. Qualitative investigations of sexual assault prevention provide valuable information about how values and attitudes can be changed to create a culture where college students take responsibility for preventing the behavioral supports that perpetuate sexual violence. Qualitative methods such as these can uncover aspects of a phenomenon not open to quantitative investigation.

Common themes across quantitative and qualitative studies pave a path for future research investigating the use of theatre of the oppressed interventions for sexual violence prevention. Findings from a study by Frazier, Valitson, and Candell (1994)assert that we need to conduct more research that evaluates theatre-based prevention interventionsso that we can establish how the intervention will work with distinct settings and communities to have a lasting impact on study participants. It is possible that more than one intervention session is needed for study participants to absorb the material and apply new knowledge into their daily behaviors; they may need exposure to values and beliefs that prevent sexual violence over the course of several months and at multiple intervals. Black and associates (2000) offered similar findings, researchers were not able to predict the long-term impact the theatre-based intervention might have on study participants, because they did not conduct a follow-up data capture. In tandem with the previous two studies, Rodriguez and associates (2006) were not able to evaluate the long-term impact that theatre of the oppressed had on study participants, because they did not conduct a follow-up data capture. However, building on previous research, Rodriguez and associates developed a measure that assessed specific variables associated with sexual assault prevention, such as empathy, ability to comfort a survivor, and emotional contagion. They were able to assess which variables were significantly affected by the theatre-based intervention.

Qualitative research that has investigated theatre of the oppressed sexual violence prevention programs does not always provide answers to questions left by many of the quantitative studies. Brigell (2010), for example, found that engaging community members in the development of a theatre of the oppressed intervention extended change beyond specific study participants, by taking this new knowledge into families and friendship networks. Pomeroy and associates (2011) analyzed why and how theatre-based prevention interventions have a more integrated and realistic impact on students versus a traditional didactic presentation. They found that theatre-based presentations illustrate through overt demonstration how they can intervene in problematic situations. Study participants have the opportunity to practice intervening exactly how they would in real life, because theatre of the oppressed draws audience members on stage to rehearse for incidents that are likely to encounter. In my own research I have delved into experiences of participants who had gained a sense of "study membership" and found that their values and perceptions were changed after experiencing the intervention (see Christensen, 2013). Participants were inspired to embody an ethic of care within their community, particularly in situations where sexual violence can occur. Study *members*, as it were, discussed how the intervention inspired them to subvert social norms that perpetuate sexual violence and said that they appreciated the opportunity to develop their own solutions to the problem, rather than have ideas handed to them by experts outside their community. The intervention inspired participants to develop key skills to assist them with preventing sexual violence in their community, and assist them with addressing social problems in a variety of settings, well beyond their experiences on a university campus.

Dialogue with Practitioners

I invited three practitioners of theatre of the oppressed to have a conversation with me about personal perspectives and unique experiences in utilizing theatre of the oppressed to prevent sexual violence. I asked each colleague to answer three questions, as mentioned below.

Shireen

The first colleague we will meet is Shireen Ghorbani, is a PhD Candidate in the Department of Communication at the University of Utah. She is currently working on her dissertation focused on organizational responses to violence in the context of campus sexual assault. Shireen has an extensive background in theatre and has been using theatre of the oppressed techniques in various capacities for many years. Shireen participated in creating revolUtion, mentioned at the beginning of this chapter, and has acted as the Joker for over a year in revolUtion performances.

1. What drew you to Theatre of the Oppressed for sexual violence prevention?
   In my undergraduate years, I studied theatre and, through the communication department, became interested in performance studies and Theatre of the Oppressed. At the same time, I started in small ways working on sexual violence prevention and education. At that time, theatre seemed like a great platform to imagine a something different. That something different might be a world where one in five college students do not experience sexual violence, where women feel safe on campus, in their homes and communities, or where LGBTQ [Lesbian-Gay-Bisexual-Transgender-Questioning] people are able to express their love without violent consequences. In some ways, we are far from that world now and I believe making communities safer for all people will require some radical and creative thinking. Theatre of the Oppressed provides the perfect platform for that kind of knowledge building and creative critical thinking.
2. Tell me why you think that Theatre of the Oppressed is an effective tool for sexual violence prevention?
   In many ways, theatre generally, and Theatre of the Oppressed specifically, help generate creative and different ways of thinking about life circumstances. In TO exercises [as *Theatre of the Oppressed* is called among practitioners], participants are often asked to focus on body awareness, word choice, tone, and other aspects of communication. Through developing that sense of awareness, students have the opportunity to see, in very plain ways, how bodies present themselves to be potentially inviting or threatening. Helping students develop a sense of awareness in social contexts is endlessly valuable.
3. Can you share one or two "success stories" about the impact that theatre of the oppressed has on sexual violence prevention?
   It can be difficult to define success stories in this line of work. I feel hopeful in presentations where, through interaction and role play, students get to explore making different choices when faced with situations that might be difficult to navigate. For example, one role play that I've used a lot deals with helping students make plans for staying in communication after a party. It might be awkward for young people to initiate conversations about picking a designated driver or leaving a party together at the end of the night. When students get to practice those conversations, they develop a sense of personal confidence in initiating that kind of talk.

Alexis

Alexis V. Arczynski is the next practitioner to respond to the questions. Alexis is a doctoral candidate in Counseling Psychology at the University of Utah. She uses a feminist multicultural approach in her clinical work, thus, activism and social change are foundational to her personal and professional lives. Alexis participated in the development and implementation of revolUtion and played the role of Andi.

1. What drew you to using Theatre of the Oppressed for sexual violence prevention?
   Most of my clinical training and practice has been focused on inter-personal violence (e.g., child abuse, sexual violence), and I wanted a chance to look at ways outside of the therapy room to create change in communities. As part of my practicum experience with the Women's Resource Center, I was given the chance to be involved with preventing violence against women. Coming from training focused on individual or group intervention, I had no idea what prevention work would look like. However, I yearned for the opportunity to prevent violence. Therefore, I jumped at the opportunity. Honestly, I was willing to do whatever the training team threw at me. When I started working with Candace [chapter author], I did not know what she would ask of me. I found that the using Theatre of the Oppressed had a better shot in hell of changing the culture on my college campus than other prevention methods. Working in revolUtion was a life-changing experience. I loved helping audience members feel empathy for the experience of sexual violence survivors. I found the experience of getting participants to see their role in rape culture a welcomed challenge. Through empathy and recognition of culpability versus blaming violence solely on the survivor or the perpetrator, participants became willing to change their behavior as bystanders.
2. Tell me why you think that Theatre of the Oppressed is an effective tool for sexual violence prevention?
   Theatre of the Oppressed allows for institutional and cultural change versus individual change. Thus, change can be more widespread than in methods focusing on the survivor or perpetrator. Theatre of the Oppressed uses peers as educators. Peers can be experts in behavioral change and can foster change in others much easier than the identified experts (e.g., presenters). It is a modality that gets people into a mindset of changing cultural and community norms and forces people to recognize the part they play in violence even if they have never been a perpetrator. Further, when engaged, participants seem to become less defensive ("Hey, I'm not a rapist, so this doesn't apply to me") and *othering* (e.g., "It's not me – it's that guy"). Participants seem to get energized by the experience which makes change happen.
3. Can you share one or two "success stories" about the impact that Theatre of the Oppressed can have on sexual violence prevention?
   Honestly, I feel that my involvement with a very small, tight-knit student group was a huge success story. Participants took an active role in changing their college campus. Some of us were scared by the opportunity to engage in Theatre of the Oppressed prevention, but each member took the role of being an agent of change seriously. As the veil of silence surrounding sexual violence and rape culture was lifted, members took charge, and I valued seeing them take ownership of engaging with same aged peers.

Rebecca

Our third practitioner is Rebecca Adelman Brown. Rebecca, the director of The Interactive Theatre Project, which she co-founded in 1999. The Interactive Theatre Project, at the University of Colorado at Boulder, uses theatre as a medium for education, dialogue and social change. She is also a long time ensemble member of Playback Theatre West, a Colorado-based theatre and improvisational company. An actor, writer and director Rebecca has performed and been involved in dozens of Colorado and New York productions. Rebecca has a MA in drama therapy from New York University.

1. What drew you to Theatre of the Oppressed for sexual violence prevention?
   The first time I ever saw a Theatre of the Oppressed performance was in NYC. It was led by Augusto Boal and, I believe, addressed sexual harassment. The room was "on fire." It was incredibly exciting. Sexual violence prevention needs to be a community conversation. Nothing changes when someone is told not to do something. They have to be challenged by their peers to think and act differently within a community context.
2. Tell me why you think that Theatre of the Oppressed is an effective tool for sexual violence prevention?
   We have a Theatre of the Oppressed performance on sexual violence prevention that we perform during student orientation at the University. It is one of the first opportunities where 350 incoming students can talk to each other rather than be "talked at" and given information. For years we performed the presentation as a question-and-answer session with characters staying in role and talking to the audience. The last several years it has been performed as a forum theatre piece with audience members coming up on the stage to take the role of a bystander and to change what is taking place at the party.
3. Can you share one or two "success stories" about the impact that theatre of the oppressed has on sexual violence prevention?
   The first one that comes to mind is one of my favorites. Many years ago we had a public performance of our piece entitled, "Just Another Party," for Sexual Assault Awareness Month in April. We had done this performance for Orientation during the summer and wanted to have another performance of it for the community [everyone on campus] and not just incoming students. At the beginning I asked people why they were at the performance. A guy raised his hand and said that he saw the performance at orientation and thought it was a load of "BS". Then he started going to parties and realized that after several months in college he had seen more situations like "Just Another Party" than he could have imagined. He came to the performance again this time with a more open mind and to further challenge his perspective. It was amazing. I wish I had it on film.
   Another favorite moment that sticks in my mind is when we were doing the performance utilizing theatre of the oppressed Forum Theatre techniques. A young man came up on stage and asked that we take the performance from the party dance moment (there is a moment when all the characters are dancing to music and then go to take shots). As the actor went to grab the bottle of booze, the young man stopped him, asked for the music to continue and grabbed the actor and continued dancing. It

was just a great moment. This young man ended up auditioning for our interactive theatre ensemble and becoming a member!

I have one more incident that is very moving to me. A young woman audience member during the debrief portion of the performance, stood and told the audience about her aunt and how her aunt had been sexually assaulted. She became overcome with emotion and couldn't speak. The audience started applauding in support of her. She took a breath and continued her story. Theatre, particularly interactive theatre, allows people to approach gender violence from a heart place, an undefended place. This openness is very important if we want change to occur.

CONCLUSION

It takes a great deal of energy, initiative, support, and community involvement to establish Theatre of the Oppressed interventions aimed at preventing sexual violence. Given that sexual violence is an epidemic world-wide, in the U.S., and in local communities, garnering energy, support, and community involvement is necessary and possible. I would encourage violence prevention scholars and practitioners to begin with a small, manageable pilot program that utilizes a few theatre of the oppressed techniques. Evaluate this program by conducting formal or informal focus groups with audience members and use this information to refine and re-focus the intervention. Community support and interest in projects will grow as the intervention is refined. Theatre of the oppressed is a well-developed theory and practice that has been used to solve social problems in communities for over 50 years. There is a growing body of research that evaluates the impact using theatre of the oppressed has on preventing sexual violence. Findings from this research support efforts to continue developing theatre-based interventions and evaluating their outcomes. The more we investigate these interventions to identify successful core elements, the more effective they will become.

In this chapter, I invited Theatre of the Oppressed practitioners to provide readers with a more personal and tangible view of how theatre of the oppressed can have impacts, by those who use it and those who experience the interventions. The three practitioners each have a unique perspective on why they feel theatre of the oppressed is an effective tool to use in sexual violence prevention. Finally, my hope is for readers to have a greater appreciation for the transformative power that theatre of the oppressed can have with communities of students as well as others whose lives who affected by oppressive conditions. These techniques inspire individuals to talk about topics normally *that are often* kept hidden and unvoiced, to devise better solutions to these serious problems, and create a safe space to rehearse solutions with feedback from community members. Practices based on theatre of the oppressed have the potential to dramatically change how we engage in violence prevention.

REFERENCES

Anderson, L. A. & Whitson, S. C. (2005). "Sexual assault education programs: A meta-analytic investigation of their effectiveness," *Psychology of Women Quarterly*, *29*, 374-388.

Archambault, J. & Lonsway, K. A. (2006). "Dynamics of sexual assault: What does sexual assault really look like?" Revised 2008 edition, End Violence Against Women International's On-Line Training Institute, Retrieved from > http://evawintl.org/onlinetraining.aspx

Babbage, F. (2004). *Augusto Boal,* New York, NY: Routledge.

Basile, K. C. (1999). "Rape by acquiescence: The ways in which women "give in" to unwanted sex with their husbands," *Violence Against Women*, *5*, 1036-1058.

Bechhofer, L. (1990), "Diverget perceptions of men and women and the risk of date rape," Paper presented at the annual meeting of Society for the Scientific Study of Sex, Minneapolis, MN.

Black, B., Weisz, A., Coats, S. & Patterson, D. (2000). "Evaluating a psychoeducational sexual assault prevention program incorporating theatrical presentation, peer education, and social work," *Research on Social Work Practice*, *10*(5), 589-606.

Black, M. C., Basile, K. C., Breiding, M. J., Smith, S. G., Walters, M. L., Merrick, M. T., Chen, J. & Stevens, M. R. (2011). *The National Intimate Partner and Sexual Violence Survey (NISVS): 2010 Summary Report*, Atlanta, GA: National Center for Injury Prevention and Control, Centers for Disease Control and Prevention.

Boal, A. (1985). *Theatre of the Oppressed*, CA McBride and ML McBride, Translators, New York, NY: Theatre Communications Group (Original work published 1973).

Boal, A. (1992). *Games for Actors and Non-Actors*, London, UK: Routledge.

Brigell, M. (2010). "Participatory theatre and the prevention of gender-based violence," *Advocate's Forum 2010,* The University of Chicago School of Social Service Administration, Chicago, IL: Retrieved from > http://www.ssa.uchicago.edu/publications/advforum/AF-2010.pdf#page=20

Briere, J. & Elliot, D. M. (2003). "Prevalence and psychological sequelae of self-reported childhood physical and sexual abuse in a general population sample of men and women," *Child Abuse and Neglect*, *27*, 1205–1222.

Burt, M. (1980). "Cultural myths and supports for rape," *Journal of Personality and Social Psychology*, *38*(2), 217-230.

Campbell, R. & Raja, S. (1999). "Secondary victimization of rape victims: Insights from mental health professionals who treat survivors of violence," *Violence and Victims*, *14*(3), 261-275.

Carmondy, M. (2006). "Preventing adult sexual violence through education?" *Current Issues in Criminal Justice*, *18*(2), 342-356.

Casey, E. (2009). *Promising Practices in Sexual Violence Prevention*, Report released by City of Seattle Government, Seattle, WA.

Centers for Disease Control and Prevention, (2010). *Injury Prevention and Control: Violence Prevention*, Atlanta, GA: Retrieved from > http://cdc.gov/ViolencePrevention/

Centers for Disease Control and Prevention, (2008). *Sexual Violence: Facts at a Glance*, Atlanta, GA: Retrieved from > http://www.cdc.gov/violenceprevention/pdf/SV-DataSheet-a.pdf

Centers for Disease Control and Prevention, (2004). *Sexual Violence Prevention: Beginning the Dialogue*, Atlanta, GA: Retrieved from > http://www.cdc.gov/ncipc/dvp/SVPrevention.pdf

Christensen, M. C. in press, "Using theatre of the oppressed to address sexual violence against women on college campuses," *Trauma, Abuse, and Violence* (accepted).

Christensen, M. C. (2013). “Engaging theatre for social change to address sexual violence against college women: A qualitative investigation,” *British Journal of Social Work* (online) Retrieved from > http://bjsw.oxfordjournals.org/cgi/content/full/bct006?ijkey=1Ds3hpm80jgYJlO&keytype=re (online)

Creswell, J. W. & Plano Clark, V. (2011). *Designing and Conducting Mixed Methods Research* (Second edition) Thousand Oaks, CA: Sage Publications.

De los Rıos Castillo, J. L. & Sanchez-Sosa, J. J. (2002). “Well-being and medical recovery in the critical care unit: The role of the nurse-patient interaction,” *Salud Mental*, *25*, 21-31.

Dimitriadis, G. & Kamberelis, K. (2006). *Theory for Education*. New York, NY: Routledge.

Dube, S. R., Anda, R. F. & Whitfield, C. L. et al, (2005). “Long-term consequences of childhood sexual abuse by gender of victim,” *American Journal of Preventive Medicine*, *28*, 430-438.

Epstein, J. & Langenbahn, E. (1999). *The Criminal Justice and Community Response to Rape: Issues and Practices*, Washington, DC: U.S. Department of Justice, National Institute of Justice, NCJ #148064.

Fisher, B. S., Cullen, F. T. & Turner, G. T. (2000). *The Sexual Victimization of College Women* (NCJ Publication Number 182369), Retrieved from > https://www.ncjrs.gov/pdffiles1/nij/182369.pdf

Frazier, P., Valtinson, G. & Candell, S. (1994). “Evaluation of a coeducational interactive rape prevention program,” *Journal of Counseling & Development*, *73*(2), 153-158.

Friere, P. (1970). *Pedagogy of the Oppressed*. New York, NY: Continuum.

Grey, M., Boland, E. A., Davidson, M., Li, J. & Tamborlane, W. V. (2000). “Coping skills training for youth with diabetes mellitus has long-lasting effects on metabolic control and quality of life,” *Journal of Pediatrics*, *137*, 107–113.

Humphrey, S. E. & Kahn, A. S. (2000). “Fraternities, athletic teams, and rape: Importance of identification with a risky group,” *Journal of Interpersonal Violence*, *15*, 1313-1322.

Joronen, K., Rankin, S. & Astedt-Kurki, P. (2008). “School-based drama interventions in health promotion for children and adolescents: Systematic review,” *Journal of Advanced Nursing*, *63*(2), 116-131. doi: 10.1111/j.1365-2648.2008.04634.x

Karjane, H. M., Fisher, B. S. & Cullen, F. T. (2005). *Sexual Assault on Campus: What Colleges and Universities are Doing about It*, National Institute of Justice, U.S. Department of Justice.

Kimmel, M. S. (2002). “Gender Symmetry,” Domestic Violence: A Substantive and Methodological Research Review (Special Topic), *Violence against women*, *8*(11), 1332-1363.

Lanier, C., Elliott, M., Martin, D. & Kapadia, A. (1998). “Evaluation of an intervention to change attitudes toward date rape,” *Journal of American College Health*, *46*(4), 177-180.

Lipscomb, G. H. et al, (1992). “Male victims of sexual assault,” *Journal of General Internal Medicine*, *19*, 485-491.

Lisak, D. & Luster, L. (1994). “Educational, occupational and relationship histories of men who were sexually and/or physically abused as children,” *Journal of Traumatic Stress*, *7*, 507–523.

Lisak, D., Gardinier, L., Nicksa, S. C. & Cote, A. M. (2010). “False allegations of sexual assault: An analysis of ten years of reported cases,” *Violence Against Women*, 16, 1318-1334.

Margalit, A. P. A., Glick, S. M. & Benbassat, J. (2004). "Effect of a bio-psychosocial approach on patient satisfaction and patterns of care," *Journal of General Internal Medicine*, *1*, 485-491.

McGettigan, P. (1999). *Radical Pedagogy: What is Radical Pedagogy?* International Consortium for Academic Publication, Retrieved from > http://radicalpedagogy.icaap.org/content/issue1_1/mcgettigan.html.

Milhausen, R. R., McBride, K. R. & Jun, M. K. (2006). "Evaluating a peer-led, theatrical sexual assault prevention program: How do we measure success," *College Student Journal*, *40*(2), 316-328.

National Center for Victims of Crime, (2008). *Acquaintance Rape*, Retrieved from > http://www.ncvc.org/NCVC/main.aspx?dbName=DocumentViewer&DocumentID=32306.

National Sexual Violence Resource Center, (2012). *Crime Reports of Sexual Violence*, (online) Retrieved from > http://nsvrc.org/sites/default/files/Publications_NSVRC_Factsheet_Media-Packet_Crime-reports-sexual-violence.pdf.

Newman, B. S. & Colon, I. (1994). "Beliefs about rape among college males: A revision of the Rape Myth Acceptance Scale," *College Student Journal*, *28*(1), 10-17.

Paulo Friere Institute UCLA, (2011). "About Paulo Friere / Work," Retrieved from > http://web.gseis.ucla.edu/~pfi//index.html.

Pomeroy, E., Parrish, D. E., Bost, J., Cowlagi, G., Cook, P. & Stepura, K. (2011). "Educating students about interpersonal violence: Comparing two methods," *Journal of Social Work Education*, *47*(3), 525-544.

Rennison, C. A. (2002). "Rape and sexual assault: Reporting to police and medical attention, 1992-2000" [NCJ 194530] U.S. Department of Justice, Office of Justice Programs, Bureau of Justice Statistics, Washington, DC: Retrieved from > http://bjs.ojp.usdoj.gov/content/pub/pdf/rsarp00.pdf.

Robbins, S., Chatterjee, P. & Canda, E. (2006). *Human Behavior Theory* (Second Edition) Boston, MA: Simon and Schuster.

Rodríguez, J. I., Rich, M. D., Hastings, R. & Page, J. L. (2006). "Assessing the impact of Augusto Boal's 'proactive performance': An embodied approach for cultivating prosocial responses to sexual assault," *Text and Performance Quarterly*, *26*(3), 229-252.

Rohd, M. (1998). *Theatre for Community Conflict and Dialogue: The Hope is Vital Training Manual,* Portsmouth, NM: Heinemann Drama.

Sampson, R. (2002). *Acquaintance Rape of College Students*, U.S. Department of Justice, Office of Community Oriented Policing, Problem Oriented Guides for Policing, Vol. *17*.

Tjaden, P. & Thoennes, N. (2006). *Extent, Nature, and Consequences of Rape Victimization: Findings from the National Violence against Women Survey*, NCJ #210346, U.S. Department of Justice (Washington, DC) Retrieved from > http://www.ncjrs.gov/pdffiles1/nij/210346.pdf.

U.S. Department of Justice, (2009). *Rape and Sexual Violence*, National Institute of Justice (Washington, DC) Retrieved from http://www.ojp.usdoj.gov/nij/topics/crime/rape-sexual-violence/welcome.htm.

U.S. Department of Justice, (2008). *Criminal Victimization in the United States, 2006 Statistical Tables: National Crime Victimization Survey*, NCJ #223436, U.S. Department of Justice (Washington, DC): Author.

Widom, C. S. (1999). "Posttraumatic stress disorder in abused and neglected children grown up," *American Journal of Psychiatry*, *156*, 1223–1229.

Widom, C. S. & Morris, S. (1997). "Accuracy of adult recollections of childhood victimization, Part 2: Childhood sexual abuse," *Psychological Assessment*, *9*, 34-46.

World Health Organization, (2002). *Sexual Violence*: *World Report on Violence and Health*, EG Krug, LL Dahlberg, JA Mercy, AB Zwi, R Lozano (Eds.) pp. 147-182 (Geneva, Switzerland) Retrieved from > http://whqlibdoc.who.int/publications/2002/ 9241545615 _chap6_eng.pdf.

World Health Organization, (2010). *Gender, Women, and Health: Sexual Violence*, Retrieved from > http://www.who.int/gender/violence/sexual_violence/en/index.html

World Health Organization, (2012). "Violence against Women: Intimate Partner Violence and Sexual Violence against Women," *Media Centre/Fact Sheets* (Geneva, Switzerland) Retrieved from > > http://www.who.int/mediacentre/factsheets/fs239/en/.

Yeater, E. A. & O'Donohue, W. (1999). "Sexual assault prevention programs: Current issues, future directions, and the potential efficacy of interventions with women," *Clinical Psychology Review*, *19*, 739-771.

Yodanis, C. L. (2004). "Gender inequality, violence against women, and fear: A cross-national test of the feminist theory of violence against women," *Journal of Interpersonal Violence*, *19*(6), 655-675.

In: Assaults
Editor: Keith V. Bletzer
ISBN: 978-1-62808-051-3

Chapter 7

CORPORAL PUNISHMENT: MINOR ASSAULT IS STILL ASSAULT

Mary Ward Pollard, Courtney Sparks and Cliff McKinney*

Department of Psychology, Mississippi State University, Mississippi State, MS US

ABSTRACT

Corporal punishment remains a controversial issue in today's society. One of the ongoing concerns has been the relationship between use of corporal punishment and its impact on a child's overall well-being and development. A thin line exists between what is considered *corporal punishment* and what is considered *assault*, as the former often escalates into the latter. Research has provided insight as to what factors might lead a parent to engage in corporal punishment, which generally includes parental, child, and environmental factors. Researchers have conducted numerous studies to determine negative effects and outcomes that are associated with corporal punishment, but little is known as to what methods of intervention will reduce public opinion that currently seems to take a position of favorability toward its use. Some studies have focused on using education to demonstrate negative outcomes associated with corporal punishment to parents, school administrators and students, and community groups. Overall, the use of corporal punishment has been shown to be ineffective and correlated with negative outcomes. Corporal punishment in schools has declined markedly in recent years due to organizational efforts and new laws. Yet corporal punishment remains a lawful form of school punishment in many districts throughout the United States. Much still needs to be done to intervene against corporal punishment in the home. Providing solid information on the harmful effects and ineffectiveness of corporal punishment to the public has been shown to be an effective method in changing people's opinions on its use and everyday practice.

Keywords: Corporal punishment, parenting, positive discipline, legal implications, prevention

* Corresponding author: Email: CMcKinney@psychology.msstate.edu.

INTRODUCTION

A child's negative behaviors require the most effective means of correction and re-direction. Research has indicated that the most positive and beneficial way is through the use of non-violent discipline rather than methods that incorporate corporal punishment. The prevalence of corporal punishment introduces a matter of concern that has been controversial with blurred boundaries, as a thin line exists between the definition of corporal punishment and assault. The former practice can too easily escalate into the latter. Use of corporal punishment draws the interest of many in today's society. Researchers add to the discourse, having found that use of corporal punishment can have a negative impact on a child's overall well-being and development (Renk, McKinney, Klein & Oliveros, 2006). Yet, some sectors of society view corporal punishment as a normal part of life and the needed response to a child's behavior that requires "discipline."

Many different factors influence parental responses to children's behavior, including but not limited to factors that pertain to the parent, the child, the family, the environment, or any combination of these. Many reasons exist as to why parents choose to employ corporal punishment as a form of discipline. The study of the factors associated with the utilization of corporal punishment, and the present prevalence rate and legality of corporal punishment in the United States, is extremely important to better understand how corporal punishment can be considered assault. Such a consideration may help parents to become better educated and adopt a positive and beneficial disciplinary plan of action that will lead to more positive child outcomes.

CORPORAL PUNISHMENT AS A PARENTING STRATEGY

Overall, the use of corporal punishment is conceptualized as a negative parenting behavior. Parents may use multiple types of responses to address a child who has not followed the rules. Parents might react to disobedience with power assertion, love withdrawal, and induction strategies (McKinney, Milone & Renk, 2011). Some examples of actions performed under the power assertion strategy include taking away privileges that a child has previously had, physical violence which basically asserts a position of parental dominance, or threats to forcefully change the behavior of the child. Examples of love withdrawal to change behavior in contrast are less direct and include ignoring or isolating the child or stating a dislike of the child. Finally, examples of induction strategies include communicating with the child what standards have been set and what expectations for proper behavior have been articulated that the child needs to follow and re-enforced, as needed, reasoning with them to get them to obey (McKinney et al, 2011). It is apparent that physical assault as well as corporal punishment is included in the power assertion strategy, and non-violent and positive forms of discipline are included in induction strategies.

Previous studies have shown that parents may not be aware how often they exercise corporal punishment to discipline their children. For example, one study demonstrated that the frequency of spanking that parents recalled during an interview was one-sixth of the actual frequency of spanking that was recorded in their own daily parenting diary (Straus & Stewart, 1999). Many different factors are included in parental support of corporal punishment. The main consideration is that corporal punishment, such as spanking, allows one parent or two parents to assert parental authority over their child or children (Hicks-Pass, 2009).

Research has provided much insight as to what factors may influence a parent's opinion of corporal punishment and what factors might lead to actual engagement in corporal punishment. These factors include younger parental age, history of physical violence between parents, lower family income, excessive alcohol use, and parental psychopathology (Straus & Stuart, 1999). All of these parental characteristics have been associated with a higher tendency to use corporal punishment as a parenting strategy to address negative child behaviors. Furthermore, parents that utilize corporal punishment as a disciplinary strategy on their child often have experienced corporal punishment themselves. Clement and Chamberland (2008), for example, found that mothers who were victims of violence in their own childhood were more likely to adopt views and attributions that favor use of corporal punishment.

Several critically important factors unrelated to a parent's opinion of corporal punishment, such as the child's age, gender, and temperament, also predict use of corporal punishment. Specifically, boys and younger children are more likely to be subjected to and receive physical and/or violent disciplinary acts than girls and adolescents. Straus and Stewart (1999) used a study design to replicate the findings of at least six previous studies that boys were hit more than girls in response to misbehavior. Following prior research, they proposed that boys are still subjected to more violent ways of socialization in today's society. The higher rates of corporal punishment among boys, however, could be due to the fact that boys have higher rates of misbehavior than girls. On the other hand, because boys have been found to be corporally punished more and at a younger age than girls, these higher rates of misbehavior might be attributed to having been exposed longer to a more violent form of socialization under the guise of punishment. A child's misbehavior is sometimes attributed to psychopathology within the child. Multiple explanations, both environmental and genetic, exist as to why such psychopathology is present in children. Recent research has indicated that parents, specifically mothers, of children with anxiety disorders are themselves more likely to be diagnosed with an anxiety disorder and in some cases the same anxiety disorder as their child (Hughes, Furr, Sood, Barmis & Kendall, 2009). Similarly, Laskey and Cartwright-Hatton (2009) found that parents who reported high levels of personal anxiety were more likely to report using high levels of discipline that were in effect ineffective, particularly harsh discipline techniques.

Parental psychopathology has been found to have a significant impact on parenting practices. Studies have shown that parents who have psychopathology are more likely to engage in negative parenting behaviors. For example, a parent who has been diagnosed with an anxiety disorder is more likely to employ ineffective disciplinary tactics, like corporal punishment, which can negatively affect a child's sense of security and thus illicit negative internalizing behaviors (Laskey & Cartwright-Hatton, 2009). Other studies have reported similar findings on increased use of corporal punishment by parents with psychopathology. Observations of mothers interacting with their children, for example, indicate that when these women are depressed they exercise angrier, more hostile and intrusive, conflicted behavior with their children than the non-depressed mothers (Kane & Garber, 2009). Similar investigations have pointed to harsher, punitive discipline of these parents with children, which were considered ineffective in resolving conflict (Goodman & Gotlib, 1999). Thus, research has consistently found that parental negativity toward children, as well as forms of ineffective discipline like corporal punishment, are more likely to be expressed in the context of parental psychological distress (see Papp, Cummings & Goeke-Morey, 2005). When we consider the role played by child psychopathology in relation to the parental use of corporal punishment, as mentioned earlier, a process of cyclical transference between parent and child is found.

EFFECTS OF CORPORAL PUNISHMENT

Positive parenting, such as being warm and demanding and using non-violent discipline, is associated with positive psychological adjustment for children in their late adolescent stage (McKinney & Milone, 2012). Corporal punishment in contrast has been shown to be ineffective and correlated with negative outcomes. It is important to consider corporal punishment not just in terms of how it affects a child in the long run, but also how effective it is in actually correcting a child's immediate behavior. Robinson, Funk, Beth, and Bush (2005) have noted that corporal punishment does not suppress negative or unapproved behavior, but instead validates and legitimizes the use of hitting or physical force as an option to solve child behavior problems. This can be seen when the child mimics the same aspects of the same physical behaviors that corporal punishment encompasses, but more importantly is the fact a child whose parents use corporal punishment receives it repeatedly over time. This means it is ineffective as a punisher or else it would be needed no more than once or very few times (Robinson et al, 2005). It has been shown that authoritative parents identified and characterized by higher levels of responsiveness as well as demandingness are less likely to inconsistently employ punitive discipline and in turn their children are less likely to break the rules set forth as expectations and more likely to adhere to them. These children are less likely to need any excessive punitive or reprimanding discipline, because the rules that were set were properly explained and, when needed, they were appropriately enforced by the parents (McKinney et al, 2011).

Studies have shown that corporal punishment is positively related to anti-social behavior, child-to-parent violence, other aggression, depression, future substance abuse, future violence against intimates, and decreased cognitive development (Straus & Stewart, 1999). Corporal punishment, then, has been shown to affect not just the child's well-being and future mental health and behaviors but also the relationship between a child and their parent(s). Mulvaney and Mebert (2010) found that some children view their parent(s)' use of corporal punishment as inter-personal aggression, and this may lead to resentment by the child.

Many studies show an association between corporal punishment and poor mother-child relationships. Other studies have found harsher parenting practices to be related to negative outcomes for the child later in life, such as externalizing disorders and drug and alcohol use. Lynch and associates (2006), for example, focused on pinpointing negative outcomes by controlling for genetic and environmental influences. Results of their study showed that in pairs of twins where one parent employed harsh punishment and the other did not, these children exhibited more externalizing and drug and alcohol-related symptoms than children where neither parent used harsh punishment. Seeking to elucidate the emotional toll of parenting through a life history recall design, Renk and associates (2006) found that physical parental punishment was related significantly to anxiety, self-esteem, and depression later in life among collegiate females.

As with any controversial matter, contradictory findings exist for the effects of corporal punishment. Some studies suggest that corporal punishment does not have negative outcomes and instead suggest that children who were spanked had less reported schoolyard fights. Sad to say, it is noteworthy that many studies that find similar findings include a disclaimer that states their findings were merely indicative of the need for possibly more complex research to specifically determine the effects of corporal punishment, which leads to the caveat their particular research and findings were not meant to be used as support or endorsement for the practice of corporal punishment (e.g., Hicks-Pass, 2009). Contradictory findings in the outcomes for studies of children who have been subjected to corporal punishment might be due to inconsistent definitions of corporal punishment. When defined narrowly, corporal punishment is not a strong predictor of negative internalizing or externalizing behaviors in children. An example of this can be seen with children whose parents spank them and in addition routinely exercise harsher, more abusive forms of punishment. For these children, spanking may be unrelated to subsequent behavioral problems in comparison to those children with parents whose punishment style is limited to and stops with "controlled spanking" (Lynch, Turkheimer, D'Onofrio, Mendle & Emery, 2006). Despite the contradictory findings, it is difficult to ignore the abundance of research that correlates harsh discipline including corporal punishment to negative outcomes including but not limited to lowered cognitive development, lowered achievement, aggression, anxiety, depression, poor social relationships, delinquency, and more.

Opponents to this viewpoint argue that the existing research is not experimental and therefore cannot be used to determine causality. Although this point is valid, when one is investigating any of these issues, complete experimental control is limited and/or impossible. However, if negative outcomes are at minimum a possible effect of corporal punishment, the question remains as to why it exists as an acceptable form of parenting behavior in various settings of society. When we take corporal punishment out of the context of parenting choices, the act of committing physical violence on an individual is looked down upon and, in some contexts, it is illegal. The answer to this question may lie in how corporal punishment is viewed within society and across various cultures.

Corporal Punishment as Assault

The debate on considering corporal punishment as assault, and therefore legally handled in this context, is centered on a notion called "reasonable force." As it stands now, the parental application of reasonable force is what separates corporal punishment from assault (Straus, 2010). Under current laws, parents may use "reasonable force" to discipline negative child behaviors. However, what is considered to be "reasonable force" can be different and controversial among different people and cultures. Hence, the definition has changed as public approval for using corporal punishment has shifted in recent decades (Coleman, Dodge & Campbell, 2010). The most common examples of corporal punishment include spanking on the buttocks, shoving, grabbing, and hand-slapping. Corporal punishment has been defined by various other publications as "the use of physical force with the intention of causing [bodily] pain, but not injury, for the purpose to correct and/or control the child's behavior" (Straus, 2010, pp.1-2). This is the practiced legal definition that protects parents from being accused of, or charged with, assault when they have employed physical force on their child in response to a negative behavior on the child's behalf.

Coleman and colleagues (2010) identify three major problems with current definitions of corporal punishment and how it pertains to the judiciary system in our society. The first issue is that the existing definition(s) do not fulfill the signaling or expressive functionality of the law, meaning they do not give adequate and clear guidance to legal actors. The second problem is that the definition(s) do not provide consistency in legal case outcomes. Finally, the third issue deals with false-positives and false-negatives as unacceptable errors that stem from the inherent vagueness and broadness of the definition(s) as they pertain to the court system. A thin line exists between the commonly used definition of Straus (2010) and what is legally and culturally considered to be assault. One example of this thin and unclear line is that the use of a hairbrush, paddle, stick, or belt can still be considered legal forms of punishment, as long as no injury occurs, or as long as no mark lasts any longer than about one day (Straus & Stewart, 2005). Although many people consider using a paddle or a belt to be physical abuse, the law does not recognize it as such, and does no more to define the line between abuse and corporal punishment than indicating the aforementioned legal guidelines of no injury or only a "mark" lasting no more than a day as a "cutoff point." Regardless, any accidentally inflicted serious injury that results from either physical assault or corporal punishment is prohibited by law.

To add further convolution to the definition of corporal punishment, corporal punishment is commonly disguised as a "'tradition' for 'discipline'" within familial and cultural contexts (Pinheiro, 2006). An example of how corporal punishment can be embedded within tradition is exemplified by the finding that parents who approve of corporal punishment as an acceptable style of discipline were submitted to corporal punishment during their childhood (Clement and Chamberland, 2008). Furthermore, in the United States, it is often the norm to consider it "family business" whenever any injury short of a serious one results from some form of corporal punishment (Coleman et al, 2010). Yet many if not all states have mandatory reporting laws whereby adults within educational institutions, such as teachers and school staff, *must report any suspicion* of child abuse or neglect, which could have originated at home through the excessive use of corporal punishment.

Corporal punishment in United States schools has declined markedly in recent years due to organizational efforts and new laws. Yet corporal punishment regretfully remains a lawful form of punishment in some states and various schools districts throughout the United States. Among the list of 'developed' countries, the United States and Australia are the only ones that still allow an adult "to paddle" a child on school premises as a form of discipline and punishment for bad behavior (Robinson et al, 2005). Specifically in the United States, it may be that cultural influences due to geographical locations are at play in places where corporal punishment is the most widely accepted and used. A poll showed that in the South, only 33% of people opposed the use of corporal punishment in schools, while 66% of people in the East opposed exercising corporal punishment in the school system. Percentages for teachers approving or disapproving of corporal punishment in the classroom were similar. As far as the parents were concerned, 53% of parents in the South endorsed using paddling in schools as a form of disciplinary practice, whereas national polls indicated that only 38% of parents approved of paddling in the classroom. Higher support and use of corporal punishment in the south (Mississippi, Arkansas, Alabama, Tennessee, Texas, Georgia, Louisiana, Oklahoma, South Carolina, and Kentucky) could be a result of generally stronger fundamental religious beliefs, biblical literalism, strong adherence to tradition, and conservative ideology (Robinson et al, 2005). What might be the most concerning outcome of these discussions is that a survey in South Carolina found that "aggressive acts" by students were considered to be appropriate in response to corporal punishment but neither the "bad behavior" or an act of counter-aggression was perceived as appropriate for an intervention with a psychologist (Robinson et al, 2005).

An argument can be made that the effort of trying to differentiate between a definition of corporal punishment and assault is arbitrary, although an escalation from the former to the latter frequently occurs. Making the distinction between 'corporal punishment' and 'assault' may be relevant and critically important within the family and societal context especially with respect to schools, where young people spend considerable time during their formative years. The way in which corporal punishment is distinguished is relevant for the personnel of organizations such as child protective services (CPS), where the staff is required to take action and intervene when a child or children in a family is at risk for and/or has been subjected to abuse. In addition, the definition of corporal punishment holds legal importance, as it is critical for courts involved in child abuse cases (Coleman et al, 2010).

Putting the aforementioned consequences of using corporal punishment aside, the observation of homicidal statistics alone produces a strong foundation against the use of corporal punishment. Pinheiro (2006) reported that the majority of homicide victims were between the ages of 15 to 17, closely followed by children with ages ranging from 5 to 14. In addition, close family members most often perpetuated the child-directed homicides, where death was often caused by injury to the head or internal organs, intentional suffocation, shaking, choking or battering (Pinheiro, 2006). Not surprisingly, the actions that account for these child-directed homicides have long been associated with the different types of corporal punishment, such as whipping, spanking, beating with an object, and shaking (Gershoff, 2002). Using this information, one can make the argument that the use of corporal punishment is inherently no different than assault. It seems the only difference between the two lies in what legislating bodies deem as assault. Knox (2010) provides a similar model on use of corporal punishment with children to the classic argument it was once legal for men to punish wives by use of physical violence. Similar to the corporal punishment controversy, legal precedent in the courts deemed that it was a man's right to correct his wife. However, in today's legal climate, the use of physical violence is considered illegal and, thus, it is discouraged. Knox (2010) points out that not surprisingly the use of violence is illegal within our society against other adults, namely, those who are institutionalized, such as prisoners and hospital patients, military personnel, persons suspected or arrested for crimes, and those in special relationships such as employer/supervisor and employee/worker. Given these arguments, it is difficult to understand why use of physical violence against children, who easily are our society's most delicate and innocent population, goes beyond consideration of being legal to place young people on the receiving end of physical violence, under the guise of sanctioned forms of corporal punishment.

Recommendations

Researchers have conducted numerous studies to determine the negative effects and corresponding outcomes associated with corporal punishment, but little is known as to what methods of intervention will reduce public favorability towards corporal punishment. It may be the case that some parents are not aware of other ways to discipline their child. To aid in the decline of the use of corporal punishment in the home, Flaskereud (2011) suggests that parents should be provided interventions, such as the behaviorally-based Parent Effectiveness Training Program, to aid them in their parenting techniques. Strategies suggested to help parents re-direct their child's misbehavior include *time-out* and *privilege removal*. Both these procedures fit the use of positive and negative reinforcement, recommended by the American Academy of Pediatrics (AAP). However, parents who believe that corporal punishment is the ideal way to handle misbehaviors of their child may not be open to the idea of being instructed on how to parent their child. As a result, information on an alternative form of discipline may not be effective when parents believe that corporal punishment is the optimal form.

Providing information on the harmful effects and ineffectiveness of corporal punishment has been shown to be more effective in changing people's opinions on corporal punishment than providing information on alternative effective disciplinary methods. Some studies have focused on using education as a method to demonstrate the negative outcomes associated with corporal punishment to parents as well as members of society. Some psychologists have reported that after the recent formation of numerous organizations aiming to abolish corporal punishment in schools, a decline in use of corporal punishment in southern schools was observed, whereas corresponding decreases in number of incidents of corporal punishment in the home were not observed during that same time (Robinson et al, 2005). These findings reiterate the fact that much still needs to be done to intervene against using corporal punishment in the home. Outlawing corporal punishment as a parental disciplinary action may help to establish a cultural norm in the United States. Similar steps toward outlawing corporal punishment have been taken in other countries and, as a result, are producing positive outcomes. For example, Sweden outlawed corporal punishment in 1979. Since the legal provision, a significant decrease has been observed in young people who get into trouble for theft, alcohol and drug use, and rape as well as those who attempt or succeed at suicide (Robinson et al, 2005).

Conclusion

Overall, the use of corporal punishment provides no social benefits for the well-being of children. In fact, the preponderance of the available research strongly demonstrates that corporal punishment inflicts greater harm than good. In society, the lines between what is considered corporal punishment and assault are blurred. Distinctions between the two are mostly legislatively arbitrary. As explained earlier, the use of corporal punishment practices can easily and too often cross a line into harsher punishment practices that can be considered assault. Although the more severe side of corporal punishment might differ greatly from occasional spanking, both include physical harm to the child. All forms of physical punishment have been shown to be associated with some type of negative outcome. As might be expected, opponents to the view of corporal punishment as an ineffective discipline strategy have buttressed their argument with the research findings that children who are spanked have positive outcomes as adults, such as lower levels of juvenile delinquency.

Instead of debating the issue, many concerned citizens question whether negative outcomes outweigh whatever might be the benefits, if any, of corporal punishment. Specifically, if corporal punishment were associated with negative outcomes as acknowledged in the existing research, then truly what debate is there? In the short-term, other aforementioned methods of discipline are as equally effective as corporal punishment and perhaps more effective in the long-term than corporal punishment (Gershoff, 2002). These alternatives to, or replacements of, corporal punishment include but are not limited to time out to provide reflection opportunity, inattention to negative behavior to deny its goal as attention-seeking, response cost, and positive reinforcement to highlight and reward expected behaviors. More significantly, non-harsh types of discipline are in no way associated with children having negative outcomes but, instead, are commonly associated with positive outcomes, such as pro-social behavior, increased achievement, increased cognitive development and moral reasoning, improved social relationships, and more. Based on these factors, possible benefits of corporal punishment become less clear. The arguments in favor of corporal punishment seem to take on a different meaning altogether. More specifically, corporal punishment may just be another form of assault that is used due to a false belief that it is effective and/or does not lead to negative outcomes. False beliefs require work to remove them but the benefits outweigh the efforts that might be required to attain success.

REFERENCES

Clément, M. & Chamberland, C. (2009). "The role of parental stress, mother's childhood abuse and perceived consequences of violence in predicting attitudes and attribution in favor of corporal punishment," *Journal of Child and Family Studies*, *18*, 163-171.

Coleman, D. (2010). "Where and how to draw the line between reasonable corporal punishment and abuse," *Law and Contemporary Problems*, *73*, 107-165.

Flaskerud, J. H. (2011). "Discipline and effective parenting," *Issues In Mental Health Nursing*, *32*, 82-84.

Goodman, S. H. & Gotlib, I. H. (1999). "Risk for psychopathology in the children of depressed mothers: A developmental model for understanding mechanisms of transmission," *Psychological Review*, *106*, 458-490.

Gershoff, E. T. (2002). "Corporal punishment by parents and associated child behaviors and experiences: A meta-analytic and theoretical review," *Psychological Bulletin*, *128*, 539–579.

Hicks-Pass, S. (2009). "Corporal punishment in America today: Spare the rod, spoil the child? A systematic review of the literature," *Best Practice in Mental Health*, *5*, 71-88.

Kane, P. & Garber, J. (2008). "Parental depression and child externalizing and internalizing symptoms. Unique effects of fathers' symptoms and perceived conflict as a mediator," *Journal of Child and Family Studies*, *18*, 465-472.

Knox, M. (2010). "On hitting children: A review of corporal punishment in the United States," *Journal of Pediatric Health Care*, *24*, 103-107.

Laskey, B. J. & Cartwright-Hatton, S. (2009). "Parental discipline behaviours and beliefs about their child: Associations with child internalizing and mediation relationships," *Child: Care Health and Development*, *35*, 717-727.

Lynch, S. K., Turkheimer, E., D'Onofrio, B. M., Mendle, J., Emery, R. E., Slutske, W. S. & Martin, N. G. (2006). "A genetically informed study of the association between harsh punishment and offspring behavioral problems," *Journal of Family Psychology*, *20*, 190-198.

McKinney, C., Milone, M. & Renk, K. (2011). "Parenting and late emotional adjustment: Mediating effects of discipline and gender," *Child Psychiatry Human Development*, *42*, 463-481.

McKinney, C. & Milone, M. (2012). "Parental and late adolescent psychopathology: Mothers may provide support when needed most," *Child Psychiatry And Human Development*, *43*, 747-760.

Mulvaney, M. & Mebert, C. (2010). "Stress appraisal and attitudes towards corporal punishment as intervening processes between corporal punishment and subsequent mental health," *Journal of Family Violence*, *25*, 401-412.

Papp, L., Cummings, E. & Goeke-Morey, M. (2005). "Parental psychological distress, parent-child relationship qualities, and child adjustment: Direct, mediating, and reciprocal pathways," *Parenting: Science and Practice*, *5*, 259-283.

Pinheiro, P. S. (2006). *World Report on Violence against Children, Independent Expert for the United Nations*. New York, NY: United Nations.

Renk, K., McKinney, C., Klein, J. & Oliveros, A. (2006). "Childhood discipline, perceptions of parents, and current functioning in female college students," *Journal of Adolescence*, *29*, 73-88.

Robinson, D. H., Funk, D. C., Beth, A. & Bush, A. M. (2005). "Changing beliefs about corporal punishment: Increasing knowledge about ineffectiveness to build more consistent moral and informational beliefs," *Journal of Behavioral Education*, *14*, 117-139.

Straus, M. A. (2010). "Prevalence, societal causes, and trends in corporal punishment by parents in world perspective," *Law and Contemporary Problems*, *73*, 1-30.

Straus, M. A. & Stewart, J. H. (1999). "Corporal punishment by American parents: national data on prevalence, chronicity, severity, and duration, in relation to child and family characteristics," *Clinical Child and Family Psychology Review*, *2*, 55-70.

In: Assaults
Editor: Keith V. Bletzer

ISBN: 978-1-62808-051-3

Chapter 8

A Multiple Pronged Approach to Decrease Assault on Hospital Nursing Staff

*Marilyn Lanza**
Edith Nourse Rogers Memorial Veterans Hospital, Bedford, MA, US

Abstract

Nurses often take care of victims and perpetrators of violence from the communities in which they live. They are our friends, families, and neighbors. Violence occurs in areas of the hospital such as emergency rooms and trauma units that are the symbols of safety and care yet have become battlegrounds where people are maimed and killed rather than cured. The upsetting but basic fact is that violence occurs everywhere in the health care system, not just psychiatric units. In fact, the general hospital has less control over the facility environment than does a locked psychiatric ward.

Homicides make national headlines, but in hospital settings verbal threats, non-fatal physical assaults, and unwanted sexual advances are often under-reported or not reported at all. Part of the problem is nurses' perception that assaults come with the territory. Most nurses would not think of reporting a patient with Alzheimer's disease who strikes out, as he's being fed. Nor would they report the girlfriend of a young man who is pronounced dead on arrival, who lashes out because, she believes, you did nothing to save him. Increased rates for both physical and non-physical violence have been identified for working in a nursing home, long-term care facility, intensive care unit, emergency room, or psychiatric/behavioral department. Providing patient care and supervising patient care, as well as working with primarily geriatric patients, resulted in increased rates for physical violence. A national Veterans Administration (VA) survey was conducted in which 48% reported at least one verbal or physical assault within a 12-month period. Many published studies document assaults, but health care institutions have a long way to go toward implementing these findings, especially as they apply to staff working conditions. I hope this Multiple Pronged Approach helps you to decrease assault on nursing staff.

Keywords: Patient assault, nursing staff, prevention, communication (verbal and non-verbal), commonsense precepts

* Corresponding author: Email: Marilyn.Lanza@va.gov.

INTRODUCTION

Nurses are often taking care of the victims and perpetrators of violence from the communities in which they live. They are our friends, families, and neighbors. Violence takes place in areas of the hospital such as emergency rooms and trauma units, which are symbols of safety and care, yet have become battlegrounds where people are maimed and killed, rather than cured. The upsetting but basic fact is that violence can occur anywhere in the health care system, not just within the psychiatric units. In fact, the general hospital has less control over the environment than does a locked psychiatric ward.

Homicides can make national headlines, but inside our nation's hospitals verbal threats, non-fatal physical assaults, and unwanted sexual advances are often under-reported or not reported at all. Part of the problem is nurses' perception that assaults come with the territory (OSHA / Occupational Safety and Health Administration, 2004). Most nurses would not think of reporting a patient with Alzheimer's disease who strikes out at her, as he's being fed. Nor would they report the girlfriend of a young man who has been pronounced *dead on arrival*, who lashes out because, she believes, "you did nothing to save him."

Increases in Hospital Assault

Increased rates for both physical and non-physical violence were identified for working environment of a nursing home, long-term care facility, intensive care unit, emergency room, and psychiatric/behavioral department. Providing patient care and supervising patient care, as well as working with primarily geriatric patients, is associated with increased rates for physical violence (Demir & Rodwell, 2012; Gerberich et al, 2004; Hesketh et al, 2002; Lanza et al, 2010; Lanza et al, 2011). Most assaults involve male patient to male patient. When hospital staff is the main target, both male and female patients can be the assailant.

Lanza, Zeiss, and Rierdan (2006) conducted a national Veterans Administration (VA) survey in which 48% of facility respondents reported at least one verbal or physical assault within a 12-month period. Lanza and associates found that there were many changes in nursing staff's response after being assaulted. These changes included: fear of returning to the scene of the assault; fear of the patient who hit them or of other patients, feeling sorry for the patient who hit them; general feelings of helplessness, irritability, resignation, anger, anxiety, shock, apathy, disbelief, dependency; denial of thoughts about or preoccupation with the assault; considering a new life-style/job or new relationship with co-workers; difficulty returning to work; self-blame for not having prevented the assault; anger toward authority, wanting protection by authority and from authority's condition; body reactions such as startle response, sleep pattern disturbance, soreness, headaches, body tension (Lanza et al, 2011). Not surprisingly, these symptoms and body responses parallel those that occur with other types of assault and aggression.

Verbal intervention may preclude the need for physical intervention. Violent patients may feel helpless, terrified of losing control, or frightened by the intensity of their own emotion, which can become magnified through their presence in a health care setting. It is important to try to establish rapport by acknowledging these feelings and focusing on verbal intervention. The aggressive person should be encouraged to talk it out or "get it off his or her chest." At the same time, it should be made clear that violence is not acceptable, and the consequences should be outlined. Threats should be met with a firm but supportive setting of limits on aggressive behavior and enforcement of these limits (Gerberich et al, 2004; Lanza, 2006).

As first documented in 1981, the rate of assault in hospitals is under-reported by as much as 80% (Lion, Snyder & Merrill, 1981) and the data at best reflect a critical measure of incidence (Lanza & Campbell, 1991; Silver & Yudofsky, 1999). In the Department of Veterans Affairs context, where I have conducted research, the majority of assaults are perpetrated by men. The operational definition for assaultive behavior includes verbal and physical aggression. The common types of assault are *verbal* (yelling, screaming, or threatening) and *physical* (hitting with part of the body or a weapon). Although most concern has been with physical violence, verbal abuse and threats have significant sequelae for staff as victims and negative consequences for the perpetrator. Killing a nurse is the most extreme type of assault and gets the most media attention. The total number of verbal and physical assaults is very large, but because death is not the usual outcome, the tendency of the media has been to ignore the fate of victims of the milder forms. On a medical unit, most physical assaults involve slapping, punching, and kicking. Verbal assaults commonly involve swearing at the victim or something more subtle such as making verbal threats.

Institutional limits must be placed on verbal as well as physical abuse. All persons must be treated with respect. This includes examining paternalism within staff. For example, in some circumstances, when patients and nursing staff are called by their first name but the doctor is addressed as "Dr. Brown," everyone understands that there is a hierarchical status among staff, so that hitting Dr. Brown is much worse than hitting a nurse. The physician can use "Dr. Brown." Most others have no recourse to titles. Or everyone can be more formal and use titles such as Mr., Miss, Nurse, etc. This includes patients and every member of the staff on the unit, including secretaries and housekeepers. The important point is that no one should have a higher risk to be assaulted, owing to work status within a staff hierarchy.

Victims often blame themselves and/or those in authority. Coworkers, albeit unwittingly, blame the *assaultee* or assailant. Finally, those in authority often view the "system" as a whole and blame the victim (Lanza, 1992). This last part of the blaming triangle is particularly important to understand, because it has profound effects on increasing the incidence of patient violence. Simply stated, if an institution assumes that fault or responsibility lies with the assaulted staff member, then the institution can deny that there is a more general problem of patient assault. As a result, there is no determination of the extent of the problem of assault or recognition that such a problem even exists. The assault of a staff member is seen as a rare occurrence and caused by some unique characteristic in that person. The bottom line is that no prevention strategies are established to cope with the problem of assault and the mythical reality is maintained that "At Institution Z we do not have a problem."

The institutional environment correlates with the increased risk of violence (Lanza, 1995, 2006) and includes the following factors: 24-hour open-door policies for patient access; decrease in available treatment for the mentally ill and substance abuse patients resulting in an increasing number of acute and chronically mentally ill being released from hospitals; availability of drugs and money in the hospital settings; prevalence of weapons among patients; current cost-cutting focus and widespread down-sizing within the health care industry; working alone during the night shift or in the early morning, which are associated with traditional staffing patterns and often low staffing levels at times of increased activity within the facility. Circumstantial factors are less suspected but have equal importance, such as unrestricted movement of the public in health care settings, presence of gang members, drug or alcohol abuse, trauma patients, distraught family members, long waiting periods, and inability to obtain expected care.

COMMONSENSE PRECEPTS

What Can We Do with What We Know?

Situations of hospital violence are preventable and have been elucidated through research. Each situation needs institutional attention.

Are all doors, whether electronic or key operated, properly secured/locked, and are the exits to offices unobstructed, not blocked by chairs, desks, or coat racks?

Are purses, wallets, keys, money, credit cards and other valuables secured in locked desks or rooms when not in use?

Is there adequate lighting of parking lots, exit door areas and pathways that are used by employees who arrive and/or depart at night?

Is there a separate interview area away from waiting and treatment areas?

Are visiting and business hours posted at main entrances used by patients and visitors?

Are all the stairwells and landings appropriately secured and/or illuminated?

Are employees required to wear ID badges?

Individual Precautions

Awareness of Surroundings

There are several commonsense strategies that you as a staff member can employ to reduce likelihood of violence, at the same they permit responsive action, should it be required. The first tactic is awareness of your surroundings. Avoid turning your back, as you do not know who is behind you or what is around you, as you move throughout the facility and when you stop to talk with someone, whether patient or staff member. At this point, the point of encounter, you should position yourself without thinking about it. Your stance should allow you to be able to stand firmly and move quickly. This should occur naturally. You should not be threatening in your demeanor. Stay at least four arm-lengths from the patient. You should keep your arms at your sides and hands outside your pockets. Folded arms communicate the message: "I am not listening." Maintain good eye contact. Know cultural differences among patients – this will develop over time and the process can be enhanced through training. Members of certain communities, for example, might become agitated with *direct contact*; others vary over preferences for direct/indirect verbal instruction, and so on. As you are perceived as a practitioner, your tone of voice should be assertive, not aggressive or provocative.

Patient Contact

With respect to patient care, intent is revealed by touch, which can be perceived as sexual or threatening to some patients. If at all possible, tell the patient that you're going to touch them, and briefly explain the reason why, before you do so. When interviewing patients, request permission to ask questions. Give the patient control over his/her situation by offering solutions or alternatives. Call the patient by name. Let other staff members know where you are. Take another person with you, if necessary. Decide whether an interview room or day-room is preferable. Your content is very important. "Are you OK?" or "What's wrong?" is not helpful. If the patient knew the answer, he or she would not be anxious. It is better to acknowledge the presence of emotions: "You look anxious." Or you might say, "Sounds as if you're upset." Basically, such phrases will tell the person that you are listening and you care.

Dress for Safety

Avoid provocative clothing. Remove loose objects: Ties, necklaces, and scarves make a ready means for choking the staff member. Remove pens, especially when they are visible.

Be Careful when Entering Wards

If doors are locked, check who may be hiding in the corner. If uncertain, wait for another staff member to accompany you. Be careful when entering elevators: Stay by the control buttons.

Be careful of Locked Rooms

Patients and staff members should both be able to leave.

Keys, alarms

Keys should be inconspicuous and worn in such a manner to avoid incidents yet be readily available when needed. Personal alarm systems must be utilized by staff members and tested as scheduled in the police station of a hospital.

Above All

Take action before anger builds up.

It is important to know and communicate your own strengths and weaknesses to coworkers *before* an assault situation arrives (Lanza, 1995). Coworkers need to know each other very well. There should not be any surprises in the middle of an emergency, such as "I cannot be the one to restrain him, I have a bad back." You do not have to give all the details of how you acquired a bad back but you do need to let everyone know how they can and cannot count on you in certain ways. There is no one who does not have a useful rule. The point is that when an emergency is called, all must know what they should do, when a particular person might be limited in physical movement.

Discuss among coworkers your own reactions to assault. Share how you and your coworkers usually handle fear, anger, denial, omnipotence, and projection onto others. For example, some staff always avoids assaultive situations. It is vital that hospital administrators and staff can be trusted. It is often the case that overt views by administration of staff reaction is positive but underneath, covertly, the administration is trying to determine "what happened," which can result in blaming the victim. It is very important to have an open and two-way discussion before an assault occurs. After several assaults, it becomes evident whether in fact there is real trust among staff and staff/administrators.

The patients and staff on a given ward make up a community of individuals who are brought and held together by commonalties of purpose. Prevailing social norms for this small but dense community can have either facilitative or inhibitory influences on a patient's potential for assault. The "community" may be any group in which there is cohesion among members. A sense of community does not have to be an individual ward. It can, for instance, be a group of visitors to a medical unit.

Certain assumptions can foster an increased level of physical aggression. Inexperienced staff and those who have trouble dealing with their own aggressive feelings may unwittingly give patients cues that they expect them to behave violently. Patients might exercise less control over aggressive impulses if they assume a diagnosis of a mental illness is exculpatory and hospitalization protects them from the consequences of untoward behaviors. Patients who fear attacks from others may strike preemptively. A clearly articulated, strongly supported norm against violence is required to minimize the intensity of these dangerous assumptions. The *norm against violence* can be promulgated by a variety of means. A patient orientation manual, treatment meetings or staff contacts with individual patients are a few of the means.

Depending on how the *norm* is developed and articulated, there is risk that it will create rather than prevent aggression. If the *norm* against violence is perceived as a heavy-handed approach by staff to maintain absolute control, sonic patients may feel challenged or provoked to test its strength. If a pronounced split exists between patients and staff, the *norm* can become a focus for contention. When this occurs, patients will accuse staff of erring, regardless of action they take following a violent episode.

To reduce the risk of backlash and patient/staff splitting, hospital staff should involve patients as much as possible in establishing and maintaining the *norm* against violence. For example, patients can be directly involved in formulating the patient orientation manual. Discussion of the *norm* can also take place in patient government meetings and in treatment meetings.

Patient-staff discussion about the *norm* should not focus narrowly on the issue of control. Discussion should stress the ultimate goal to be served by observing the norm: creation of a living and working ambience that is sufficiently safe and trustworthy to allow patients and staff to work effectively on treatment issues. It is not possible for patients to deal with inner conflicts while they are frightened of being assaulted. Any dangerously aggressive act must be regarded as a community event. Although only one or two individuals may have acted violently, the incident will reverberate with negative reactions. Patients will assume that prevention of violence is the province of staff only.

Counseling

Nurses who are assaulted report conflict between their role as a professional and feeling they are a victim (Bailien, Rodriquez, de Witte, Notelaers & Moreno-Jiminenez, 2011; Lanza, 1992). Nurses are not socialized to expect to ever be assault victims, and most do not receive education to prepare them for such a fate. Formal training usually comes through employment in a facility. There is intense conflict between conflicting realities when a nurse is assaulted (Lanza, 1992; Lanza et al, 2005). He or she generally believes that nurses are not assaulted:

yet it has occurred. There is divided loyalty between allegiance to one's professional functioning – putting the patient's needs first – and attention to one's own needs as a victim (Demir & Rodwell, 2012; Lanza, 1992). For example, the nurse is hit by a patient and required to continue working, because staffing is inadequate to permit going home. Children question why their mother or father works in "such a place." The victim often defends the institution to family members and denies his or her own feelings of victimization. Nurses are in the somewhat unique position of needing to provide extensive care for the person who assaulted them. For example, the patient may require continuous observation by the nursing staff, after assaulting one of the nursing staff members. In summary, victims experience intense emotional reactions, want someone to speak to about their reactions, yet feel that it is "unprofessional" to do so. Victims do not expect to receive support from hospital administrators despite the victim's loyalty to the institution.

What Can be Done?

One may ask if administrators should not be more public in acknowledging that assault by patients is a problem. On closer inspection, that might create a conflict for administrators. If they admit that patient assault is a problem at their institution, they may find themselves blamed for the problem. For example, the assumption could be made that patient assault is a problem, because of poor administration. It might be suggested that if patients become violent, it is because they are mistreated. As mentioned earlier, issues of patient rights and safety measures to prevent violence are often presented as adversarial. That is, to institute safety measures, patients' rights are considered at risk, when the more global approach suggests that only when safety exists can anyone, that includes staff and patients, have rights.

The last dilemma to be faced in publicizing the existence of patient assault is that such knowledge may arouse fear in the community and inhibit the discharge of non-violent patients. This is particularly true for any patient with a history of mental illness, who might be seen as too dangerous to live outside of the hospital, a long-held belief that mental health professionals have valiantly tried to eradicate.

Given that coming to terms with the problem of patient assault may arouse ambivalent feelings and conflict-laden situations, there are steps that administrators can take to support nursing staff in dealing with assaultive situations.

Programs Helpful in Coping with Aggression

A specific protocol for assaulted employees such as that instituted at Edith Nourse Rogers Memorial Veterans Hospital (Bedford, MA) can be developed, which outlines rights and services available for an employee who is assaulted (Lanza, Keefe & Henderson, 1996). Guidance for such a protocol is part of the *OSHA Guidelines for Preventing Workplace Violence for Healthcare and Social Service Workers*.

Planning such a protocol should be structured. Fifteen members of the nursing staff, for example, met with the author for one hour a week for 12 weeks. For the first 15 minutes, the leader talked about a particular topic involved in being or having been assaulted, such as blame. For the next 45 minutes, the group discussed the topic and the personal experiences and responses of the staff, and emphasized any positive changes in how they were feeling. These discussions resulted in a more valid and practical guide (for more information, see Lanza, Demaio & Benedict 2005).

Assertiveness Training

The author has given an assault prevention course to both staff and patients several times. It helps people be more direct, honest, and open. The last point is of particular importance: to be able to hear what the other person is saying and not be absorbed by what you yourself are going to say in return – to learn to listen. The result is fewer "U" statements and more "I" statements. You as the speaker are not blaming another person but are learning to say to others how you feel. A study was done at the Edith Nourse Rogers Memorial Veterans Hospital and found no difference between male and female staffing in terms of assault, nor were age or work shift factors (Lanza, Kayne, Guilliford, Hicks & Islam, 1997). The only difference was an inverse relationship between the number of assault and length of time spent with patients: the lower the hierarchical position, the higher the likelihood of being assaulted. This means that the higher you are in the "food chain," so to speak, the less likely you are to be assaulted. Nursing assistants are, therefore, the staff that suffers the most assaults, because they have more frequent and more direct contact with patient care.

Violence Prevention Community Meeting

The Violence Prevention Community Meeting (VPCM) was pilot-tested and as a result, a nationwide study has been finished. The important point for this chapter is that the VPCM takes the form of a regular community meeting but the discussion is focused only on assault. If an assault whether verbal or physical has just occurred, how could it have been prevented? What led up to it? What occurred and why? The discussion must include the effect on staff and patients, who were on the ward, but did not actually observe the assault. Finally, what could have been done differently?

If there has not been a recent assault, the committee should still meet and the discussion should focus on what is going on that prevents assaultive behavior. It should be emphasized for all situations how being verbally respectful can lead to a decreased likelihood of physical aggression.

Concentric Interactive Psychodynamic Group

This format for training staff to cope with aggression was developed by the author as a psychodynamic / psychotherapy group rather than an anger management group. Each 75-minute Concentric Interactive Psychodynamic Group (CIPG) meeting consists of three phases, which involve three differently constituted participant groups. In the first part, the patient-centered phase (45 minutes) – closest to a traditional psychodynamic therapy group – patients form a group, led by two co-leaders. Staff participants observe from the perimeter of the inner group.

In the second part of the group (15 minutes), the staff-centered phase, staff participants form a group with the two co-leaders, and discuss their reactions to the patient's psychotherapy group as well as to the interactions within their own group. The staff participants-observers are encouraged to voice their perceptions regarding evidence of intra-psychic processes, inter-personal processes, and the dynamics among themselves and co-leaders, and to acknowledge disagreement when it arises. In this phase, patients become the observers of the interactions of the staff from the perimeters of the group.

In the last phase of the group (15 minutes), the integrated-group phase, all participants including patients, co-leaders and staff participants form one integrated group, where all may speak as they discuss their intra-psychic, inter-personal, and group-related reactions to the observed and experienced first and second parts of the group (Lanza, 2007; Lanza & Schmidt, 2008).

CONCLUSION

The multiple pronged approach[1] is directed to both staff and patients. Each institutional unit makes a "community." From the multiple people and multiple places where I worked and consulted, I have explored dynamics about patient assault (Lanza, Zeiss & Rierdan, 2009). The article proposes a *360-Degree* model that allows a clinical comparison of perspectives of assailant, victim, victim's peers and victim's supervisor. The accounts will vary greatly from one to another. It is the hope this paper will do the same in building sensitivity skills and responsiveness toward persons who are gravely ill and temporarily/permanently immobile, who provide us the opportunity for greater understanding among people. The process requires time and effort, and begins with planning. From my experience – I am always planning – this makes life interesting.

REFERENCES

Bailien, E., Rodriquez, A., de Witte, H., Notelaers, G. & Moreno-Jiminenez, B. (2011). "The Demand-Control Model and target's reports of bullying at work: A test within Spanish and Belgian blue-collar workers," *European Journal of Work and Organization Psychology*, *20*(2), 157-177.

Demir, D. & Rodwell, J. (2012). "Psychosocial antecedents and consequences of workplace aggression of hospital nurses," *Journal of Nursing Scholarship*, *44*(4), 376-384.

Einarsen, S., Hoel, H., Zapf, D. & Cooper, C. L. (2011). "The concept of bullying and harassment at work: The European Tradition," in S Einersen, H Hoel, D Zapf, CL Cooper (Eds.), *Bullying and Harassment in the Workplace: Developments in Theory, Research and Practice* (3-39), Boca Raton, FL: CRC Press.

Gerberich, S., Church, T., McGovern, P., Hansen, H., Nachreiner, N. & Geisser, M. S. et al, (2004). "An Epidemiological study of the magnitude and consequences of work related violence: The Minnesota Nurses' Study," *Occupational Environmental Medicine*, *65*, 495-503.

Hesket, K., Duncan, S., Estabrooks, C., Reimer, M., Giovannetti, P. & Hyndman, K. et al, (2003). "Workplace violence in Alberta and British Columbia hospitals," *Health Policy*, *63*, 311-321.

[1] Material in this chapter is based upon work funded by the Department of Veterans Affairs Central Office and is supported by the Edith Nourse Rogers Memorial Veterans Hospital, Bedford, MA 01730.

Lanza, M. L. (1992). "Nurses as patient assault victims: an update, synthesis, and recommendations," *Archives of Psychiatric Nursing*, *6*(3), 163-171.

Lanza, M. L. (1995). *Education Program in Dealing with Assault*, Course taught at ENRM Veterans Administration Hospital, Bedford, MA.

Lanza, M. L. (2006). "Violence in nursing," in EK Kelloway, J Barling, JJ Hurrell, Jr. (Eds.), "*Workplace Violence*," 147-167, Thousand Oaks, CA: Sage Publications.

Lanza, M. L. (2007). "Modeling conflict resolution in group psychotherapy," *Journal of Group Psychotherapy, Psychodrama and Sociometry*, *59*(4), 147-158.

Lanza, M. L. & Campell, D. (1991). "Patient assault: A comparison study of reporting methods," *Journal of Nursing Quality Assurance*, *5*(4), 60-68.

Lanza, M. L., Demaio, J. & Benedict, M. (2005). "Assault support group: A beginning," in JP Morgan (Ed.), *Psychology of Aggression* (87-99), New York, NY: Nova Science Publishers, Inc.

Lanza, M. L., Kayne, H. L., Gulliford, D., Hicks, C. & Islam, S. (1997). "Staffing of in-patient psychiatric units and assault by patients," *Journal of the American Psychiatric Nurses Association*, *3*(42), 42-48. Doi: 10.1177/107839039700300204.

Lanza, M. L., Keefe, J. & Henderson, M. C. (1996). "Assaulted and/or battered employee policy," *Guidelines for preventing workplace violence of healthcare and social service workers* (OSHA 3148, Revised edition, 1998), Occupational Safety and Health Administration, U.S. Department of Labor.

Lanza, M. L., McMillan, F. & Demaio, J. (2011). "Support our staff (SOS) – A unique program to help deal with patient assault," *Perspective in Psychiatric Care*, *47*(3), 131-137.

Lanza, M. L., McMillan, F., Demaio, J. & LeFebvre, T. (2010). "Assault from the top down," in V. Nardi (Ed.), *Women and Leadership* (179-186), New York, NY: Nova Science Publishers.

Lanza, M. L. & Schmidt, S. (2008). "Group work with aggressive men: Group within a group within a group," *Journal of Contemporary Psychotherapy*, *38*(4), 197-203.

Lanza, M. L., Zeiss, R. & Rierdan, J. (2006). "Violence against psychiatric nurses: Sensitive research as science and intervention," *Contemporary Nursing*, *21*(1), 71-84.

Lanza, M. L., Zeiss, R. & Rierdan, J. (2009). "Multiple perspectives on assault: The 360-Degree interview," *Journal of the American Psychiatric Nursing*, *14*(6), 1-8.

Lion, J. R., Snyder, W. & Merrill, G. (1981). "Underreporting of assaults on staff in a state hospital," *Hospital & Community Psychiatry*, *32*, 497-498.

Occupational Safety and Health Administration, (2004). *Guidelines for Preventing Workplace Violence for Health Care and Social Services Workers*, retrieved December 9, 2012 from www.osha.gov.

Silver, J. M. & Yudofsky, S. C. (1999). "Propranolol treatment of chronically hospitalized aggressive patients," *Journal of Neuropsychiatry and Clinical Neuroscience*, *11*(3), 328-335.

In: Assaults
Editor: Keith V. Bletzer

ISBN: 978-1-62808-051-3

Chapter 9

OUTCOMES OF TORTURE BY INTENTIONAL BURN

***Kishore Kumar Das*[1,*], *Sazzad Khondokar*[1], *Anjana Chakraborty*[2], *M. Quamruzzaman*[3] *and Rashidul Haque*[1]**

[1]Dhaka Medical College Hospital, Dhaka, Bangladesh
[2]Bangabondhu Sheikb Mujib Medical University, Dhaka, Bangladesh
[3]National Institute of Cancer and Research, Dhaka, Bangladesh

ABSTRACT

Many forms of torture exist. One of them is a burn that leaves marks on the skin in addition to physical impediments and mental trauma. The physical damage and outcome of an intentional burn is often worse than an accidental burn. When available, the hospital history is important for diagnosis and management of cases of injury by burns. Identifying the features of an intentional burn and correlating them with tools of harm that were used, motives and the victim's associated socio-economic status, makes it possible to discern injuries that are non-accidental, whether perpetrated by the injured individual or another person. Acids among which is sulfuric acid are the most used chemicals for attack. Motives vary for why a person or group might intentionally inflict burns on another individual. However severe the injuries might be, particularly for women and/or children, the burns usually are inflicted by persons known to the victim. Contact burns on servants might occur for punishment or to obtain a confession of an alleged theft. Some victims have psychological impairment before they are burned, while repeated assault leads to psychological disorder in others. Assault by burning leads to a risk of death and disability from physical/psychological scarring. For legal purposes injury certificates from the hospital can provide strong assistance to victims. As they are poor and often without resources, these victims fare poorly in seeking justice from perpetrators that have higher social ranking; for them, the process of justice is difficult and complicated. Legal and social support for victims and families are frequently inadequate to compensate for losses. A statement from a qualified doctor regarding the nature and causation of the burn wound would be a major assistance for them in seeking justice and compensation.

Keywords: Assault by burn, post-burn psychosis, reactive depression, legal and psychological support

[*] Corresponding author: Email: kishorek50@hotmail.com.

INTRODUCTION

The inhumanity of human beings to other human beings has been pertinent in every civilization. Presently, torture is being reported in 159 countries across the globe. Reported incidence rates range from three to 10 percent and are calculated using data from burn centers in Germany, Hong Kong, and the United States (Amnesty International 2010; Krob, Johnson and Jordan, 1986; Stone, 1988; Theodoru et al, 2009). Apart from 'torture' when used as a state-engineered mechanism, these same procedures can be found among general populations, taking place as an 'assault' by one person or group against another.

Several demographic characteristics set apart these victims of burn assault from burn patients that are hospitalized for non-intentional (accidental) causes. Skin lesions left after a burn might manifest as an acute burn with pain, inflammation and infection, chronic lesions with scars that might cause cosmetic disfigurements or functional impairments if they involve a joint (Daneielsen & Rasmussen, 2006). Appropriate medical history, meticulous examination and proper documentation are important. Care must be exercised to determine the presence of skin disease and non-torture lesions that can produce similar sorts of injury. This will help to determine the cause of the injury. It is extremely important that the doctors emphasize the degree of consistency of the lesion with any history of torture, as there have been incidents of false accusation (Daneielsen & Rasmussen, 2006). Self-harm surprisingly is as common as torture and assault burns. Thus, its detection requires the careful elicitation of a case history.

Based on our joint experience in institutional settings where patients arrive and/or are transported for medical treatment, we provide background information on the forms that burn assaults take, before describing the motives, the tools used by the perpetrator, consequences to victims and possible legal outcomes against the attacker or attackers. We focus on the country of Bangladesh and include comparative data from other parts of the world. We use photographic images taken at the time of presentation to a medical facility to show the extent of damage caused to the body and include illustrations created for prevention literature used in Bangladesh to advise people and increase awareness of the risk of potential assault. Those cases with unclear clinical evidence of the burn source, which usually are those believed caused by acid, were excluded from analysis.

OBSERVATIONS

Attack with Chemicals

Generally, an attack with chemicals is designed not to bring about death but to cause severe bodily disfigurement and grave impairment of the senses, when the face is targeted, such as blindness. When the intent is to maim and scar but not to kill, chemicals are preferred over more lethal weapons that generally are difficult to obtain (Bari & Chowdhury, 2002; Yeong, Chen, Lin & Engav, 1997; Branday, Arscott, Smoot, Williams & Fletcher, 1996; Asaria et al, 2004). In a majority of cases, a chemical analysis finds no remnants of acid, particularly when the patient reports late in the hospital or delays in reporting to the police. By this time circumstantial evidence of the harmful substance has been destroyed. Chemical analysis is usually done from burnt clothes and acid left in pots used by the attacker or attackers. An analysis on a wound by litmus paper shows no results, when patients come to the hospital too late and/or they have already used water on the wound. Rinsing with water is a well-known method of first aid in chemical burns – however, it removes the source of the injury. Although patients often claim they have had acid thrown on them, it is also common to find that lime water and rice water (*mar*) that has been heated were used in an attack, particularly against elderly persons following a verbal altercation.

The number of acid attack victims is declining in Bangladesh, since the inception of the 'Acid Crime Control Act 2002' and 'Acid Control Act 2002'. This proves that a strong law can improve a situation that affects persons who often lack legal recourse (Hossain, no date; Acid Survivors Foundation, 2011; Bari & Chowdhury, 2002).

Tools

Most types of attacks with chemicals are acids that are readily available in local markets, where the cost is minimal and restrictions generally do not apply. Bangladesh has the highest prevalence of attacks with acids. These burn incidents constitute 60% of the globally reported cases of intentionally inflicted burns. More readily accessed by means other than commercial outlets, an attacker can secure acid from car batteries. Most commonly used in burn assault is sulfuric acid, because of its inexpensive availability. The sulfuric acid used to replace dry lead–acid batteries, for example, is unregulated, cheap and readily available in many areas of Bangladesh, as well as some countries in Africa. Nitric acids and hydrochloric acid, and chemicals such as kerosene oil or other caustic solutions, are additional substances that are commonly used in burn assaults.

Features

The face is the most common target for an acid attack (Figure 1), which can result in ophthalmic injuries ("eyes"). The long-term consequences can include but are not limited to eyelid damage, synblepheron, ectropion, corneal opacity, and even destruction of the eyeball (ASF / Acid Survivors Foundation, 2011; Bari & Chowdhury, 2002). Other facial features can be severely damaged and impair such actions as eating and speaking, and affect the senses of smelling (nose and nostrils) and hearing (ears).

In acid assaults the depth of injury depends on concentration of the acid as well as the length of water irrigation (if any). Color and pliability of the skin helps in assessing depth of burn. Deep burns become darker and the skin loses elasticity. Conventional methods of assessing depth by color and capillary blanching as occurs in a flame burn do not apply in chemical burns. Putting running water immediately on the wound significantly reduces the depth and extent of an acid burn, and skin color becomes light brown (Figure 2).

The majority of chemical burn victims suffer less than 5% damage to bodily surface areas. Bari and Chowdhury (2002) have observed that cases where the percentage of damaged surface area increased to around 40%, the perpetrators were closely related to the victim, such as spouse or in-laws, who had greater opportunity and more occasions of frequent proximity in which to pour large amounts of acid onto the victim.

Figure 1. Acid attack, owing to denial of love proposal. Face is the most common target, as the skin surface is visible and uncovered. Artistic portrayal used for Prevention Education Campaign.

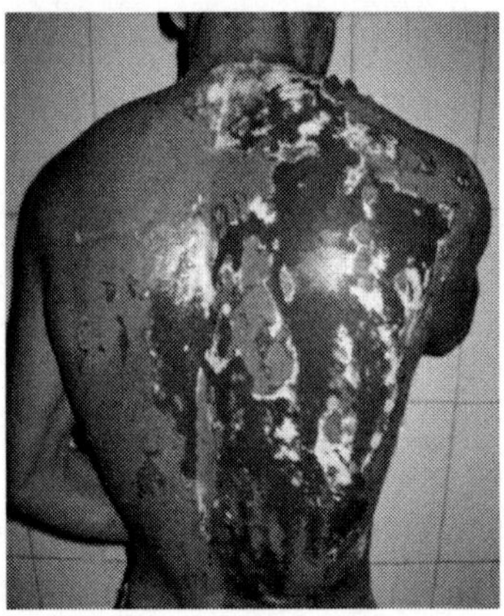

Figure 2. Mixed thickness acid burn exacerbated by pouring water on burn, showing alteration of skin color and deep dermal characteristics.

Secondary sites also are impacted. The chemical trickles down from the site of skin contact and "drops" produce sprinkling over the body, particularly on its flat surfaces. Deeper burn areas are found in crevices and curves of the body, where the chemical accumulates. Given the appearance of these injuries, sometimes diagnosis is not straightforward. In such cases, a case history can be helpful, including chemical analysis from the victim's clothes and any container or carrier that might have been used by the attackers.

Demography

Females are more commonly victims (58%) of acid attacks than male. Most of the attacks take place in and around the home (Bari & Chowdhury, 2002). All age groups are affected. The highest incidence occurs between 26 and 30 years of age (22%) which is followed by persons between 11 and 15 years (16%). Adolescent girls and recently married women are the most frequent victimized group. Children constitute 7.6% of all acid burn cases. In two studies in Bangladesh, however, the mean age of the attack victims were 22.5 and 20.4 years (Bari & Chowdhury, 2002; Mannan, Ghani, Sen, Clarke & Butler, 2004) which means that a sufficient number of young adults as victims elevated the mean age.

Most acid attacks occur in rural areas (74%). Over 45 % of the acid attacks in Bangladesh, for example, take place during the summer months (April through June) when people leave a window open, while asleep, and do not use a blanket or quilt. Thus, the face and most parts of the body can be targeted, owing to their visibility (Figure 3). Incidents occur less during the winter months (December through January), owing to the greater likelihood that windows and doors will be kept closed, and warm clothing is worn.

Motives

Worldwide a variety of motives have been identified for assault via chemical injury. In Taiwan, for example, domestic disputes over money were the dominant trigger (80% of cases nationally). In Jamaica the assailant was commonly a female perpetrator with a significant number of attacks on other women, owing to alleged or real infidelity by a spouse. In Uganda, robbery and burglary accounted for 47% of all chemical attacks (Asaria et al, 2004; Yeong et al, 1997; Branday et al, 1996). In Bangladesh, land dispute is the most common reason for an acid attack. Family disputes and those between neighbors were the second most common, usually following a quarrel.

In countries where female children are unwanted, they become frequent victims. Other motives for attack with acids include issues that arise in relation to marriage, usually for young girls where plans have been proposed or arranged for marriage. In instances of a couple recently married, the husband might have traveled abroad and someone within the immediate or extended family seeks to make sexual advances on the wife who was left behind. If she refuses she might become a victim. Dowry disagreements and divorces are also common as motives to inflict burn injuries, as well as inter-personal disputes over money lending. Some disputes might have political origins that motivate an acid attack.

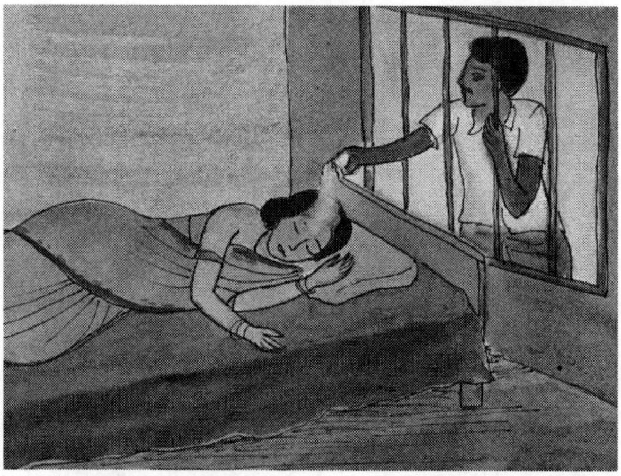

Figure 3. Night attack, acid thrown into house through open window. Because windows are opened because of heat, this form of attack is most common in summer months (April – July) and less frequent in winter (December – January) (Prevention Campaign).

In some cases the attacker intends to throw acid onto one person and it lands on another who was not the actual target. Usually children become the extra victims, owing to their proximity to the actual targets. In a number of cases the victim does not know the cause of the attack and the attacker remains unidentified. Some victims are assaulted physically prior to an attack with acid. Elderly persons and those who are psychiatric patients sometimes throw hot rice water (*mar*) or hot cooking oil onto a targeted victim, and these can be difficult to differentiate from a true acid assault.

Self-inflicted chemical burns happen as a means to punish another person, blackmail family members and/or antagonize political opponents. Clinical features in those cases usually do not correlate with the story that is told on how the injury took place. In these cases where the story is suspiciously inconsistent, care in eliciting a case history is important.

Burn by Fire, Flame and Heat

In the Indian subcontinent, bride burning has become a variant of domestic violence, as it has been outlawed and is currently handled as culpable homicide. Continuous harassment and physical abuse by husbands and in-laws, nonetheless, can lead a woman to commit suicide (Amnesty International, 2010), sometimes through self-immolation, that is, body burning. However, many of these alleged suicides are actually homicides (United Press International, 1997)._ENREF_67

Tools

Any number of hot fluids can be used as "tools," where burn injuries are caused by fire, flame or objects heated to extreme temperatures. These tools usually include everyday materials that are found in and around homes, such as hot scalding water, lentil soup (called *Dal*), hot rice water (called *Mar*), as well as various teas, hot cooking oil, and heated objects such as hot pot or bottle, lighted cigarettes, laundry irons, heated rods and pipes, electric cigarette lighter, kitchen utensils of various kinds, and even cooking herbs (Figures 4A, 4B and 4C).

A B C

Figure 4A (left). Superficial burns from hot lentil soup, healed spontaneously (compare Figure 2).
Figure 4B (center). Cooking utensils, heated red-hot to inflict contact burn; easily available.
Figure 4C (right). Intentional arm burns caused by lighted cigarettes, perpetrated by husband.

Features

Intent to inflict homicidal burning by fire always produces a major injury, as the victims are often tied or held in some fashion to prevent them from resisting (Figure 5). Hot oil or kerosene is then poured over the body, before it is lit to burn. Usually there is no one to medically rescue the target person and the case arrives too late in the hospital. These cases result in an almost 100 percent mortality, because of the severity of injury and the delay in seeking medical treatment.

Hot liquids such as soup or rice water or oil produce a burn that has the appearance of "rain drops" that mimic an acid burn. Sometimes a person will claim that such injuries were caused by acid. The only differentiating point is that those burns are superficial to mid-dermal burns, where thickness of the burn varies from the central point of contact to periphery. In periphery burns the wounds are more superficial. In the case of acid burns, however, such transitions usually do not take place and the burn depth is more or less uniform. The deeper burn is produced in body furrows, where acid has trickled down and accumulated. Hot objects and cigarette burns produce a characteristic shape. Cigarettes, for example, produce a circular burn of some 5 to 20 mm in diameter, where the depth of the burn depends on the length of time the cigarette was applied to the skin (Daneielsen & Rasmussen, 2006; Wolf, Davidovici, Parish & Parish, 2010). Complaints for cigarette burns are usually made against the husband.

Demography

Most the victims are female, burned by family members or in-laws, whereas a few are boys or men, where the burn injury has been inflicted owing to disputes over property and/or politics. When the victim is a man, the result of the burn incident is often homicide. In some cases kerosene oil is poured over the body of a victim before ignition. Incidents of this type can happen in the house of the in-laws, where the husband's relatives burn the victim, when demands for dowry are not made. In a few cases both the victim and the igniter are minors. Older children have been known to put fire to the clothes of younger ones.

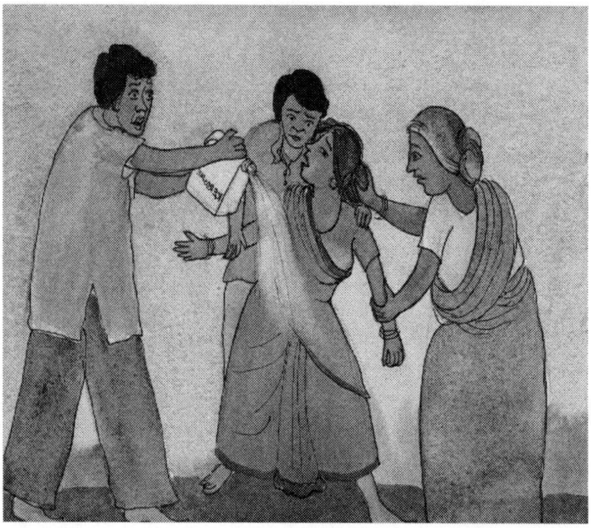

Figure 5. Dowry burn, husband and in-laws holding the victim increases burn severity and eminent death, close to 100% mortality (Prevention Campaign).

Medical staff have observed that the location of cigarette burns is a clue to whether an injury has been self-inflicted, especially in cases where the burn is located on a medial aspect of non-dominant forearm versus the more frequently used, dominant arm.

Motives

Similar to the motives for injuries sustained through chemical contact, burns through the use of hot liquids and/or everyday objects commonly involve disputes among persons known to each other. These disputes might involve a dowry, denial of an expression of love or unwillingness to agree to marriage, or divorce. Burn incidents for these cases often have a history of other forms of assault, prior to the burn injury. Sometimes a failed seduction or attempted rape might lead to a burn injury as retaliation against the unwilling person. Young girls forced into prostitution, when they become pregnant, or if they try to escape or shirk job responsibilities, sometimes are burnt to death. Other motives include family quarrels and village disagreements, where the latter usually are related to land ownership, debts and personal finances, and claims to property. During periods of political unrest the passenger buses, taxies and cars are set ablaze and the people inside become trapped and receive burns that are severe enough to cause death.

Because of the severity of injury and coverage by current law, the victims initially might lie about the incident, when they are brought to the hospital by the husband's relatives. They are afraid and seek to save the husband for the future of the child. They generally do not fully recognize the severity of their injuries, which often brings death. Later on when their parents enter the situation, the actual story is revealed. By this time it is too late. Police in the meantime have accepted the victim's statement and the story ends with her death. No one gets punished. However, the conflicting double statement sometimes is recorded and the outcome is altered.

Cases also have occurred among domestic servants who are working overseas. Whether the victim is living outside the country or working close to home, fractures and bodily deformity often have accompanied the burn injury in these domestic servants. Servants sometimes are made to suffer through burning to mete out punishment for an alleged indiscretion in performance of their domestic duties and as a means to force a confession regarding a perceived theft or related act of missing property while in the service to the sponsoring household. Refusal to engage in prostitution for the benefit of the patron also can become a motivating factor in burn injuries.

Psychological Aspects of the Burn Victims

Torture by burn causes both physical and psychological trauma. Most cases, the physical trauma is highlighted and managed but the psychological impact of a burn injury on the victim is ignored when services are delivered. The psychological aspects of burn injury have been researched in different parts of world. According to data secured through the Burn Unit of Dhaka Medical College Hospital, the overall psychiatric morbidity among both accidental and intentional burn victims is 47.6%, whereas it affects 70.6% of non-accidental burn patients. Regarding the patterns shown within the psychiatric morbidities experienced by burn victims, anxiety disorder (AD) has the highest percentage at 54.24%, followed by depressive disorder (DD) at 35.6%, acute stress disorder (ASD) at 3.4% and post-traumatic stress disorder (PTSD) at 5.1% and psychotic disorder at 1.7%. Victims suffering from reactive depression were found in a few of these cases.

It is apparent from observations at local medical facilities in Bangladesh that low socio-economic conditions, less education and unmarried status parallel manifestation of psychiatric disorder, following a burn. Large body surface areas often are involved in the patients with multiple sites of burn injuries, especially around the head, neck and face. Burn injuries that evolve and become increasingly greater can also produce mild to serious psychiatric disorders. Suicidal burn patients in contrast usually have a pre-existing psychiatric disorder.

Legal Issues

Twenty-one laws currently exist in Bangladesh to protect women and children against violence (Hossain, no date). To ensure the effective prevention of violence by acid injury and by fire or heated objects, it is important that all the known perpetrators are brought into the justice system. A parallel strategy is administratively monitoring the availability of various "tools," including the illegal use of acid. Implementation of these laws, however, has not always been effective. According to the central monitoring group of the Bangladesh Ministry of Home Affairs, among the reported cases of intentional burn injuries, 9.6 % have resulted in a conviction that has not been over-turned. Of the 1,693 burn cases that have been reported in Bangladesh since 2002, 39% of the cases were accompanied by a final police report, resulting in some 1,017 persons who were formally charged with a crime. Among those found guilty and formerly convicted of an intentional burn injury, thirteen were given a death sentence (AAB, no date; ASF, 2011).

Discussion

In Bangladesh, victims of torture by burn are typically female, whereas in many countries it is men who more commonly are victims. In South Africa, non-domestic arguments frequently precede assaults by fire and scalding liquids, and two-thirds of the assailants are male. In Hong Kong, the number of assaults by fire comprises 43% of all burn victims who were treated at medical facilities (Bari & Chowdhury, 2002; Yeong et al, 1997; Branday et al, 1996).

Self-immolation in low-income countries is particularly common among young women whose living situations are characterized by marital discord and family conflict. In Iran, these women are beset by poverty, illiteracy and limited access to mental health treatment. These experiences can be especially devastating, given the high incidence of adjustment disorders, depression and post-traumatic stress syndrome among both men and women (Ahmadi & Ytterstad, 2007).

The victims of acid burns have less mortality from their injuries but their morbidity rate is high. The scar left by the acid burn typically is not deep. Nonetheless, victims suffer their whole life by becoming the burden of the family, as well as the larger society and nation. Most the victims experience a dramatic change in lifestyle, which includes social isolation and debilitating damage to their self-esteem and corresponding economic difficulties (Zafreen, Wahab, Islam & Rahman, 2010). The psychological recovery of a burn patient is seen as a continual process, which is divided into three stages: (a) critical stage or *resuscitation*, (b) acute stage and (c) the rehabilitation stage, which typically takes the longest time. Not surprisingly, the psychological needs of burn patients differ at each stage (Shelley, Wiechman & Patterson, 2004).

Simultaneous evaluation and management of psychiatric disorders in torture burn patients are important. Extent of burn has been found associated with psychological impairment. Worldwide among intentional burn victims, the prevalence of depression has been reported at 58% and anxiety at 82% (Krug, Mercy, Zwi & Lozano, 2002). Full syndrome and acute post-traumatic stress disorders (PTSD) were found in 20 to 30 percent of these patients with burns, while in the hospital and/or after medical discharge (Levenson, 2007). In another study, post-traumatic stress disorder was diagnosed in 7% of the patients at time of their discharge and found in more than 22% of patients at four months follow-up (Roca, Spence & Munster, 1992).

The intentional burn patient is subjected to the stress of uncertainty during early management of their injury, which commonly affects both physical and psychological recovery (Levenson, 2007). In addition to the high demands of physical and psychological rehabilitation, patients must deal with social stressors, including family strains, accommodations when returning to work, sexual dysfunction, change in body image, and disruption of customary routines in daily life. Many people continue to have vivid memories of the incident, which exacerbate periods of distress. Cognitive and emotional status of patients and their families play an important role in the success or failure of burn treatment at each stage of the recovery process. Social support is an important buffer against recurrence of continuing psychological difficulty (Shelley, Wiechman & Patterson, 2004; Duminy & Hudson, 1993).

Some outcome investigations of pediatric burn cases have indicated that child survivors have adjusted well. Other studies in contrast have appeared which suggest that some 20 to 50 percent of pediatric burn cases experience psychological maladjustment that includes but is not limited to the inter-locking symptoms of depression and anxiety (Delilah, Noronha & Faust, 2007; Shelley, Wiechman & Patterson, 2004). These psychological symptoms are similar to those appearing in adults with the additional burden of having these complications at critical developmental stages in childhood and adolescence.

Even with strict national laws, the annual figures of reported incidents of acid violence remain high. Several reasons have been proposed for delay in legal justice. Studies show that victims of acid violence are more likely to be from a lower socio-economic class and in most cases the perpetrators are more influential and economically well-off and thus able to influence the family of the survivor to withdraw the case. Most survivors find it difficult to secure witnesses willing to testify in court. In many cases even the treating physician is reluctant to go to court to provide evidence. Importantly, the constant delays in trial process frustrate the victim and their family; they often lose faith in the justice system, because they are unable to bear the costs of frequent travel to court and time away from a job. Delays are often caused by lack of sufficient judges and judicial officers in the lower courts, prolonging the time to a hearing, which results in cases not heard on time or those that remain pending.

Challenges faced in the stages of investigation include inadequacies in First Information Report (FIR), partial and flawed investigation, deficient charge sheet, distorted framing of the charge, the appearance of ambiguous or incorrect medical reports, and the lack of perpetrator identification (AAB, no date; ASF, 2011).

CONCLUSION

Torture and assault by burn is brutal and can be severely damaging to both the external body and an individual's sense of inner personhood. The events of intentional harm infliction by chemical burns, fire, flame or heated objects could easily be preventable through the creation of social and political awareness, enforcement of the existing laws, public education and stronger enforcement of corrosive substance controls and distribution. Easy availability and casual use of acid at numerous factories and even at home, for example, was found alarmingly commonplace. Survivors of torture by burn often face social isolation and experience mistrust and public stigmatization, which further damages their sense of self-esteem and impairs their capacity to work, which in turn might alter their socioeconomic status. These aspects of injury by intentional burn prevent the victim from living an independent life, resulting in a situation of structural vulnerability and continuing social-economic dependency that can endure a lifetime.

REFERENCES

Ahmadi, A. & Ytterstad, B. (2007). "Prevention of self-immolation by community-based intervention," *Burns*, *33*(8),1032-1040.

Amnesty International, (2010). *Annual Report*, Retrieved from > https://www.amnesty.org/en/region/iran/report-2010.

AAB / Action Aid Bangladesh, no date, *Final Report*, Retrieved > http://www.preventionweb.net

Asaria, J., Kobusingye, O. C., Khingi, B. A., Balikuddembe, R., Gomez, M. & Beverige, M. (2004). "Acid burns from personal assault in Uganda," *Burns*, *30*, 78-81.

ASF, (2011). *Acid Survivors Foundation Annual Report*, Retrieved from > http://www.acidsurvivors.org

Bari, S. M. & Chowdhury, I. M. (2002). "Acid burn in Bangladesh," *Annual of Burns, Fire and Disasters*, *14*, 115-118.

Branday, J., Arscott, G. D., Smoot, E. C., Williams, G. D. & Fletcher, P. R. (1996). "Chemical burns as assault injuries in Jamaica," *Burns*, *22*, 154-155.

Daneielsen, L. & Rasmussen, O. V. (2006). "Dermatological findings of after alleged torture," *Torture*, 108-127.

Das, K. K., Quamruzzaman, M., Tareque, A. A., Islam, M. R. & Sen, S. L. (2011). "Chemical burns: A tertiary burn unit experience in Bangladesh," *Journal of Plastic Surgery*, *2*(2), 27-32.

Delilah, O. & Noronha, J. F. (2007). "Identifying the variables impacting post-burn psychological adjustment: A meta-analysis," *Journal of Pediatric Psychology*, *32*(3), 380-391.

Duminy, F. J. & Hudson, D. A. (1993). "Assault inflicted by hot water" *Burns*, *19*(5), 426-428.

Hossain, A. (no date). "Institutional approach to combat violence against women in Bangladesh," Retrieved from > *www.mspvaw.org.bd/filedownload.*

Krob, M. J., Johnson, A. & Jordan, M. H. (1986). "Burned-and-battered adults," *Journal of Burn Care and Rehabilitation*, *7*(6), 529-531.

Krug, E. G. D. L., Mercy, J. A., Zwi, A. B. & Lozano, R. (2002). *World Report on Violence and Health*, Geneva: World Health Organization, Retrieved from > *whqlibdoc.who.int/hq/2002.*

Levenson, J. L. (2007). "Psychiatric disorders among burn patients," *Psychiatry Weekly*, *2*(29) (online).

Mashreky, S. R., Rahman, A., Svanstrom, L., Khan, T. F. & Rahman, F. (2011), "Burn mortality in Bangladesh: Findings of the National Health and Injury Survey," *Injury – International Journal of Care of the Injured*, *42*(5), 507-510.

Mannan, A., Ghani, S., Sen, S. L., Clarke, A. & Butler, P. E. M. (2004). "The problem of acid violence in Bangladesh," *The Journal of Surgery*, *2*(1), 239-243.

Roca, R. P., Spence, R. J. & Munster, A. M. (1992). "Post-traumatic adaptation and distress among adult burn survivors," *American Journal of Psychiatry*, *149*, 1234-1238.

Shelley, A., Wiechman, R. & Patterson, D. R. (2004). "ABC of burns psychosocial aspects of burn injuries," *British Medical Journal*, *329*(7462), 391-393.

Stone, M. J. (1988). "Assault by burning and its relationship to social circumstances," *Burns*, *14*(6), 461-467.

Theodorou, P., Spanholtz, T. A. & Amini, P. (2009). "Cologne Burn Centre experience with assault burn injuries," *Burns*, *35*(8),1152-1157.

United Press International, (1997). "Kitchen fires" kill Indian brides with inadequate dowries, Retrieved from > http://www.hartford-hwp.com/archives.

Wolf, R., Davidovici, B. B., Parish, J. L. & Parish, L. C. (2010). *Emergency Dermatology, Cambridge University Press, New York*, 313-317

Yeong, E. K., Chen, M. T., Lin, T. W. & Engrav, L. H. (1997). "Facial mutilation after an assault with chemicals: Fifteen cases and literature review," *Journal of Burn Care and Rehabilitation*, *18*, 234-237.

Zafreen, F., Wahab, M. A., Islam, M. N. & Rahman, M. A. (2010). "Socio-demographic characteristics of acid victims in Bangladesh," *JAFMC Bangladesh*, *6*(1), 12-15.

In: Assaults
Editor: Keith V. Bletzer
ISBN: 978-1-62808-051-3

Chapter 10

Sexual, Physical and Psychological Aggression Linked to New Means of Communication: Child Pornography, Cyber-Grooming and Cyber-Bullying

Sébastien Prat [1,2]* ***and Carol Jonas*** [2]
[1]Forensic Department, University Hospital Center of Tours, France
[2]Psychiatry Department, University Hospital Center of Tours, France

Abstract

New means of communication have made it easier to communicate worldwide. They enable contact in real time, irrespective of distance and borders. However, these new means of communication have been diverted from their primary use to feed deviant fantasies or to satisfy a need of superiority. There are particular situations that can directly affect people: child pornography, grooming and cyber-bullying. The Internet is the main tool that is used in these three situations. However, the extensive use of cell phones should not be overlooked. In all three situations, the essential factors that explain the growth of offences are virtual aspects of communication and anonymity. Apart from child pornography, the main victims of cyber-grooming and cyber-bullying are adolescents, as, by definition, the victim must be able to establish virtual contact with an aggressor and thus have the capacity to master telecommunication tools. Likewise, the appeal of these tools for adolescents inevitably leads to their deviant use by other young people who are not always aware of the danger of virtual contacts and do not always recognize the impact of bullying. Criminal and victim profiles have been identified. Dematerialized aspect of these offences makes it difficult to apprehend the perpetrators. States must take steps to deal with cyber-criminality. New methods need to be set up to apprehend the perpetrators and protect the victims.

Keywords: Internet, child pornography, cyber-bullying, cyber grooming, offender, victim

* Corresponding author: Email: sebastienprat@hotmail.fr.

Introduction

Changes in society have led to significant shifts in behavior. New electronic means of communication enable messages to be sent instantaneously anywhere in the world and reach a very large number of people (Çetin, 2011). This has had an impact on both sexual violence and other forms of aggression, such as bullying. The victims are usually minors, who are not always aware of the dangers of the Internet and are unable to restrict their use of this tool, which they see as an important social asset (Bryce, 2009). These new means of communication help young people develop social relationships and allow them freedom of thought (Quayle, 2011). For the aggressors, use of these methods is linked to recurrent online contacts with reduced offline social relationships; the anonymity provided by these tools gives them an impression of domination (Appel, 2012). Three particular offences mediated by virtual communication are of particular concern: child pornography, online grooming, and cyber-bullying. Child pornography and online grooming are both sexual offences. However, child pornography does not necessarily lead to contact with an actual victim, unlike online grooming and cyber-bullying, which involve a specific link between the aggressor and the victim. Each of these three behaviors has its own specific characteristics, both by nature of the offence and profile of the perpetrators and the victims.

Child Pornography

Child pornography is the production of pornographic or erotic material involving use of children or adolescents (Chase, 2005; Howitt, 2007; Taylor, 2001). Tackling this phenomenon is complicated, owing to the range of child-pornography material and the diversity of criminal justice proceedings in different countries (Endrass, 2009; Kierkegaard, 2008; Prat, 2012, 2012a; Tirelli, 2008; Tyler, 1985). The first photographs go back to 1862 (Tyler, 1985). For many years, child pornography was limited to written texts and photographs (Burke, 2002; Frederick, 1996). Some aspects were perceived as artistic. In France, for example, Tony Duvert received a literary award in 1972 for his book "*Paysage de fantaisie,*" which can be perceived as an *apologia* for child pornography. Technological progress has gradually increased the possibilities of representing pedophile fantasies. Not only did the arrival of the Internet assist revised production of child pornography, it also allowed it to be disseminated more widely. It was not until the end of the 20th century that various nation-states began to pass laws to deal with the problem (Tyler, 1985).

Characteristics of Child Pornography Images

Actualization of child pornography is reprehensible. At present, no court has penalized pedophile fantasies, as long as they are not disseminated. Child pornography is a lucrative market. It mainly involves photographs and video recordings. Some written texts exist, but these generally accompany an image. The law had to be changed at the beginning of the 2000s to counter the growing industry, owing to use of new electronic means of communication and technologies (Prat, 2012). These new technologies facilitated the production and dissemination of pedophile images. The specific characteristic of this practice lies in the content of the images. As explained above, it does not necessarily involve a pornographic picture. The COPINE Project or *Combating Paedophile Information Network in Europe Project* drew up a classification of images, based on their suggestive or actually sexual aspects, also adding notions of sexual violence (Krone, 2004; Quayle, 2000; Quayle, 2006; Taylor, 2001; Taylor, 2003). Ten different types of image were identified, which varied in the degree of violence of the fantasies: 1) *Indicative*, 2) *Nudist*, 3) *Erotic*, 4) *Posing*, 5) *Erotic posing,* 6) *Explicit erotic posing,* 7) *Explicit sexual activity,* 8) *Assault,* 9) *Gross assault,* 10) *Sadistic-Bestiality*. Other aspects of these images should be considered, notably the fact they do not necessarily involve real aggressions. There is in effect a scale of images (Mirkin, 2009; Tate, 1992).

There are also so-called virtual or pseudo-photographs, created from collages or by computer graphics (Kleinhans, 2004; Krone, 2004). This aspect raises legal problems, as creating these images does not involve any actual abuse. Additional legal measures were thus introduced to tackle the issue. In many cases, people make large collections of images. In 1992, Lanning described six characteristics of child-pornography collections (Taylor, 2001): 1) *size* (number of images), 2) *consistency* (a specific topic), 3) *organization* (image classification), 4) *permanence* (preservation over time), 5) *secret nature* (images kept safe in protected places), 6) *sharing* (images pooled on pedophile sites). These images constitute an effective bargaining chip between child pornographers, who form networking groups to exchange advice, or find a minor. Interest in the images does not lie in stimulating fantasies, but rather in their use as a means of networking between collectors, of disinhibiting children for online and offline contacts, of rationalizing the adult's deviant behavior, and in some cases performed for financial gain (Quayle, 2003; Quayle, 2006; Taylor, 2001).

Child Pornography Users

A number of authors have described the profiles of child-pornography users. Generally, classifications mix simple child pornography users who do not contact a minor with people who solicit minors on the Internet with the intent to make contact online or offline. Burgess and associates (2005), for example, identified three categories: 1) *Traders* (people who collect child pornography via the Internet), 2) *Travelers* (people who seek to communicate with children), 3) *Traffickers* (people who participate actively in child trafficking with the aim of exploiting them sexually). Elliott and associates (2009) described four typologies: 1) *Periodically prurient* (people who show curiosity but without any actual sexual interest in children), 2) *Fantasy only* (people who are content with gratifying their fantasies virtually, without any real or virtual contact), 3) *Direct victimization* (people seeking real or virtual contact with minors), 4) *Commercial exploitation* (people interested only in the financial aspect). Krone (2004) drew up a more detailed description with eleven categories: 1) *Browsers* (people who come across images by accident, but knowingly save them), 2) *Private fantasists* (people who access images for their own interest and do not wish to share them), 3) *Trawlers-sexually omnivorous* (people who consume all types of pornographic material, including child pornography), 4) *Trawlers-sexually curious* (people who have experimented with child pornography but have not pursued it), 5) *Trawlers-libertarian* (people who believe that they are free to access all types of material), 6) *Non-secure collectors* (people who download and exchange images from openly available sources that do not impose security barriers), 7) *Secure collectors* (people who download and exchange images, taking precautions to limit the risks of being caught), 8) *Online groomers* (people who use child pornography with the intention of establishing contact with a minor), 9) *Physical abusers* (people who use child pornography both as part of actual abuse and to gratify their craving when they have no actual victim), 10) *Producers* (people who produce images involving either a real abuse, or pseudo-images), 11) *Distributors* (people who supply the pedophile network but who do not necessarily have pedophile fantasies themselves).

From these classifications, we can see that child pornographers, who are mostly seen as users as opposed to producers and distributors, do not use child pornography for the same purposes. Child pornography is not a clear-cut phenomenon and its use varies according to these profiles. One of the main notions to consider is pedophile attraction; a number of authors have shown that images are not always downloaded purely for pedophile sexual arousal (Elliott, 2009; Krone, 2004; Prat, 2012b). In some cases, this type of image is accessed as a way of defying a taboo. In this situation, the individual also displays an interest in other images of violence, war, among others. In general, studies of child-pornography users do not differentiate between people who do or do not establish virtual contact with a minor, even though direct communication adds to the risk of actual abuse. However, there does not appear to be a correlation between consuming pedophile images and the risk of committing an offline offense (Endrass, 2009). By contrast, studies generally differentiate between virtual and real contact (Deirmenjian, 2002; Gillispie, 2007). In sum, the use of child pornography can either constitute an end in itself or be a means of carrying out an offline abuse.

Typically, child pornography users are almost exclusively educated, professional men between the ages of 25 and 50. Overall, there are as many married users as single. On the whole, they are in a consensual adult sexual relationship, although they might not experience it as satisfactory (Beech, 2008; Burgess, 2005; Burke, 2002; Fortin, 2006; Frei, 2005; Prat, 2012b, 2013; Quayle, 2006). In general, there is no history of previous psychiatric disorder. In most cases, there is no prior conviction for a sexual offense. The rate of recidivism for child pornography users is relatively low, emerging one and a half to six years after conviction (Babchishin, 2011; Eke, 2011; Seto, 2011; Wakeling, 2011). With regard to their psycho-pathological functioning, we can observe a cognitive distortion, generally similar to that of a pedophile who has committed actual abuse, although they may have more empathy with their victims (Babchishin, 2011; Burgess, 2005; Marziano, 2006; Seto, 2011). This can be explained by the fact that the borderline between the virtual and the real is sometimes tenuous and that many child-pornography users have clearly pedophile fantasies, even if they only gratify them virtually.

Child Pornography Victims

Victims of child pornography can be divided into two categories (Prat, 2013; Varnhagen, 2007): minors who have been subjected to an actual assault and minors whose image has been falsified for sexual purposes (pseudo-images). With regard to distribution of child-pornography imagery, what is important is the process of perpetual victimization (Prat, 2013). Even if the assault actually occurred once or not at all in the case of a pseudo-image, victimization continues indefinitely with the transmission of the image depicting a minor in an erotic or pornographic scene. Moreover, the aggressors can put pressure on victims through the pictures they have taken, either telling them they must keep it secret or subjecting them to further abuse under threat of diffusing the images (Tate, 1992).

Interpol maintains a database of 520,000 images, involving 680 victims. The Internet Watch Foundation identified 2,755 Internet domains involving child-pornography images. Almost 80% of these images involve young girls (Elliott, 2009). This high percentage of female victims could explain the low rate of recidivism, as a higher rate of recidivism occurs among extra-familial homosexual pedophiles. In the 80,000 photographs and 400 video recordings identified by the COPINE Project, there were as many boys as girls (Quayle, 2000; Taylor, 2001; Taylor, 2003). UNICEF (2009) released a report stating there were more than four million Internet sites and that more than 200 new images were posted every day (Maala, 2009). At the end of 2011, the Interpol database contained 2,500 victims from 46 countries (Aiken, 2011). In general, children of all ages are involved, including infants, pre-pubescent children and adolescents. These categories of victims provide significant psycho-pathological information about the users of these images, notably to setting up appropriate prevention measures (Elliott, 2009). It is the apparent age of the victims in the image that is generally used by the courts to determine whether or not child pornography is involved. In some cases, the images involve adults dressed up as children. Under these circumstances, the protagonist's status changes from victim to accomplice (Prat, 2013a).

The attitude of the victims in the pictures is an important issue. Most images show children looking cheerful or neutral (Burke, 2002). This plays a role in the cognitive distortions of pedophile-customers, as they have the impression that these scenes are not unpleasant for the children, who must be enjoying themselves, reinforcing the idea that there is no coercion involved.

Child pornography is a complex deviant behavior. Users are not always satisfied with "fuelling" their fantasies through the images, but may seek contact with a minor, even if only virtually.

Online Sexual Grooming

Online grooming is a way of establishing contact with another person for sexual purposes. It corresponds to legal practice, when two adults establish a relationship on the Internet to satisfy reciprocal desires and an illegal practice when an adult seeks to satisfy his/her sexual cravings with a minor. There is a close link with child pornography, as pedophile images are often used to establish online and then offline sexual contact (Chase, 2005; Quayle, 2003; Quayle, 2006; Taylor, 2001). The adult may take pictures of the assault, which he can then use later to attract other minors (Prat, 2013). The use of telecommunication devices enables the perpetrator to identify and make contact with a "target" child (Tate, 1990; Taylor, 2003). Before the arrival of the Internet, establishing contact between a pedophile and a minor involved a direct relationship with no way of falsifying identity. The perpetrator used specific means of persuasion to establish a close relationship or resorted immediately to violence. Emergence of the Internet made it possible for the perpetrator to remain anonymous and falsify his identity, thereby making it easier to establish a relationship through online grooming (Burgess, 2008; Quayle, 2003).

Characteristics of Online Grooming

Online grooming developed at the same time as cyber-sex (Quayle, 2003). Development of the Internet made it easier for pedophiles to realize their fantasies. Distance communication made it possible to reach large numbers of people. As mentioned in the Introduction, possibilities of distorting reality provided by virtual contact has a significant effect on the occurrence of online grooming (Deirmenjian, 2002). There are two significant aspects of online grooming. First, it can simply be a means of identifying vulnerable minors that sets the stage for a meeting, without waiting for the minor's consent. Secondly, it can involve establishing a complicit contact between adult and minor, leading the minor to engage in sexual activity with an adult without coercion. When the Internet and virtual communication technologies first emerged, the aggressor had to gain the victim's confidence for the discussion to take on a sexual connotation. Nowadays, with the growth of social networks, very detailed information, including a photograph, enables an aggressors to make more rapid and targeted contacts (Quayle, 2011). In particular, they can target minors living in their neighborhood, thereby opening a possibility of establishing an offline contact faster and more easily. Likewise, personal details make it easier to identify vulnerable minors likely to be more receptive to and less suspicious compliments made by the adult.

Anonymity afforded by the Internet and electronic communication devices is a critical element in *virtual assault*. In particular, it allows identity and age to be collapsed and/or falsified, a method commonly used to obtain the child's confidence. It also has an impact on the aggressor, notably in terms of disinhibition (Quayle, 2003). Various aspects of disinhibiton have been identified. For example, Whittle and associates (2012) referred to a study in 2004 by Suler, who identified six underlying factors: 1) *dissociative anonymity*, corresponding to not being identifiable online, 2) *invisibility*, whereby virtual abuse is facilitated by not having to worry about social appearances, 3) *asynchronicity*, whereby the time lag imposed by these methods of communication impairs normal reactions, 4) *solipsistic introjections*, whereby lack of face-to-face communication can allow one person to conjure up a false image of the other with an impression of being able to read their mind, 5) *dissociative imagination*, whereby there is a split between the online and offline *persona*, allowing the abuser to live in a fictional world, 6) *minimization of authority*, whereby the person does not feel that he is committing any offence because there is no real contact.

New means of communication enable instantaneous discussions to take place at a distance. This makes fantasies seem almost real (Quayle, 2011; Whittle, 2012). Two of three profiles identified by Elliott and Beech (2009) can be found among online groomers: 1) *browsers*, who seek to communicate virtually, 2) *cruisers*, who adopt a sexual language in order to establish offline contact, 3) *pornographers*, whose specific interest is in pornographic material, without seeking any personal contact. It is this third profile that corresponds most to the child pornography users whom we have described. However, one should not overlook the impact of child pornography on the functioning of the online groomer, as we have shown with its use for attracting minors (Krone, 2004). This material enables adults to join discussion groups, thereby making it easier to identify minors able to meet their needs. A study in California found that 30% of sexual assaults involved the Internet (Gillispie, 2007). These assaults mediated by the Internet mainly involved men. In most cases, victims were aware that they were communicating with an adult (Quayle, 2011; Wolak, 2008).

Online Groomers

Davidson and associates (2011) defined an online groomer as someone who initiates contact with a child through the Internet with the intention of establishing a sexual relationship, involving cyber-sex or sex with physical contact (Davidson, 2011; Quayle, 2011). The term covers a heterogeneous group, as is generally the case for child sexual offenders (Prat, 2013; Whittle, 2012). Studies indicate that time spent prior to the offline meeting varies, usually around one month. However, it should be noted that in some cases the contact occurs less than 24 hours after the first online discussion (Quayle, 2011). The literature does not provide a specific profile, unlike child-pornography users where grooming does not have a direct sexual aim (Prat, 2012b, 2013). By contrast, two groups appear to emerge: *contact-driven group* comprising people who are looking for a real offline contact and *fantasy-driven group* composed of people who are looking for cyber-sex with no offline contact (Briggs, 2010; Quayle, 2011).

The *fantasy-driven group* like those who download pedophile images (characteristics often found in the same person), unlike the perpetrators of sexual assault, generally show few criminal characteristics (Quayle, 2011). They spend a lot of time on the Internet, which allows them to avoid real social relationships. These virtual contacts allow them to gratify their sexual urges. It is possible that these individuals are inhibited, and/or have a social phobia, explaining the low criminal aspect and low rate of recidivism (Barron, 2000; Prat, 2012b, 2013; Quayle, 2003). This inhibition could thus be considered a protective factor, keeping them away from the risk of carrying out actual abuse. For these individuals, the online contact is a way of gratifying a fantasy that child pornography material cannot do. The characteristics of this group are broadly similar to those of users of child pornography: relatively young with a good education and no criminal record. It is possible that people who consume child pornography gradually become *fantasy-driven*. It could therefore be considered an escalation of the pedophile process, and should thus be treated as a potential risk of offending.

Individuals in the *contact-driven group* target children and then create links with them as a precursor to assault. This method of virtual communication allows them to establish a non-coercive contact (Guan, 2009; Quayle, 2004; Tyler, 1985). The non-coercive aspect of an assault on a minor is an important element. In fact, not all child sexual offenders act with violence and force. Some seek the child's approval, as part of their way of operating. Pedophile attraction can in fact be linked to other cognitive distortions, such as the impression the act is not deviant and the child is willing (Babchishin, 2011; Burke, 2002; Howitt, 2007; Marziano, 2006). Indeed, some pedophile groups militate for release of people imprisoned following a sexual relationship with a minor not involving coercion (Tyler, 1985). Their argument is based on the child's consent. The difficulty in explaining this consent, even when it is clearly expressed by the child, is biased first by the child's emotional immaturity and secondly by the possibility the child is psychologically disturbed. Online groomers are generally younger than offline offenders (Babchishin, 2011; Prat, 2013). This can be explained by the recent emergence of these means of communication. Previously, in order to gratify fantasies, offenders had to find their victims in the real world. They therefore set up specific mechanisms to attract victims, such as showing an interest in children living in the neighborhood, obtaining their parents' confidence, among other tactics. As these mechanisms work for them, they have not needed to change their behavior. Now, thanks notably to the

Internet, pedophiles can be more circumspect and can establish contact without having to communicate with people close to the child, making it more difficult to identify and apprehend them (Krone, 2004).

Victims of Online Grooming

Victims of online grooming are generally adolescents between the ages of 14 and 17 (Willis, 2002). This can be explained by the fact the victims must themselves be connected to the Internet and know how to use it. Within the general population, between 13 and 17 percent of children have been victims of online solicitation (Whittle, 2012). Half the children reported these events to an adult (Varnhagen, 2007). Wolak and associates (2004) found that one child in seven who used the Internet had experienced a sexual solicitation; 4% were aggressive and 34% involved exposure to pornographic material. These children must be able to understand objectives of the adult, particularly when the latter seeks to establish a sexual contact without coercion. Unfortunately, it is very likely that the average age of the victims will fall in coming years due to the fact that the Internet is being used by increasingly younger children and there is a certain form of liberalization of behavior, as parents do not always restrict access nor monitor their children's interactions. The victims are generally psychologically distressed (Willis, 2002). They often have self-image problems that can be linked to previous abuse or flawed family structure. They are more likely to respond to advances made by individuals who often offer comfort. They are therefore willing to establish a relationship, particularly if it boosts their self-esteem, which no other person has done. These children can then become victims of child pornography, if they are filmed or photographed during their abuse. Fortunately, as pointed out by Wolak and associates (2008), not all children who use the Internet are at risk.

The advent of social networks has changed the identification and profile of potential targets. Previously, victims were approached in online *chat rooms*. Contact was established around a particular topic in which the child participated. The groomer showed a passing interest in this topic in order to establish a special relationship with the child, pretending to share a common interest. Increasingly, with the rise of social networks, children seek to extend networks to prove their popularity, driving them to reveal information about themselves without worrying about potential risks. Giving personal information, particularly details that enable a child to be located, which could lead to sexual discussion, incurs a greater risk of receiving aggressive messages and of suffering an offline assault (Mitchell, 2007; Quayle, 2011). Furthermore, some messages left on the child's personal page describe her/his distress and hence vulnerability. Fortunately, this concerns a low percentage of children, as observed by Quayle and Taylor (2011) quoting a study by Ybarra and associates (2007). A study by Dowell and associates (2009) reported that 20% of adolescents who put photos on line were at risk (Dowell, 2009).

Online grooming has a real psychological impact, even if no actual abuse occurs. The other type of cyber-violence involving a real victim is cyber-bullying.

Cyber-Bullying

Bullying is a wide-spread phenomenon found in all areas of social life and affecting people of all ages. Underlying factors motivating this behavior are complex. Like the two offences described above, the use of new means of communication has transformed this phenomenon. Previously, harassment or intimidation involved specific characteristics, such as need for a victim, an aggressor and a bystander. Now, the bystander is no longer systematic and yet impact is just as great. Bullying tactics were rarely possible without a real contact. When leaving school or the work-place, the victim could feel a sense of security, because of the absence of the aggressor, whereas now these destabilizing tactics lack boundaries and there can be no refuge. Moreover, the fact that messages are sent anonymously renders them even more destabilizing, and the victims do not know which way to turn.

The Characteristics of Cyber-Bullying

Olweus (1995) defined bullying through three criteria: 1) showing aggressive behavior towards an individual or group, 2) it is repetitive, 3) there is a clear power imbalance between "bully" and "victim" (Baughman, 2012; Huang 2010; Kowalski 2007). A fourth criterion can be added, namely, 4) the intention to harm the victim (Baughman, 2012). Cyber-bullying removes the physical aspect, leaving only the so-called verbal (insults, rumors) and emotional (exclusion, social alienation) aspects of the aggression (Çankaya, 2010; Kowalski, 2007). In traditional bullying, physical aggression could be a major component with some bullies using insults to provoke a victim to react violently. Bullying involves distinct behaviors: direct insults, indirect insults, exclusion, rumors. There is a difference between cyber-stalking and cyber-harassment. In cyber-stalking, the victim fears a credible threat likely to result in real physical injury. Cyber-stalking thus provokes more psychological disturbance and is more difficult to put aside than cyber-harassment (Dimond, 2011). Cyber-bullying can be broken into indirect and direct aggressive behavior. Direct aggression harms the victim without attacking them personally, for example, sending hoax messages, indecent photos or making threats. Indirect aggression no longer consists of physical assault but involves disseminating personal information or spreading false rumors, which can have a direct impact on the victim's reputation (Betz, 2011). Most studies on cyber-bullying involve cohorts of adolescents and/or students. Few studies have described the practice of cyber-bullying among adults. Children who bully or become victims of bullying are generally over ten years of age, which is related to the use of electronic means of communication such as the Internet and cell-phones that have become a popular way of aggressing someone close, especially among young people. Before advent of these devices, the main places where bullying occurred was school or university. This geographical limit of bullying provided a degree of emotional protection in that the victim had a possibility of avoiding these places. Now, the specificity of cyber-bullying has removed these temporal and spatial boundaries. The victim can thus be reached at any time – at school, university, work or home.

The Internet has modified the forms of bullying but the number of bullies does not seem to have increased (Dimond, 2011; Kumazaki, 2011). By contrast, the specific nature of these new means of communication is that it enables virtual relationships, whereby some adolescents only know each other through the Internet. Addiction to the Internet seems to encourage the spread of cyber-bullying, associated notably with a reduction in social relationships (Çankaya, 2010). Thus, as stated above, it is sometimes impossible to identify the aggressors, and even when they are known, they remain intangible, leading to a sense of estrangement, and dispossession of the self (David-Ferdon, 2007; Stassen Berger, 2007). In a study by Li (2007), half the students had already heard of someone being cyber-bullied. It is a well-known but under-estimated, phenomenon. In a study carried out by Patchin and Hinduja (2006), 11% of participants had been aggressors, 29% had been victims, and 47% witnesses. In some ways, this phenomenon is similar to malicious calls in that it involves repeated, anonymous attacks.

With regard to the actual organization of the aggression, there remains the question of the form that it takes. At what point can one consider oneself the victim of aggression? When it involves a repeated message, notably on social networks, does a message posted by the same individual constitute a new aggression, or is it part of a single aggression? If someone else takes part in the conversation, are they considered to be a second aggressor? (David-Ferdon, 2007). Initially, bullying required the existence of a group. People could harass an individual alone, but in this case the profile was generally one of gratifying sadistic urges, while the main characteristic of bullying is that the aggressors feel superior in the eyes of peers by belittling another person. With cyber-bullying, the power of the aggressor is no longer a question of physical strength or notoriety, but lies rather in the possibility of constantly harassing someone with no restriction of time or space. Phenomena have thus emerged that could be described as individual, in that the aggressor no longer requires a group to find satisfaction in the harassment which now only involves two people. Group cyber-bullying exists, notably through open discussions on social networks, which have enabled traditional offline bullying to be recreated on the Internet.

Cyber-Bullies

The perpetrators of cyber-bullying, mainly children or young adults, generally show relationship difficulties with their parents. There are two types of bully: those who bully gratuitously to gain notoriety and those who bully as a reprisal and can thus be described as bully-victims. The latter often react impulsively to a previous real or imagined aggression. Among adolescents, this tends to concern boys more than girls, with the reverse trend among adults (Stassen Berger, 2007). Girls have a greater tendency to reveal secrets and spread rumors, while boys generally have more direct, less insidious behaviors (Çetin, 2011; Huang, 2010). Unlike girls, boys tend to attack people of the same sex (Betz, 2011). Finally, these behaviors seem to overlap and can occur offline, where boys show proactive aggressive behavior, while girls behave in a more indirect fashion. Anonymity increases the power of the aggressors, who therefore feel stronger (Çetin, 2011). Wolak and associates (2007) observed the proximity that is often found between the aggressor and his/her victim; in 57% of cases the aggressor is a known peer and in 43% of cases is unknown. The impact on the victim is generally under-estimated by the perpetrator due to the online contact and the lack of physical aggression.

The virtual aspect of this aggression has modified the profiles of bullies. Some are described as inhibited, without social ties, and generally addicted to the Internet, at the same time needing stimulation and personal satisfaction that they find through harassment, notably for the sense of power it gives them (Kowalski, 2007). Previously, bullies were described as people certain notoriety in their group. Their behavior was never explained as possible psychological disorder. Now, there is concern about psychological disorders shown by these bullies and cyber-bullies, notably narcissistic disorders and suicidal ideation (Betz, 2011; Kubiszewski, 2012). Aggressive behavior such as harassment does indeed reflect a mental disorder that can only be externalized by attacking others.

There appears to be a link between the aggressive attitude of a child and the likelihood that he/she will become a bully in adolescence. An aggressive child is generally rejected, while an aggressive adolescent is often feared and respected (Stassen Berger, 2007). Behavior that can be a manifestation of mental suffering thus becomes a solution for finding notoriety and respect, and it is therefore difficult for the bully to stop this apparently beneficial behavior. The role played by the other peers is critical in the way the bullying behavior develops. Some bystanders can easily become bullies themselves, thinking that it will bring them notoriety or simply as a way of pleasing the aggressor. This phenomenon is found in cyber-bullying where there is not always an audience, but when an aggressor can find personal satisfaction in the action this brings an impression of narcissistic aggrandizement. It was initially thought that bullies had problems with social skills, which explained their behavior. Baughmann and associates (2012), however, demonstrated they had good scores on social intelligence, notably with capacities for empathy that made their intimidation more effective. By contrast, what emerged were anti-social traits. Bullies also have better scores on social cognition tests than victims and observers, which enables them to anticipate the behavior of others (Baughman, 2012). However, in some cases, an individual may act merely in a spirit of revenge in the anonymous environment afforded by cyber-space which appears safe and secure, thus becoming a cyber-bully in response to previous offline harassment (Baker, 2010).

Victims of Cyber-Bullying

There is a continuum in the process of victimization between bullying and cyber-bullying. David-Ferdon and associates (2007) found that 68 to 97 percent of online victims were offline victims, and between 2 and 76 percent had experienced physical violence. Two categories of victim have been identified: *passive* and *aggressive*. *Passive victims* are generally weak and submissive. They have few relationships with peers, very low self-esteem, which reinforces the intimidation, but good contact with adults, both parents and teachers. They often have the fatalistic impression that these people will not be able to help them, giving the aggressor a powerful hold over their defense mechanisms. *Aggressive victims* on the other hand are impulsive. They generally have previous psychological disorders that give rise to stigmatization, which is the starting point of the harassment. They adopt ineffectual reprisal behavior but find no support among adults (Stassen Berger, 2007). As in conventional harassment, aggressive victims will attempt to retaliate, but their impulsiveness may aggravate a situation, as they do not realize the impact of new communication such as the Internet. Their response may thus be out of proportion with the initial aggression, and the image they present is thus more that of aggressor than victim.

The virtual aspect has given rise to a third category, corresponding to victims who could be defined as neutral and who are sometimes chosen at random. At the outset, these victims do not present any psychosocial characteristics associated with vulnerability or any physical or psychological features that could give rise to stigmatization. The fact they become victims is due to their reaction to the aggression. The principal behind bullying and cyber-bullying is its repetitive nature. The way the victim reacts will thus either give credit to the rumor or encourage the aggressor to repeat the malicious messages.

Many psycho-social problems have been identified among victims of bullying and cyber-bullying, including stress, depression and social anxiety, declining academic performance, narcissistic disorders among girls and delinquent behavior among boys (Baughman, 2012; Kubiszewski, 2012). The prevalence of depression is three times higher than that reported in the general population (Baker, 2010). Some victims have even been found at school with a weapon, which appears to be the only way they can feel safe. These problems can be treated readily with strong family support, determined effort to stamp out the process, particularly when the child seeks the help of an adult. In a study by Wolak and associates (2007), 12% of the victims told their parents of the incident and 9% told another adult. There are several causes for this lack of communication with parents. First, there may be difficulty confiding in a parent linked to the typical conflicts found during adolescence. Another factor that is frequently reported in the scientific literature concerns the child's fear their use of the Internet will be restricted, because they consider this means of communication so essential for well-being (Appel, 2012). In half the cases, it seems that the child is also afraid the parent may make the situation worse. In general, although it is not always effective, the child will seek support from his/her peers. Only peers who are popular within the child's social group can help stop the harassment (Fenaughty, 2012). The most effective criterion to stop this phenomenon is for the child to seek the help of an adult more than actual assistance, by adopting a passive attitude (Fenaughty, 2012; Stassen Berger, 2007). Other strategies used to tackle the problem appear to be ineffective, such as passively ignoring it, or confrontation, which merely seems to boost the bully's ego and stimulate aggressiveness (Fenaughty, 2012).

Over and above the possible help of others, the victims' own characteristics will affect their ability to extricate themselves from an aggressive situation. They must have sufficient social skills to identify risky situations, know how to get rid of messages, and alert the people who are in a position to help them (Betz, 2011). In a study by Smith and associates (2004), 72% of victims had stopped being victims two years later, because they had been able to modify their social environment. For a person no longer to be considered as a victim of cyber-bullying, two criteria must be met; first, bullying behavior has effectively stopped, and second any psychological disorders caused by the behavior have disappeared. While bullying has been modified by cyber-phenomenon, main targets are still the most vulnerable people on account of physical appearance or psychological vulnerability. An inability to overcome psychological disorders, linked to bullying, will lead to the long-term continuation of these disorders, and will aggravate the victims' vulnerability, making them more susceptible to future attack. The term *cyberbullicide* was coined to describe suicide, influenced by virtual intimidation (Betz, 2011). It is not always easy for victims to escape from the harmful environment when cyber-bullies act via a communication tool that is indispensable to their victims, even if the latter have good social skills (Dimond, 2011).

Cyber-bullying is the ultimate non-sexual cyber-aggression. It includes a wide range of behaviors, whose negative consequences are not always immediate.

Conclusion

New electronic means of communication have opened up considerable changes in terms of violence, notably the emergence of *virtual violence*. In some cases, virtual violence can lead to very real physical and sexual abuse. The other feature inherent in the virtual aspect concerns attacks that can be qualified as “hidden.” Some victims of child pornography know nothing about dissemination of their image as part of a pedophile fantasy. Likewise, victims of online grooming are not aware of the other person’s sexual interest in them and victims of cyber-bullying do not always know the identity of their attacker. Development of these offences has therefore required specific measures. Speed and ease of communication, together with lack of frontiers, has obliged many countries to change existing or create newer legislation. With regard to cyber-bullying, this offence does not generally cross national borders. Legal procedures in contrast to deal with use/distribution of child pornography and online grooming, two very similar practices, had to be modified, as the networks frequently involved several countries. Various police actions, notably by Interpol and Europol, have led to the arrest of members of some networks (Dombrowski, 2004; Gillespie, 2010; Kierkegaard, 2008; Krone, 2005; Prat, 2012a). However, certain police practices, notably sting operations, are allowed in some countries but not in others.

These three deviant online behaviors mainly affect children. They lead to what can be called ‘rebound’ or ‘time-bomb’ phenomena (Bryce, 2009). The aggression is not always immediate, the victim is not always aware of it and it has delayed psychosocial consequences. The general public must therefore be made aware of these phenomena and the very real risks to young people of using electronic means of communication in general, and the Internet in particular.

References

Aiken, M., Moran, M. & Berry, M. J. (2011). “Child abuse material and the Internet: cyberpsychology online child related sex offending,” *29th Meeting of the INTERPOL Specialist Group on Crimes against Children Lyon, France*, 1-22.

Appel, M., Holtz, P., Stiglbauer, B. & Batinic, B. (2012). “Parents as a resource: Communication quality affects the relationship between adolescents’ internet use and loneliness,” *Journal of Adolescence*, *35*, 1641-1648.

Babchishin, K. M., Hanson, R. K. & Hermann, C. A. (2011). “The characteristics of online sex offenders: A meta-analysis,” *Sex Abuse*, *23*, 92-123.

Baker, Ö. E. & Tanrikulu, I. (2010). “Psychological consequences of cyber bullying experiences among Turkish secondary school children,” *Procedia - Social and Behavioral Sciences*, *2*, 2771-2776.

Barron, M. & Kimmel, M. (2000). “Sexual violence in three pornographic media: Toward a sociological explanation,” *Journal of Sex Research*, *37*, 161-168.

Baughman, H. M., Dearing, S., Giammarco, E. & Vernon, P. A. (2012). “Relationships between bullying behaviours and the Dark Triad: A study with adults,” *Personality and Individual Differences*, *52*, 571-575.

Beech, A. R., Elliott, I. A., Birgden, A. & Findlater, D. (2008). "The Internet and child sexual offending: A criminological review," *Aggression and Violent Behavior*, *13*, 216-228.

Betz, C. L. (2011). "Cyberbullying: The virtual threat," *Journal of Pediatric Nursing*, *26*, 283-284.

Briggs, P., Simon, W. T. & Simonsen, S. (2010). "Internet initiated sexual offenses and the chat room sex offender: Has the Internet enabled a new typology of sex offender," *Sex Abuse*, *22*, 72-94.

Bryce, J. & Klang, M. (2009). "Young people, disclosure of personal information and online privacy: Control, choice and consequences," *Information Security Technical Report*, *14*, 160-166.

Burgess, A. W. & Hartman, C. R. (2005). "Sexually motivated child abductors: Forensic evaluation," *Journal of Psychosocial Nursing and Mental Health Services*, *43*, 22-28.

Burgess, A. W., Mahoney, M., Visk, J. & Morgenbesser, L. (2008). "Cyber child sexual exploitation," *Journal of Psychosocial Nursing and Mental Health Services*, *46*, 38-45.

Burke, A., Sowerbutts, S., Blundell, B. & Sherry, M. (2002). "Child pornography and the Internet: Policing and treatment issues," *Psychiatry, Psychology and Law*, *9*, 79-84.

Çankaya, İ. H. & Tan, Ç. (2010). "Effect of cyber bullying on the distrust levels of pre-service teachers: Considering Internet addiction as a mediating variable," *Procedia - Social and Behavioral Sciences*, *9*, 1634-1640.

Çetin, B., Yaman, E. & Peker, A. (2011). "Cyber victim and bullying scale: A study of validity and reliability" *Computers and Education*, *57*, 2261-2271.

Chase, E. & Statham, J. (2005). "Commercial and sexual exploitation of children and young people in the UK - a review," *Child Abuse Review*, *14*, 4-25.

David-Ferdon, C. & Hertz, M. F. (2007). "Electronic media, violence, and adolescents: An emerging public health problem" *Journal of Adolescent Health*, *41*, S1-S5.

Davidson, J., Grove-Hills, J., Bifulco, A., Gottschalk, P., Caretti, V., Pham, T. & Webster, S. (2011). "Online abuse: literature review and policy context," *European Commission Safer Internet Plus Programme*.

Deirmenjian, J. M. (2002). "Pedophilia on the Internet," *Journal of Forensic Sciences*, *47*, 1090-1092.

Dimond, J. P., Fiesler, C. & Bruckman, A. S. (2011). "Domestic violence and information communication technologies," *Interacting with Computers*, *23*, 413-421.

Dombrowski, S. C., LeMasney, J. W., Ahia, C. E. & Dickson, S. A. (2004). "Protecting children from online sexual predators: Technological, psycho-educational, and legal considerations," *Professional Psychology: Research and Practice*, *35*, 65-73.

Dowell, E. B., Burgess, A. W. & Cavaunaugh, D. J. (2009). "Clustering of Internet risk behaviours in a middle school student population," *Journal of School Health*, *79*, 547-553.

Eke, A. W., Seto, M. C. & Williams, J. (2011). "Examining the criminal history and future offending of child pornography offenders: An extended prospective follow-up study," *Law and Human Behavior*, *35*, 466-478.

Elliott, I. A. & Beech, A. R. (2009). "Understanding online child pornography use: Applying sexual offense theory to Internet offenders," *Aggression and Violent Behavior*, *14*, 180-193.

Endrass, J., Urbaniok, F., Hammermeister, L. C., Benz, C., Elbert, T., Laubacher, A. & Rossegger, A. (2009). "The consumption of Internet child pornography and violent and sex offending," *BMC Psychiatry*, *9*,43.

Fenaughty, J. & Harré, N. (2012). "Factors associated with young people's successful resolution of distressing electronic harassment," *Computers and Education*, *61*, 242-250.

Fortin, F. & Roy, J. (2006). "Profils des consommateurs de pornographie juvénile arrêtés au Québec : L'explorateur,le pervers et le polymorphe" *Criminologie*, *39*, 107-128.

Frederick, D. (1996). "Defending pornography," *Political Notes*, *124*, 1-4.

Frei, A., Erenay, N., Dittmann, V. & Graf, M. (2010). "Paedophilia on the Internet – A study of 33 convicted offenders in the Canton of Lucerne" *Swiss Medical Weekly*, *135*, 488-494.

Gillespie, A. (2010). "Legal definitions of child pornography" *Journal of Sexual Aggression*, *16*, 19-31.

Gillispie, J. F. (2007). "Cyber shrinks : Expanding the paradigm," in Gackenbach J (Ed), *Psychology and the Internet: Intrapersonal, interpersonal, and transpersonal implications* (245-273), London, UK: Elsevier/Academic Press.

Guan, S. –SA. & Subrahmanyam, K. (2009). "Youth Internet use: Risks and opportunities," *Current Opinion in Psychiatry*, *22*, 351-356.

Howitt, D. & Sheldon, K. (2007). "The role of cognitive distortions in paedophilic offending: Internet and contact offenders compared," *Psychology, Crime and Law*, *13*, 469-486.

Huang, Y. Y. & Chou, C. (2010). "An analysis of multiple factors of cyberbullying among junior high school students in Taiwan," *Computers in Human Behavior*, *26*, 1581-1590.

Kierkegaard, S. (2008). "Cybering, online grooming and ageplay," *Computer Law and Security Report*, *24*, 41-55.

Kleinhans, C. (2004). "Virtual child porn: The taw and the semiotics of the image," *Journal of Visual Culture*, *3*, 17-34.

Kowalski, R. M. & Limber, S. P. (2007). "Electronic bullying among middle school students," *Journal of Adolescent Health*, *41*, S22-S30.

Krone, T. (2004). "A typology of online child pornography offending," *Trends and Issues in Crime and Criminal Justice*, *279*, 1-6.

Krone, T. (2005). "International police operations against online child pornography," *Trends and Issues in Crime and Criminal Justice*, *296*, 1-6.

Kubiszewski, V., Fontaine, R., Huré, K. & Rusch, E. (2012). "Le cyber-bullying à l'adolescence : Problèmes psycho-sociaux associés et spécificités par rapport au bullying scolaire" *L'Encéphale*, *39*, 77-84.

Li, Q. (2007). "New bottle but old wine: A research of cyberbullying in schools," *Computers in Human Behavior*, *23*, 1777-1791.

Maala, N. M. (2009). "Promotion and protection of all human rights, civil, political, economic, social and cultural rights, including the right to development," In Human Rights Council of the United Nations (Ed.), *Report of the Special Rapporteur on the Sale of Children, Child Prostitution and Child Pornography* (1-27).

Marziano, V., Ward, T., Beech, A. R. & Pattison, P. (2006). "Identification of five fundamental implicit theories underlying cognitive distortions in child abusers: A preliminary study," *Psychology, Crime and Law*, *12*, 97-105.

Mirkin, H. (2009). "The social, political, and legal construction of the concept of child pornography," *Journal of Homosexuality*, *56*, 233-267.

Mitchell, K. J., Finkelhor, D. & Wolak, J. (2007). "Online request for sexual pictures from youth: Risk factors and incident characteristics," *Journal of Adolescent Health*, *41*, 196-203.

Patchin, J. W. & Hinduja, S. (2010). "Changes in adolescent online social networking behaviors from 2006 to 2009," *Computers in Human Behavior*, *26*, 1818-1821.

Prat, S., Kalonji, A. & Jonas, C. (2012). "Evolution des aspects juridiques de la pornographie infantile en France," *La Revue de Médecine Légale*, *3*, 157-161.

Prat, S. & Jonas, C. (2012a). "How to catch child pornographers in France? The entrapment," *Legal Medicine*, *14*, 276-277.

Prat, S. & Jonas, C. (2012b). "Characteristics of French users of child pornography: description of a cohort subjected to forensic evaluation," *Medico-Legal Journal*, *80*, 162-166.

Prat, S. & Jonas, C. (2013). "Psychopathological characteristics of child pornographers and their victims: A literature review," *Medicine, Science and the Law*, *53*, 6-11.

Prat, S., Bertsch, I., Chudzik, L. & Réveillère, C. (2013a). "Developping software to estimate age in child pornography images for forensic purposes: Relevance and limitations in psychocriminology," *Journal of Forensic Sciences*, *58*, 845-846.

Quayle, E., Holland, G., Linehan, C. & Taylor, M. (2000). "The Internet and offending behaviour: A case study," *Journal of Sexual Aggression*, *6*, 78-96.

Quayle, E. & Taylor, M. (2003). "Model of problematic Internet use in people with a sexual interest in children," *CyberPsychol and Behavior*, *6*, 93-106.

Quayle, E. (2004). "The impact of viewing on offending behaviour," in M Calder (Ed.), *Child Sexual Abuse and the Internet: Tackling the New Frontier* (25-36), Dorset, UK: Russell House.

Quayle, E., Erooga, M., Wright, L., Taylor, M. & Harbinson, D. (Eds), (2006). "Abuse images and the Internet," In *Only Pictures?:Therapeutic Work with Internet Sex Offenders*, 1-11, Dorset, UK: Russell House.

Quayle, E. & Taylor, M. (2011). "Social networking as a nexus for engagement and exploitation of young people," *Information Security Technical Report*, *16*, 44-50.

Seto, M. C., Hanson, R. K. & Babchishin, K. M. (2011). "Contact sexual offending by men wit online sexual offenses," *Sex Abuse*, *23*, 124-145.

Smith, J. D., Schneider, B. H., Smith, P. K. & Ananiadou, K. (2004). "The effectiveness of whole-school anti-bullying programs: A synthesis of evaluation research," *School Psychology Review*, *33*, 547-560.

Stassen Berger, K. (2007). "Update on bullying at school: Science forgotten?," *Developmental Review*, *27*, 90-126.

Tate, T. (Ed.), (1990). *Child Pornography: An Investigation*, London, UK : Methuen.

Tate, T. (1992). "The child pornography industry: International trade in child sexual abuse" in C (Ed.), *Pornography: Women, Violence and Civil Liberties*, 203-216, Oxford, UK: Oxford University Press.

Taylor, M., Holland, G. & Quayle, E. (2001). "Typology of paedophile picture collections," *The Police Journal*, *74*, 97-107.

Taylor, M. & Quayle, E. (Eds), (2003). *Child Pornography: An Internet Crime*, East Sussex, UK: Brunner-Routledge.

Tirelli, L. A. (2008). "La répression pénale des consommateurs de pédopornographie à l'heure de l'Internet: Etude de droit comparé et de droit suisse" (Thesis). Université de Lausanne, Lausanne, Switzerland.

Tyler, R. P. T. & Stone, L. E. (1985). "Child pornography: Perpetuating the sexual victimization of children," *Child Abuse and Neglect*, *9*, 313-318.

Varnhagen, C. (2007). "Children and the Internet," in Gackenbach J (Ed.), *Psychology and the Internet: Intrapersonal, Interpersonal, and Transpersonal Implications*, 37-54, London, UK: Elsevier/Academic Press.

Wakeling, H. C., Howard, P. & Barnett, G. (2011). "Comparing the validity of the RM2000 scales and OGRS3 for predicting recidivism by Internet sexual offenders," *Sex Abuse*, *23*, 146-168.

Whittle, H., Hamilton-Giachritsis, C., Beech, A. R. & Collings, G. (2012). "A review of online grooming: Characteristics and concerns," *Aggression and Violent Behavior* (in press, corrected proof).

Willis, B. M. & Levy, B. S. (2002). "Child prostitution: Global health burden, research needs, and interventions," *The Lancet*, *359*, 1417-1422.

Wolak, J., Finkelhor, D. & Mitchell, K. (2004). " Internet-initiated sex crimes against minors: Implications for prevention based on findings from a national study," *Journal of Adolescent Health*, *35*, 424. e11-424.e20.

Wolak, J., Mitchell, K. J. & Finkelhor, D. (2007). "Does online harassment constitute bullying? An exploration of online harassment by known peers and online-only contacts," *Journal of Adolescent Health*, *41*, S51-S58.

Wolak, J., Finkelhor, D., Mitchell, K. J. & Ybarra, M. L. (2008). "Online 'predators' and their victims: Myths, realities, and implications for prevention and treatment," *American Psychologist*, *63*, 111-128.

Ybarra, M., Mitchell, K., Finkelhor, D. & Wolak, J. (2007). "Internet prevention messages: Targeting the right online behaviors," *Archives of Pediatrics and Adolescent Medicine*, *161*, 138-145.

In: Assaults
Editor: Keith V. Bletzer
ISBN: 978-1-62808-051-3

Chapter 11

SEXUAL ASSAULT: MEDICO-LEGAL ISSUES

Massimo Lancia**, *Ludovica Pieroni*[1] and *Valentina Rosati
Section of Legal Medicine,
University of Perugia, Italy

ABSTRACT

Sexual assault is a current problem that reaches public awareness, owing to the presence of improved documentation of violence-related injuries. Specialists assist victims of sexual assault face several difficulties, where a comprehensive examination must evaluate physical and mental health of the victim, circumstances of the assault, and a possible relationship between the victim and the perpetrator. Managing victims of sexual assault means, first, provision of medical care for their health and, second, facilitation of forensic assessment. Nevertheless, the juridical necessities are significant and therefore they must not be disregarded. Actions that aim to restore the victim's health must be performed with effective procedures to acquire useful information of forensic significance. This management needs to be advantageous beyond healing the victim. Correct collection of evidence, even if it is not the immediate purpose, can become the all-important "cultural capital" that is used in a courtroom trial.

The elaboration and introduction of a standard procedure is crucial, whereby it standardizes collection of evidence and management of the victim in the immediate setting. It is essential that an accurate case history is combined with blood tests, including research of toxics, drugs and microbes, as well as different types of sampling for sperm detection. These analyses are necessary because in most cases the medical examination and genital inspection do not reveal specific evidence of violence. Moreover, the earlier that examinations and tests are performed, the more useful and reliable the information (e.g. sperm in the vagina can be retrieved up to 72 hours, whereas toxics and drugs remain for a limited time in blood and urine). Therefore, for these same reasons, it is important to prove genital and extra-genital injury that may heal in a short time and lose its evidential validity. The importance of a proper methodology to obtain objective information stems from psychological and emotional consequences to the victim, caused by the trauma or, possibly, to drugs that could make the victim's deposition unreliable.

* Corresponding author: Email: lancia.massimo@libero.it.

The professional consultant who faces a sexual assault victim for medical assistance should, first of all, provide immediate health care and psychological support and, secondly, provide for documentary evidence by preserving the victim's clothes, sampling the appropriate body fluids and photographing possible wounds. In conclusion, it is essential that specialists be highly trained and knowledgeable regarding the effective approach in working with a victim of sexual assault and as contributing member of the multi-disciplinary cooperation team.

Keywords: Sexual assault, forensic assessment, medical examination, multi-disciplinary collaboration, victim needs

INTRODUCTION

Sexual assault is a serious problem. Public awareness is growing, insomuch as those who verify the presence and substance of violence-related injuries increase public knowledge. Sexual assault currently has a high prevalence. It is widespread across all social classes and occurs in all countries of the world. Strict categorization is not possible, because it encompasses women and men of any age, appearance and skin color. Anyone might be assaulted at any time of the day or night. Male victims of sexual assault are less common than women. For both men and women, however, the psychological impact of assault is so unbearable that it results in an under-reporting and, thus, under-estimation of the phenomenon by statistical enumeration.

Specialists who provide assistance to sexual assault victims face several difficulties. The specialist in a comprehensive examination must evaluate the physical and mental health of the victim, circumstances of the assault, and a possible relationship between victim and perpetrator. Physical and psychological consequences on the victim's health, as well as juridical ones, must be considered. Following tenets of a multi-disciplinary approach, each professional who gives assistance to the victim for sanitary or investigative reasons, and/or to offer psychological support, should first attend to the victim's primary needs. In this way, having met an obligation to the victim, the professional's work will better integrate with the practice of other professionals in forensic examination.

Managing the victims of sexual assault means, first, to provide medical care for their health, and, second, to facilitate forensic evaluation (Tschudin, 2005). For this reason, medico-legal practice becomes subordinate to medical care that re-establishes the victim's health. Nevertheless, the juridical necessities are basic and therefore must not be disregarded: those operations whose aim it is to restore the victim's health should be conducted with concomitant and adequate procedures in order to acquire useful information of significance. This type of management could be advantageous. The collection of adequate and correct evidence, even if it is not the immediate purpose of contact with the victim, is like having "cultural capital" with respect to a criminal trial.

Because the victim is the main witness in legal proceedings, forensic, medical and biological findings are essential throughout the period of investigation through the legal process of trial. Thus, each sample collected for medico-legal evaluation should be carried out in the right manner as soon as possible, given the importance of timing in relation to bodily processes. This means that it must be done by qualified personnel, well-trained for the best collaboration, in order to guarantee an appropriate intervention through medical care, first, and, second, the means to proceed effectively to trial.

Elaboration and introduction of a uniform procedure permits standardization in collection of evidence and clinical management of the victim. This is superimposed by the crucial immediacy of direct concern for the victim's health and well-being. Diffusion and adoption of a victim management protocol in each health care district allows forensic teachers to prepare professionals for managing and answering the initial needs of women, as well as adolescents and children who increasingly are becoming victims of sexual violence.

It is essential that an accurate case history is combined with the completion of blood tests that include a laboratory appraisal on toxics, drugs and microbes, as well as different types of sampling for sperm detection. These analyses are necessary because in most cases medical examination and genital inspection do not reveal, with any certainty, "evidence" of violence. This might be explained by the fact that most victims do not resist, usually for fear of dying. The earlier the examinations and tests are performed, the more useful and reliable is the information that they obtain (e.g., sperm within the vagina can be revealed up to 72 hours; toxics and drugs only remain in blood or urine for a limited time). Therefore, for the same reason it is important to prove the presence of genital and extra-genital injury which heals the quickest, before it loses its evidential validity. Early management of the victim is important to minimize associated risks to health, such as sexually transmitted disease (STD), pregnancy and psychological after-math consequences. All these need to be documented through good forensic specimens (Williams, 2004).

The importance of a proper methodology allows the medical team to obtain objective data. Established procedures permit needed intervention, related to the psychological and emotional difficulties that the victim might have experienced, which were caused by the trauma. Furthermore, members of the medical team identify the drugs that likely might have affected the victim in multiple ways, which can, for example, make the victim's deposition unreliable, during the early stages of her navigating and traversing the health care system.

The professional consultant who first faces a sexual assault victim for medical assistance should provide immediate health care (Stene et al, 2010) and psychological support and, secondarily, provide documentary evidence, by preserving the victim's clothes, sampling designated body fluids and photographing possible wounds. This type of approach can facilitate identification of the assailant and piece together the facts, as part of the criminal investigation.

Working with the victims of sexual violence requires a strong motivation and an awareness of difficulties that one might face every day with persons who have experienced structural vulnerability if not structural/symbolic violence. It is essential for specialists to be highly knowledgeable regarding correct approaches to the victim of sexual assault from a heath care and criminal justice standpoint, as well as techniques to ease anxiety over their participating in a multi-disciplinary co-operation. Practitioner knowledge and professional demeanor should also include a basic understanding of other disciplinary procedures that are utilized in daily participation with patients and members of a team of multi-disciplinary professionals.

Health Care of the Victim of Sexual Assault

Owing to its multi-disciplinary complexity, medico-legal evaluation of sexual assault requires adequate capabilities and procedures, drawing from forensic pathology, psychiatry, criminology, forensic genetics and toxicology. As described, sexual abuse represents a violation of both physical and psychic integrity, and thus justifies a multi-disciplinary approach to acquire useful medico-legal and diagnostic data, once the victim's needs have been met. A multi-disciplinary public center for adult and adolescent victims of sexual assault can offer professional medical and psychological treatment as well as capacity for forensic evidence collection and documentation (Ingemann-Hansen et al, 2009). Thus, it would be advantageous to adopt protocols, flow-charts and/or guidelines to orient the medical team on care of the victim to obtain the necessary information to provide a correct clinical and medico-legal judgment on the victim's condition. This is paramount in relation to prognosis for recovery, fulfillment of the possible need for rehabilitation and/or counseling, and legal advice in relation to the prosecution of the assault perpetrator.

Basic aims of medico-legal assessment are to minimize physical and psychological trauma experienced by the victim, maximizing probability of collecting and preserving adequate evidence for potential use in procedures of the legal system (Young et al, 1992). Protocols, flow-charts and guidelines should be structured in different phases, which include the following:

- Acceptance that sets the intervention tone, including informed consent of victim
- Case history that emphasizes assault details and prior condition before the assault
- Clinical examination focused on a victim's psychic and physical condition general and local, with photographic documentation of injuries and medical records (case notes)
- Precautionary measures that include post-coital contraception & prophylaxis against potential post-incident infection by sexually transmitted diseases (STD)
- Laboratory tests on specific genetic, toxicological and infectious dimensions
- Therapy including both psychological counseling and physical rehabilitation
- Patient advocacy and follow-up procedures

Acceptance of the Victim of Sexual Assault

An attitude of *acceptance* toward the victim is the first therapeutic necessity of intervention. This crucial first step is the foundation for all the steps that follow. In particular, the first step before the case history is victim consent to medical intervention. To increase relevance, the *acceptance* of the victim should be achieved in a reserved, quiet place. *Acceptance* should be carried out by a qualified and trained staff member, because an empathic, comprehensive, helpful and non-judgmental approach will lead the victim into a more comfortable mood and assure her/his cooperation. This may facilitate adequate collection and clarification of remaining information from the examination.

A climate of confidence must be created and nothing should be done without full consent and comprehension of the victim that includes the all-important dimension that the woman can halt her examination at any point. Written consent is secured. A woman who understands the information can make a fully informed decision to undergo a medical forensic examination and thereby assure the adequacy of forensic information, improve the likelihood she will benefit from counseling, and take steps to offer post-assault services, according to the model proposed by Du Mont and associates (2009). Development of this model through an investigation found that most women referred to their center were overwhelmingly satisfied with interactions with the specially trained examiners and felt their physical and emotional needs were addressed satisfactorily.

Post-rape trauma can influence a woman's ability to choose consciously and independently whether or not to undergo examination (Du Mont et al, 2009). Some studies have drawn on perceptions of health care providers on what the process was like for women. A survey of 110 sexual assault programs in the United States, for example, reported that a substantial proportion of nurse examiners believed that many victims found the pelvic examination and the act of disclosing details on the sexual assault the most distressing (Campbell et al, 2006). A study of 118 sexual assault nurses in Ontario, Canada, found that almost one fourth of respondents believed that collection of evidence was akin to a second assault (Du Mont & Parnis, 2003) and almost three-fifths thought the process could "re-victimize" at the same time it was "therapeutic" (Du Mont et al, 2009). A few studies have shown that women examined by health care providers with specialized instruction in working with sexual assault victims, in specialized sexual assault centers, have been more favorable about the medical forensic examination experience. Moreover, most the women sought medical attention and/or counseling. Sometimes collection of evidence was considered less important than provision of health care (Du Mont et al, 2009). Moreover, a possibility the victim might refuse participation in some, or all, the offered procedures that would allow her to re-establish a threshold of self-comfort already "overshot" and obliterated by sexual assault.

Otherwise, treatment, therapy and prophylaxis for sexually transmitted diseases bring back the victim's sense of self-integrity and help "to ride over" any feelings of inadequacy produced through sexual assault violence. Exercising personal choice in the aftermath of sexual assault is the "primary curative step for her to take in resuming personal authority over her own life" (Du Mont et al, 2009, p. 779). For this reason it is important that each victim not feel *judged* or *blamed* for the traumatic experience. The medical forensic examination can offer women an opportunity to "do something" positive. The process becomes important in helping assault victims to regain a sense of self-efficacy and self-worth. Du Mont and associates noted some women have suggested that forensic examination was empowering with respect to better understanding how to hold an assailant legally responsible.

Some victims might report, in addition to the assault details, experience with related situations of vulnerability, such as drug or alcohol addiction, or condition of homelessness, or psychiatric disease, which must not be under-estimated for importance in continuing the process to establish *acceptance* of the victim. Briefly, the phase of *acceptance* is based on the following:

- Honest availability, empathetic listening and inter-personal accessibility
- Comfortable setting without dramatizing or trivializing victim's behavior
- Non-judgmental behavior toward the victim and the experience
- Options to best disclose the case history and/or whether to undergo treatment

Intervention at this all-important acute phase requires the examiner to know how to responsibly and effectively face the victim's anguish, suffering and pain, and her most immediate concerns. For this reason, it is crucial that the program prepare a well-trained, multi-disciplinary staff that includes professional female figures that set the tone for medico-legal assessment to make the victim feel more comfortable.

Case History

The victim of sexual violence is the main source of evidence that might include physical lesions and biological traces, which confirm the act of assault. At the same time she is the main witness to the act, therefore, during the medico-legal examination the case history with care to elicit possible prior experience with sexual abuse is often the most important part of the overall evaluation (Adams et al, 2007). The goals of the medical evaluation are:

- To obtain the history from the individual who was the victim, i.e., the person "harmed"
- To consider alternative explanations for any physical sign or clinical symptom of concern
- To identify and document all possible evidence for extent of injury or presence of infection
- To diagnose and treat any medical conditions that might have resulted from prior abuse
- To identify and treat medical conditions which appear, unrelated to abuse or the assault

These are basic to collecting an adequate history from adults, adolescents and children, as stated above.

Further considerations, however, are required for any individual who is a minor. We add these here for a minor to provide the reader with a sense of the care taken to assure confidentiality, while collecting pertinent data, amidst the basic concern to have all the victim's needs met (Adams et al, 2007).

- History of prior episodes of abuse: Besides the child's history once assent is secured, it is advantageous to collect a parallel history on the child from a parent and/or guardian;
- To assess the child for any developmental, emotional, or behavioral problems that need further evaluation or assessment, and treatment, and make referrals, as necessary;
- To document findings in such a way that information can be effectively and accurately presented, if it has been requested by a social service or law enforcement agency;
- To assess the child's safety and report to child protective services if needed;
- To re-assure the child and the family, as appropriate to the circumstances;
- To help to ensure, above all, the well-being of the child and/or adolescent

A medical history is taken to determine the woman's present state of health and any physical and psychological needs that may require immediate attention. A history of the sexual assault is also taken for the purpose of guiding the evidentiary examination (Du Mont et al, 2009). In fact, the medical examiner should inquire specific to the circumstances of the assault, as well as the clinical and gynecological history of the victim. It must be considered how information regarding personal aspects of the alleged assault described by the victim might be deficient, because of her stress, tiredness and/or intoxication (Ingemann-Hansen et al, 2009).

It is important to specify time and place of the assault, if the assailant was more than one, if there were witnesses, if weapons were used to threaten and/or inflict harm, and whether drugs or other substances were used by the assailant "to facilitate" the assault. Studies have shown that adolescents pre-assault were less likely to have used drugs or alcohol than adults and more likely to be assaulted by acquaintance or relative. With young adolescent victims and children, the assailant was more likely to be a member of the minor's extended family. Adolescents were more likely to delay seeking care after rape and sexual assault, compared with adults (Jones et al, 2003). Young children might not know how to report an incident of assault. It is important to report if there was complete or incomplete penetration, if male ejaculation occurred, as well as provide a precise description of the type of penetration and whether it was vaginal, anal and/or oral. It is advisable to record with detailed accuracy, all of the physical symptoms such as headache, facial-thoracic-abdominal pain, difficult urination or defecation, pelvic disturbances, as well as expressions of psychological suffering reported by the victim. During the gathering of the forensic and corresponding case history, the examiner must pay close attention and report every possible psychological symptom, mentioned by the victim and/or manifested and observed, to create a correct evaluation of the victim's psychological status and to identify, whether present, any pre-existing psychiatric disorder. In summary, the case history record should include:

- Number of assailants and, if known, possible information about him/them
- Time and place of the assault with accurate details on unusual features
- The presence or absence of witnesses with their contact information
- Loss of consciousness by the victim and/or any others on the scene
- Use of weapons, alcohol and/or drugs "to facilitate" the assault
- Complete or incomplete penetration, or absence of penetration
- Type of penetration whether it was vaginal, anal and/or oral
- Contraceptive use, attempted or not: condom or other forms
- Whether or not ejaculation has occurred

Collecting an exhaustive record throughout the case history represents a guide for the medical examiner in the search for bodily traces and injuries appearing with the assault, as well as to analyze the compatibility between the history that was elicited and any of physical/clinical evidence that was collected.

Medical Examination

The main goal of the medical examination is to identify and record all the revealing signs that occurred with the assault, by including a general physical examination to locate extra-genital injuries as well as the all-important local genital examination, carefully inspecting all parts of the lower body, including the area between anus and genitalia ("perineum"). It is rare to discover one or more injuries that can unequivocally refer beyond a doubt to the occurrence of sexual assault, because in most cases physical findings are not pathognomonic and therefore they might refer to other types of violence and harmful modalities that have been the victim's experience, prior to the assault. On the other hand, the absence of physical injuries whether genital or extra-genital, does not mean conclusively that an assault did not occur.

Importantly, research and reported clinical experience of numerous practitioners underscore that the absence of trauma does not prove consent nor does consent preclude the absence of physical trauma (Larkin et al, 2012; Maguire et al, 2009). Slaughter and associates (1997), for example, reported that the frequency of anal-genital signs that often included redness and swelling, decreased from 89 percent at less than 24 hours to further decrease to 46 percent over more than 72 hours after the assault (Jones et al, 2003; Adams et al, 2001). This is a particular concern among young victims, who might not have reported their assault in a timely fashion (Jones et al, 2003).

Before initiating the medical examination, it is important to record with case history notes the period that has passed between assault and examination and/or whether the victim has undergone previous examinations in another health facility and/or has taken medicines, changed clothes and/or washed any areas of the body, with special attention to areas of interest where injuries might have occurred such as the perineal area. Finally, it should be recorded if the victim had consensual sexual intercourse before and/or after the assault, in order to discriminate by genetic analysis comparing the assailant's profile and that of a person unrelated to the incident. Moreover, the range of normal genital findings and those associated with consensual intercourse must be distinguished from genital findings specific to the assault under investigation to enable a correct interpretation (Lincoln, 2012). If the methods of genital examination employed are not the same as those used to examine a range of non-sexual assault victims, comparison and interpretation are further limited (Lincoln, 2012). Thus, the most appropriate genital examination and its interpretation should be done by experienced professionals.

Evidence of genital or non-genital trauma can be associated with significant findings and result in a successful legal outcome (Rambow et al, 1992). Collection and documentation of forensic evidence cannot by themselves reveal whether an examined case of sexual violence is a *crime* against the complainant (victim). Nor can this judgment rest on the complainant's credibility alone or the prosecutor's assessment of a likelihood of the available evidence to result in conviction. Therefore, as circumstances in sexual assault cases most often involve the complainant and the accused perpetrator, the third party most likely will be the forensic medical examiner, who serves in capacity of a reliable witness (Ingemann-Hansen et al, 2008). By using a standardized examination and severity scale, the forensic examiner is better able to tangibly categorize a continuum of external genital findings. At the conclusion of every sexual assault forensic examination, the ultimate question asked of the forensic examiner is, "are the physical findings consistent with the history given?" (Larkin et al,

2012). These are important guiding principles in conducting an effective medico-legal assessment.

General or Extra-genital Medical Examination

A complete physical examination of a victim requires accurate general inspection, which is particularly important in children, victimized by sexual assault, to verify the presence of signs of child abuse, either co-present or singularly observable. Some studies show that less physical coercion will be reported by adolescents (Jones et al, 2003; Jänisch et al, 2010), thus young victims most likely will have fewer non-genital injuries, whereas the adult female sexual assault cases were associated with more non-genital injuries (Jones et al, 2003). Nevertheless, general examination or extra-genital medical exam should be determined by a history from the victim. Paying particular attention to areas where the body could have been seized or struck, the aim is to search, find and record all injuries. Each should be photographed and described in detail by place, shape, color and/or dimension. Topographic localization of injuries is significant, because the most frequently injured body areas include the head, neck, breast, and internal part of thighs. Injuries from defending the body are generally localized on hands, forearms and legs. These 'defense injuries' will be absent if the victim was unconscious during the assault. Types of injuries most frequently found are abrasions, bruises, lacerations and fractures caused by a weapon or impact of the victim's body surface against a hard surface. By studying injury characteristics, the examiner should try to identify its pathogenic mechanism and modality used to produce it. All the many useful elements are carefully scrutinized for re-constructing events that led to, and culminated in, the assault under investigation. Sometimes, a general extra-genital examination is able to reveal more information than the genital examination, because it allows the examiner to find signs that took place within an act that occurred under restraint, challenged and contested by acts of aggressive resistance, such as bites on the skin or the fingered ecchymosis that might appear on the wrists and/or the thighs.

Medical-forensic examination provides a solid basis for documentation, and re-construction and interpretation of medical findings, which otherwise would not be available until later. The task of the forensic medicine specialist is to verify whether the samples obtained are consistent with the victim's statement (Jänisch et al, 2010). Because some cases have more extra-genital injuries than others, a complete physical examination is advisable to confirm the veracity of the victim's testimony (Jänisch et al, 2010).

Local Medical Examination

Identification of alterations in the perineum has a different meaning in adults than young female victims. Adolescents and young adults (18 to 24 years old) are four times more likely to be the victim of sexual assault than women in all the other age groups (Jones et al, 2003). Compared with the adults, adolescent sexual-assault victims have a greater frequency of anal-genital injuries (Danielson et al, 2004). Genital-anal injury is more prevalent in younger (less than 20 years) and older (greater than 49 years) women, compared with victims between the ages of 20 and 49 years-old (Sugar et al, 2004; Hilden et al, 2005).

Clinical forensic examination includes systematic documentation of physical injuries and the sampling of biological evidence for legal purposes. The examination should be performed as soon as possible after the assault to avoid loss of important trace evidence (Stene et al, 2010; Maguire et al, 2009; Sugar et al, 2004). As the general examination, inspection of the genital and perineal areas aims to provide documentary evidence that the act was committed under physical restraint. In reality, the types of injuries most frequently encountered are not indicative of sexual assault, and this is one of the main limits of local examination. As said before, injuries predominantly found are those of the external anal-genital area, which generally include dermatological tears and/or soft tissue lesions (Schröder et al, 2011).

Genital injuries often found in women who already have had consensual sexual intercourse are not that severe as to be interpreted as those that accompanied the assault. For this reason it is difficult to differentiate whether genital trauma was caused by consensual or non-consensual sexual intercourse. In the literature, the prevalence of injury following consensual sexual intercourse is typically reported at approximately 10 percent (Sommers, 2007). Adams and various associates (1996, 2001) documented the most frequent types of genital injuries in adolescent women after sexual assault. The most common injury sites recorded were tearing of posterior fourchette, erythema of the labia minora / hymen / cervix / posterior fourchette, and swelling of the hymen, where time from the assault to the examination was highly correlated with the degree of the injury observed (Adams et al, 2000). Timely examination of an adolescent victim is important to document assault-related injuries, preferably within 72 hours, although many victims should have non-specific findings when observed later than three days (Adams et al, 2000; Adams et al, 1996).

A useful aid to gynecological inspection is *colposcopy*. The colposcope is an instrument that permits a magnified view of internal genitalia; when used in association with a coloring substance (toluidine blue), it shows minor injuries that are not otherwise visible to the naked-eye. Toluidine blue dye adheres to nucleated cells, which normally are absent in the superficial and undamaged layers of mucosae, such as that which are found with female genitalia. Therefore, the dye adheres to areas of abraded skin and micro-lacerations, where the squamae in deeper epidermal layers are nucleated (Sommers, 2007). Studies that used colposcopy and toluidine blue staining for diagnostic purposes have found a considerably higher rate of genital-anal injury (Sugar et al, 2004; Hilden et al, 2005; Sommers, 2007; Slaughter et al, 1997).

Advances in clinical forensic medicine show that trained examiners using colposcopy obtain evidence of anal-genital trauma in 87 to 92 percent of victims, if they are seen within 48 hours of the assault (Slaughter et al, 1997). Assault victims without prior sexual intercourse experience had significantly more anal-genital injuries that were documented, compared with victims who previously had intercourse, regardless of age (Jones et al, 2003). In children and younger adolescents, using a Foley's catheter during the gynecological inspection can facilitate visualization and examination of the hymen, especially the fimbriated type, in order to aid in the correct interpretation of findings.

Laboratory Tests

Every effort must be made to preserve retrievable forensic evidence. Ideally the patient should not eat, drink, or carry out oral hygiene (e.g., brush teeth, rinse mouth) until oral samples are taken, if indicated. Similarly, defecation, urination and showering should be deferred until appropriate samples are obtained. On the other hand, it is important to emphasize that, if the victim has been severely injured, such injuries must be treated as a priority. Forensic medical examination can be performed after clinical stabilization of the patient-victim. For the same reason, if a temporary loss of cognitive capacity occurs, owing to intoxication from alcohol or drugs, the examination will need to be deferred until such capacity has returned in order to consent and respond to questions (Eogan et al, 2012).

Genetic Analysis

In most sexual assaults a large exchange of biological material occurs between assailant and victim. The role of genetic analysis is growing in relation to the evidence found in the medico-legal evaluation, because advancements in technology provide a concrete potential to identify the assailant. For this reason, during general and local examination, the examiner should assure the proper collection of samples, such as sperm, blood, saliva or hair on the victim's body or clothing. Sampling, classification and conservation that precede the genetic analysis are crucial. Not taking care to do them properly might lead to a procedural mistake that can invalidate evidence that might appear during a court trial. Therefore, every sample of biological material must be preserved in a structure that is equipped with a freezer, for correct preservation and traceability of evidence.

Samples should be dried, placed in a paper container and preserved at a temperature of 4°C for a short time (3 to 5 days) or -20°C for longer periods. Biological traces present on the victim are commonly found in certain parts of the body (skin) and in cavities such as mouth, vagina and anus. Hence, the importance of an accurate inspection of the whole body surface, including these important orifices and cavities, consistently leads to a secure case history through evidence based on specific data. Samples of biological traces also can be found on clothing worn by the victim and/or other materials such as bed sheets, blankets, towels, discarded clothing, and so on. Nevertheless, sampling from objects is characterized by weaker association with demonstrable evidence for asserting that the crime of sexual assault has occurred, than proper sampling from the victim's body. This weakened association occurs because of a possible indirect transfer of biological material.

The issue of indirect transfer is extremely significant, especially for an inspection of the crime scene, repeatedly performed by multiple professionals. This repetition increases risk of contaminating the evidence, also by transferring biological materials (Ricci et al, 2006). In sexual assault cases, it is very common to find mixed traces, where the assailant's DNA is mixed with the victim's. For this reason, genetic analysis begins with identification of the type of biological material found (namely, blood, sperm, saliva, urine and epithelial cells settled after harmful actions such as slaps or punches) followed by *profile typing*. Depending on the time passed between the assault and the examination, the usual procedure is using two sterile sanitary tampons in order to collect the assailant's biological material on different body areas of the victim, especially the vagina, posterior fourchette, rectum and oral cavity. For instance, the persistent presence of sperm in different areas can change over six hours in the oral cavity, 1-3 days in the rectum or external genitalia, and 7-10 days in the cervix.

If the victim was conscious during the assault and tried to defend herself (or himself), it is important to sample biological material that is found under the victim's fingernails. The nails should be cut and preserved, similar to preservation of the other samples. If this is not possible, other biological material can be sampled using the sterile tampons. The types of traces most frequently observed on the victim's skin are sperm and saliva. Salivary traces permit identification of a genetic profile, only if they contain oral mucosa exfoliated cells. For this reason, genetic analysis of a sample from a bite on the victim's body might lead to the identification of the assailant, even if later it is compromised, because the cutaneous area examined was previously disinfected.

Toxicological Tests

A significant number of sexual assaults involve the consumption of pharmacologically active compounds, which affect the central nervous system. Ethyl alcohol was the first substance used "to facilitate" assault, which in time was followed by the addition of other substances in recent human history. Those substances that share with ethyl alcohol similar effects can be divided into two groups. The first type of effect is to decrease attention level and victim awareness, thus reducing or abolishing inhibition and self-control, which often leads to substantial victim passiveness. The second type of effect is that of the pharmacological mechanism of one or more substances and the potential of serious side-effects such as amnesia, all of which very much work against the victim in favor of the assailant.

As a group, these substances are sometimes called, *Date Rape Drugs* (DRD). Apart from alcohol's classic use as a social lubricant, others include benzodiazepine (flunitrazepam in particular), ketamine, gamma-hydroxybutyric acid (GHB), methylenedioxymethamphetamine (MDMA) and the analogous effects from morphine, cocaine and the cannabinoids. Among the class of benzodiazepine substances utilized, flunitrazepam is the most common. Standard clinical use of benzodiazepine is indicated for anxiety disorders and insomnia treatment. However, flunitrazepam is increasingly used by drug habitués in association with alcohol and morphine compounds. It is important to say that every drug in the benzodiazepine class can be used as a date rape drug to sedate the victim, wherein most of them have an anterograde amnesia side effect (Uzun et al, 2010). Flunitrazepam, among them, is frequently used because it is sold as a colorless and flavorless liquid solution, and is easy to mix with any type of drink. At higher doses, this drug can cause a loss of consciousness (Smith et al, 2002). The acronym GHB identifies gamma-hydroxybutyric acid, as well as its potassium and sodium salts. This drug has a depressant effect on the central nervous system. For this reason standard clinical use was an anesthetic to treat sleep disorders (Stein et al, 2011). GHB is a metabolite of the neurotransmitter gamma-aminobutyric acid (GABA) and for this reason its traces can be found in the body (Schep et al, 2012). GHB is rapidly absorbed by the oral route with peak blood concentrations usually occurring within one hour. It has a relatively small volume of distribution and transfers rapidly across the blood-brain barrier. GHB is metabolized primarily in the liver and it is eliminated with a reported 20-60 minute half-life. Any dosage taken whatever its amount is fully eliminated within 4-8 hours (Schep et al, 2012). Moreover, it can be colorless, flavorless and odorless, thus easy to mix with any type of drink, similar to flunitrazepam. Because of the depressant effect of GHB on the central nervous system and rapid elimination (reported 20-60 minute half-life), the victim is less likely to seek health care with sufficient time to allow for detection of the drug in biological fluids (Schep et al, 2012). Clinical features of GHB-related poisoning include sleepiness, dizziness, nausea, amnesia, hallucination, hypotension, bradycardia, hypothermia, myoclonus, respiratory depression and at the extreme, death.

Ketamine is another chemical frequently used to facilitate sexual assault. It is a dissociative anesthetic compound that originally was used primarily in veterinary practice. It may be injected into the blood stream, swallowed orally, snorted nasally and/or smoked to where its vapors are inhaled. Ketamine interacts with the N-methyl-D-aspartate channel (Smith et al, 2002). Analgesic effects occur at lower doses and confusion, hallucination and amnestic effects at higher doses. Cardiovascular and respiratory toxicity may occur, as well as confusion, hostility, and delirium.

For all above mentioned substances, forensic toxicology is a major means of assisting in the medico-legal evaluation, where research of the main substances and their metabolites can augment an interpretation of the results of the toxicological tests. Careful practice is essential in these tasks.

Infectious Diseases Tests

Clinical and laboratory tests allow for the diagnosis of sexually transmitted diseases, where their onset might be related to the sexual assault. The onset of a sexually transmitted disease is particularly significant in children and young adolescents with no previous history of sexual intercourse. This absence of prior experience increases validity of the hypothesis that assault took place. At this point in the process of health care of the victim and the medico-legal evaluation, screening tests for the most common sexually transmitted diseases are performed. Results lead the pharmacological prophylaxis. Vaginal and cervical tampons should be utilized, in addition to blood samples, in order to identify the most common pathogens, which usually include the following:

- Neisseria gonorrhoeae
- Trichomonas vaginalis
- Chlamydia trachomatis
- Human Immunodeficiency Virus (HIV)
- Treponema pallidum
- Hepatitis C and B virus

As stated before, while the successful result in children and young adolescent is significant for sexual assault, in adults interpretation is controversial when the prior heath condition of the victim is unknown. In the case of children it is extremely difficult to differentiate between an infection resulting from the recent claim of sexual assault and any other possible previous experience.

CONCLUSION

Sexual assault produces varied consequences, direct and indirect, within a broad-spectrum of gravity. Psychological trauma and acquisition of sexually transmitted infections that include Human Immunodeficiency Virus (HIV) are the serious health-related consequences of sexual assault (Sommers et al, 2012). Particular attention must be paid to psychological trauma and related assault outcomes, because this healing process is longer and more complex than that for the physical injuries. Rape Trauma Syndrome, for instance, is a psychological reaction to the event characterized by a fragmentation of personality and subversion of relational capabilities (Burgess et al, 1974). Counseling is important for all victims of sexual assault, as psychological consequences are more common than physical injuries (Mein et al, 2003). In fact, psychological trauma caused by sexual assault cannot be assimilated to other traumatic events because it involves aspects of daily inter-personal relationships, namely, body of the victim with its sense of sexuality, self-confidence, trusting people especially men, emotional bonds with socially significant others, and other relationships especially those concerning life plans.

In the long-term, psychological disturbance might become chronic, leading to drug-addiction, eating disorder, self-injurious behavior, sexual dysfunction, and possible personality disorder. There is an elevated risk of suicide ideation and attempted suicide (Maguire et al, 2009). It is important to note that consequences of sexual assault vary from victim to victim. First, they depend on characteristics of each personality. Second, external factors play a role such as circumstances of the event and how it was interpreted by the victim and her significant others, assault modality and, importantly, whether the assailant was known by the victim. In fact, if it is not dealt with by re-elaboration through some form of counseling (see related chapter, this volume), the psychological trauma caused by sexual assault can become more complex with severe repercussions and devastating consequences on a victim's life. This is most probable when the assailant is an acquaintance, who is related to the victim by a working or confidential relationship such as friendship or family ties. Breaching trust can have devastating consequences.

For all these reasons, sexual assault represents a significant health problem in today's world because of its potential for physical and psychological consequences. According to the World Health Organization, these consequences might range from those that are minor, such as mild injury and pregnancy (Table 1) to those more severe and devastating which result in loss of life, such as potential for homicide and risk of suicide and prenatal mortality, following pregnancy (Table 2).

Table 1. Consequences of sexual assault with non-fatal outcome

Effects on physical health	Effects on mental health
• Minor or major injuries • Pregnancy • Gynecological disturbances • Miscarriage • Sexually transmitted diseases • Pelvic inflammatory disease	• Anxiety disorder and depression • Sexual dysfunctions • Eating disorders • Obsessive compulsive disorder • Post-traumatic stress disease • Alcohol or drug addiction

Table 2. Consequences of sexual assault with a fatal outcome

Fatal Outcome
• Suicide • Homicide • Prenatal mortality

References

Adams, J. A., Girardin, B. & Faugno, D. (2001). "Adolescent sexual assault: Documentation of acute injuries using photo-colposcopy," *Journal of Pediatric and Adolescent Gynecology*, *14*(4), 175-180.

Adams, J. A., Girardin, B. & Faugno, D. (2000). "Signs of genital trauma in adolescent rape victims examined acutely," *Journal of Pediatric and Adolescent Gynecology*, *13*(2), 88-89.

Adams, J. A., Kaplan, R. A., Starling, S. P., Mehta, N. H., Finkel, M. A., Botash, A. S., Kellogg, N. D. & Shapiro, R. A. (2007). "Guidelines for medical care of children who may have been sexually abused," *Journal of Pediatric and Adolescent Gynecology*, *20*(3), 163-172.

Adams, J. A. & Knudson, S. (1996). "Genital findings in adolescent girls referred for suspected sexual abuse," *Archives of Pediatrics and Adolescent Medicine*, *150*(8), 850-857.

Burgess, A. W. & Holmstrom, L. L. (1974). "Rape trauma syndrome," *American Journal of Psychiatry*, *131*(9), 981-986.

Danielson, C. K. & Holmes, M. M. (2004). "Adolescent sexual assault: An update of the literature," *Current Opinion in Obstetrics and Gynecology*, *16*(5), 383-388.

Du Mont, J., White, D. & McGregor, M. J. (2009). "Investigating the medical forensic examination from the perspectives of sexually assaulted women," *Social Science and Medicine*, *68*(4), 774-780.

Eogan, M., McHugh, A. & Holohan, M. (2012). "The role of the sexual assault centre," *Best Practice and Research Clinical Obstetrics and Gynaecology* XXX(2012), 1-12.

Hilden, M., Schei, B. & Sidenius, K. (2005). "Genitoanal injury in adult female victims of sexual assault," *Forensic Science International*, *154*(2005), 200-205.

Ingemann-Hansen, O., Brink, O., Sabroe, S., Sørensen, V. & Charles, A. V. (2008). "Legal aspects of sexual violence – does forensic evidence make a difference?," *Forensic Science International*, *180*(2-3), 98-104.

Ingemann-Hansen, O., Sabroe, S., Brink, O., Knudsen, M. & Charles, A. V. (2009). "Characteristics of victims and assaults of sexual violence – improving inquiries and prevention," *Journal of Forensic and Legal Medicine*, *16*(4), 182-188.

Jänisch, S., Meyer, H., Germerott, T., Albrecht, U. V., Schulz, Y. & Debertin, A. S. (2010). "Analysis of clinical forensic examination reports on sexual assault," *International Journal* of *Legal Medicine*, *124*(3), 227-235.

Jones, J. S., Rossman, L., Wynn, B. N., Dunnuck, C. & Schwartz, N. (2003). "Comparative analysis of adult versus adolescent sexual assault: Epidemiology and patterns of anogenital injury," *Academic Emergency Medicine*, *10*(8), 872-877.

Larkin, H. J., Cosby, C. D., Kelly, D. & Paolinetti, L. A. (2012). "A pilot study to test the differential validity of a genital injury severity scale, in development for use in forensic sexual assault examinations," *Journal of Forensic Nursing*, *8*(1), 30-38.

Lincoln, C. (2001). "Genital injury: Is it significant? A review of the literature," *Medicine, Science and the Law*, *41*(3), 206-216.

Maguire, W., Goodall, E. & Moore, T. (2009). "Injury in adult female sexual assault complainants and related factors," *European Journal of Obstetrics and Gynecology and Reproductive Biology*, *142*(2009), 149-153.

Mein, J. K., Palmer, C. M., Shand, M. C., Templeton, D. J., Parekh, V., Mobbs, M., Haig, K., Huffam, S. E. & Young, L. (2003). "Management of acute adult sexual assault," *Medical Journal of Australia*, *178*(5), 226-230.

Rambow, B., Adkinson, C., Frost, T. H. & Peterson, G. F. (1992). "Female sexual assault: Medical and legal implications," *Annals of Emergency Medicine*, *21*(6), 727-731.

Ricci, U., Previderè, C., Fattorini, P. & Corradi, F. (2006). *La prova del DNA per la ricerca della verità. Aspetti giuridici, biologici e probabilistici*, Milano, Italy: Giuffrè Editore.

Schep, L. J., Knudsen, K., Slaughter, R. J., Vale, J. A. & Mégarbane, B. (2012). "The clinical toxicology of γ-hydroxybutyrate, γ-butyrolactone and 1, 4-butanediol," *Clinical Toxicology (Philadelphia, PA)*, *50*(6), 458-470.

Schröder, A. S., Güzel, M. O., Seifert, D., Püschel, K. & Anders, S. (2011). "Injuries of the female genitalia in cases of sexual assault," *Archiv für Kriminologie*, *228*(1-2), 1-10.

Slaughter, L., Brown, C. R., Crowley, S. & Peck, R. (1997). "Patterns of genital injury in female sexual assault victims," *American Journal of Obstetrics and Gynecology*, *176*(3), 609-616.

Smith, K. M., Larive, L. L. & Romanelli, F. (2002), "Club drugs: Ethylenedioxymetham phetamine, flunitrazepam, ketamine hydrochloride, and gamma-hydroxybutyrate," *American Journal of Health-System Pharmacy*, *59*(11), 1067-1076.

Sommers, M. S. (2007). "Defining patterns of genital injury from sexual assault: A review," *Trauma, Violence, and Abuse*, *8*(3), 270-280.

Sommers, M. S., Brown, K. M., Buschur, C., Everett, J. S., Fargo, J. D., Fisher, B. S., Hinkle, C. & Zink, T. M. (2012). "Injuries from intimate partner and sexual violence: Significance and classification systems," *Journal of Forensic and Legal Medicine*, *19*(5), 250-263.

Stein, L. A., Lebeau, R., Clair, M., Martin, R., Bryant, M., Storti, S. & Monti, P. (2011). "A web-based study of gamma hydroxybutyrate (GHB): Patterns, experiences, and functions of use," *American Journal on Addictions*, *20*(1), 30-39.

Stene, L. E., Ormstad, K. & Schei, B. (2010). "Implementation of medical examination and forensic analyses in the investigation of sexual assaults against adult women: A retrospective study of police files and medical journals," *Forensic Science International*, *199*(1-3), 79-84.

Sugar, N. F., Fine, D. N. & Eckertc, L. O. (2004). "Physical injury after sexual assault: Findings of a large case series," *American Journal of Obstetrics and Gynecology*, *190*, 71-76.

Tschudin, S. (2005). "Immediate care for women after sexual and physical assault," *Ther Umsch*, *62*(4), 223-229.

Uzun, S., Kozumplik, O., Jakovljević, M. & Sedić, B. (2010). "Side effects of treatment with benzodiazepines," *Psychiatria Danubina*, *22*(1), 90-93.

Williams, A. (2004). "Managing adult sexual assault," *Austrian Family Physician*, *33*(10), 825-828.

Young, W. W., Bracken, A. C., Goddard, M. A. & Matheson, S. (1992). "Sexual assault: Review of a national model protocol for forensic and medical evaluation – New Hampshire Sexual Assault Medical Examination Protocol Project Committee," *Obstetrics and Gynecology*, *80*(5), 878-883.

In: Assaults
Editor: Keith V. Bletzer

ISBN: 978-1-62808-051-3

Chapter 12

Possible Strategies for Reducing Alcohol-related Assault: Community-Based Methodology in Cairns, Tropical North Queensland (Australia)

***Shane Boris Pointing*[1,*], *Charmaine Hayes-Jonkers*[2] *and Alan Clough*[2]**

[1]Cairns Institute, James Cook University, Cairns, Australia
[2]School of Public Health, Tropical Medicine and Rehabilitation Sciences, James Cook University, Cairns, Australia

Abstract

Objective: To refine boundaries and characteristics of the late-night entertainment precinct in Cairns to facilitate refined measurement of alcohol-related assaults, assess stakeholder perceptions regarding interventions to reduce them and explore the contribution that this process can make to sustainable interventions.

Methods: 29 semi-structured interviews incorporating cognitive mapping techniques, 12 focus groups with key service providers, and community-action research methodology to elicit feedback on preliminary findings.

Results: The rate and severity of violence in the Cairns precinct has fallen over time; reducing alcohol availability would further reduce violence but have negative economic consequences. A generational culture of 'drinking to get drunk' exists. Community-level education programs addressing this are important. A majority of interventions identified by stakeholders were situational and environmental. Participants generally agreed on a defined precinct boundary, at the same time they highlighted unexpected violence 'hot-spots'. Coordination and communication between relevant stakeholders is essential.

Conclusion: The precinct is viewed as a safe place by stakeholders and they expect to continue working together to reduce violence. The emphasis on stakeholder communication endorses current government programs to address alcohol-related violence. Independent community-action research facilitates information transfer and is a

* Corresponding author: Email: boris.pointing@jcu.edu.au.

key strategy to coordinate data collection, and in implementing and monitoring coordinated interventions.

Implications: This study supports the importance to stakeholders of defined precincts for enhanced data collection to measure alcohol-related assaults, and previous studies indicate the importance of research as an independent driver to reducing this sort of violence. The methodology is a foundational stage of establishing scientific veracity in studying this public health issue, and in guiding policy and research directions.

Keywords: Violence, assaultive behavior, alcohol-related injury, methods, precincts, qualitative research

INTRODUCTION

The majority of policy responses by Australian governments to reduce the incidence of alcohol-related assaults (ARAs) have primarily focused on environments in and around licensed premises (Loxley, Gray, Wilkinson, Chikritzhs, Midford, & Moore, 2005). A rigorous research design to measure the rate and severity of assaults occurring in these *late-night entertainment precincts* (LNEPs) has been a challenge for many years, partly due to difficulties in obtaining location data for incidents occurring within LNEPs that are precise enough for reliable monitoring. There is substantial evidence that coordinated, collaborative community-wide interventions are most effective in reducing reported assaults in these precincts with a high density of licensed premises (Loxley et al, 2005; Hauritz, Homel,McIlwain, Burrows, & Townsley, 1998; Law Justice Safety Committee, 2010; Brennan, Moore, & Murphy, 2011; Jones, Hughes, Atkinson, & Bellis, 2011). This approach has previously been effective in Cairns, but it is, however, challenging to sustain collaborative community-wide public health interventions (Hauritz et al, 1998, p. 6), particularly for partnerships to reduce assaults in LNEPs (Loxley et al, 2005; Law Justice Safety Committee, 2010; Brennan, Moore, & Murphy, 2011; Jones et al, 2011; Fawcett, Schultz, Watson-Thompson, Fox, & Bremb, 2010).

In 2011, the Queensland Government legislated approval to trial test 'Drink Safe Precincts' incorporating high density areas of licensed premises in three major cities (Law Justice and Safety Committee, 2010). The precincts in each city are less than one kilometer square (<1km^2) and highly problematic in the rate of ARAs reported to police (Holmila, Holder, Andréasson, Baklien, & Rossow, 2008). The test uses tighter regulation specific to the LNEP as the basis for intervention; precinct boundaries are defined by legislation, courts have the power to ban individuals from a 'Drink Safe Precinct' (Bligh & Lawlor, 2010) and local stakeholder committees have been established to prepare 'precinct management plans'. Additional funding has been provided to implement activities identified through these plans. The city of Cairns is not included in the 'Drink Safe Precincts' trial test, although the boundary of the LNEP in Cairns has similarly been defined by government regulation and Cairns is the subject of separate research to reduce ARAs in the LNEP (e.g., Pointing, Hayes-Jonkers, Stone, Brinn, & Clough, 2011). This chapter documents the exploratory research processes used to refine stakeholder definition of the Cairns LNEP, identify environmental factors associated with ARAs within the precinct and assess the scope and feasibility of collaborative community-wide interventions identified by the stakeholders to reduce this sort of violence. This chapter demonstrates the use of a community-action research methodology to establish part of a scientifically defensible research design and documents characteristics identified by stakeholders as necessary to sustain these collaborative interventions. Implications for more reliable monitoring of violent incidents in LNEPs and embedment of collaborative strategies to target these incidents are discussed.

In addition to University ethics approval, a Memorandum of Understanding was developed and signed between the University and the Cairns City Licensees Safety Association around the provision and use of confidential information. The Queensland Police Service required a similar agreement. Focus group respondents stated that this contributed to perceptions regarding the independence of the research.

METHODS

Setting

The coastal city of Cairns in tropical north Queensland has been accredited as an International Safe Community (Promotion WCCCS, 2011). The residential population is approximately 164,000 persons (Regional Population Statistics, 2011). Its LNEP has 26 venues licensed to serve alcohol after midnight on weekends. Tourism is a major economic contributor to the city with over 550,000 visitor-nights annually, including a significant backpacker market (Queensland TTN, 2010). Given the magnitude of these activities, inter-sectorial forums have been established to address community safety issues.

Participants

Twelve focus groups comprising stakeholders were conducted between January and December 2010. These focus groups comprised interview respondents and other stakeholder representatives. The purpose of the focus groups was to provide feedback of progressive results and comments on the veracity of the trial test in the Cairns LNEP.

To recruit participants, twelve stakeholder organizations were identified from community registers that had formal responsibilities to prevent and/or respond to ARAs in the Cairns LNEP. Twenty-nine persons from these organizations with strategic responsibilities were identified. These agencies include: regulatory and enforcement agencies, licensed venue associations, primary and allied health services, legal representatives and the regional local government council. To achieve saturation, during interviews each participant was asked to refer us to other key persons, whom they believed had similar roles, were similarly knowledgeable and experienced, and could comment on the issues under investigation.

Agencies and positions of those who were interviewed are listed in Text Box 1. Most these professionals were drawn from agencies staffed by "first responders," such as Emergency Department (ED), Queensland Police Service and Queensland Ambulance Service, as well as others with other forms of strategic roles, such as the Cairns Regional Council, liquor regulatory office, private security firm, and the licensed venue industry association. The local 24-hour medical clinic and other security providers were approached, but declined to take part in the study. An additional 18 venue owners and managers regularly attended the licensees' focus group through the Cairns City Licensees Safety Association (CCLSA), which was a formal liquor accord, and they in turn were provided with the opportunity to comment or provide feedback on study methodology and results through that forum or in private. The length of time that each interview respondent had been in Cairns varied between six months and 17 years.

Text Box 1. Semi-structured Interviews with Representatives from the Cairns LNEP

Agencies with key responsibility for preventing and/or responding to ARA in the Cairns LNEP	Professionals with key responsibility in relation to ARA who were interviewed for this study
Regulatory and Enforcement Agencies. Queensland Police Service.	N=7 District Inspector, Officer in Charge of the City Police beat station and officers from the liquor enforcement, intelligence, tactical and first response sections.
Queensland Office of Liquor and Gaming regulation (responsible for licensing and monitoring of venues).	N=2 District Manager and one field officer.
Venues Owners, management and security providers.	N=2 One venue owner (President of Cairns City Licensees Safety Association) and Operations Manager of security providers to the majority of venues.
Health Queensland Ambulance Service.	N=1District Operations Manager of the Queensland Ambulance Service.
Cairns Base Hospital Emergency Department.	N=4 Emergency Department four nurses, two doctors, and the data manager.
Drug and Alcohol Brief Intervention Team.	N=3 Three staff from the Drug and Alcohol Brief Intervention Team (DABIT).
Non-government Service Delivery Organizations	
Victims of Crime Support Service.	N=1 Manager.
Youth Substance Misuse Service.	N=1 Manager.
Transport and Other Business Public transport bus service. Sole Taxi Company. Solicitor.	N=1 Manager. N=1 Operations Manager. N=1 One solicitor (Chair of the CBD Safety Summit).
Media	N=2 The crime reporter and chief of staff from the sole commercial local newspaper.
Cairns Regional Council	N=2 Two community safety positions. N=1 Inner-city facilities manager.

Interview Questions

Twenty-nine semi-structured interviews were conducted. Participants were asked to consider "person-to-person physical contact with violence" linked to licensed premises, excluding sexual assault owing to its different social pathology. Using a cognitive mapping strategy, a base map of Cairns was provided and participants were asked to draw the boundaries of the area they believed to be of greatest concern with respect to ARAs, to mark particular localities of concern within these boundaries, and to explain their reasons. Participants were then asked to comment on the main ARA issues impacting their agency, knowledge of existing interventions to address the issue, routine data collection procedures and the potential for sharing this data, the level and outcomes of formal and informal collaboration around the issue of ARA, and views on opportunities for and barriers to developing and implementing targeted collaborative interventions.

DATA ANALYSIS

Using a modified cognitive mapping approach applied to assess health risks that were linked to alcohol outlets in urban environments (see Basta, Richmond, & Wiebe, 2010) hand-drawn maps from each of the 29 focus group participants were traced to image files. Initial comparisons were made by overlaying image boundaries around each participant's defined area of concern. The commonality of boundaries was identified by consensus among the authors. The "hot-spots" identified by participants were examined by tallying the frequency with which they were mentioned. As occurs with other forms of qualitative research, key themes in the mapping were assessed, as they emerged.

Using a standard thematic data analysis (Braun & Clarke, 2006), the interview data were transcribed and analyzed by key theme searches. These initial interpretations were provided to focus groups of key stakeholders for confirmation and feedback. Participant comments were summarized, such as "Current practices or intervention strategies recognized" and "Intervention strategies recommended." Ethics approvals were provided by the Queensland Health Cairns and Hinterland District, James Cook University Human Research Ethics Committee, and the Queensland Police Service Research Committee (Ethical Standards Command).

RESULTS

Environmental Characteristics of the LNEP

The theme identified as most important to understanding and addressing ARAs in the designated LNEP is more informed co-operation to address the issue (Text Box 2). There is a high willingness to collaborate that is combined with an incomplete picture of the issue, because no single agency sees all the assaults, and a mixed level of awareness exists regarding current interventions that are both internal and external to the agencies. A high degree of agreement was found regarding the LNEP boundary and 'hotspot' locations (see Figures 1a and 1c). The emphasis on pedestrian *egress pathways* from the LNEP (Figure 1b) was an unexpected finding, arising spontaneously as a result of participants being asked to define the boundary of the LNEP. Identified violence 'hotspots' were places where patrons mixed from venues catering to different clientele, either at congregation points around food, transport hubs or pedestrian cross-flows.

Most assaults are perceived as occurring Friday and Saturday nights (Text Box 2), which complements the literature on assault prevalence. The majority of the participants reported that the LNEP is safer now than ten years ago, although this varied depending on where the participant worked and their period of residence in Cairns. For example, all participants from the Emergency Department (ED) had resided in Cairns for less than ten years and all felt that the entire LNEP was an unsafe place. Most non-ED participants noted which venues had implemented a number of management improvements to reduce violence.

Text Box 2. Key Themes from the Focus Group Interview Data

Information about the Issue
Recognition that licensees have worked to enhance patron safety
No one agency sees all the assaults – picture is incomplete
Friday and Saturday nights (rolling to early morning) are main source of incidents
Mixed awareness of existing partnered projects to address issue
Mixed level of internal initiatives to address issue
Low marketing of internal projects to potential partners (with exceptions)
High willingness to collaborate for coordinated interventions and data sharing
Regulatory and Police visibility important, but not the only thing

Rate and Level of Violence
Cairns CBD relatively safe, depending on where the participant had worked
Operation Amazon and successors have made a positive impact
CCTV (television), security guards and radio network have made a positive impact
Rate and level of crime dropping from 10 years ago
The research project is valuable "honest information broker" role

Themes around Pre-cursors to Incidents
Alcohol availability – shortening trading hours is required
Poly-drug use a problem
People 'liquoring up' before coming into town
Quick exit from CBD is important
Enforcement of responsibly serving of alcohol
Responsible drinking
Attitudinal – less respect for others and for authority than in the past
People drink to get drunk – Australian culture
Underage drinking an increasing issue
"Tide is turning" in regulation and government
Education at a young age is a key ('Thinking Drinking' initiative valued)
More violence occurs between women now than in the past

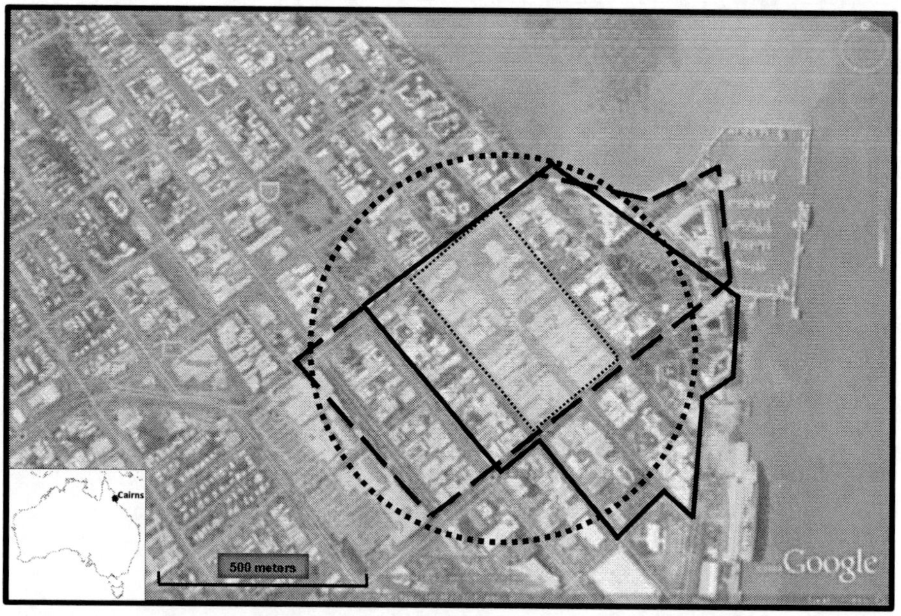

Figure 1a. Border of the CBD Defined by 29 Participants. Examples of four maps with different areas depicted. The central area was identified as one single "hot-spot" by 10 respondents, including five of the seven Emergency Department staff, and taxi management. Ten respondents identified hotspots within the Late Night Entertainment Precinct (LNEP) that they felt had no boundary. The unbroken line was identified as the boundary by a venue owner and security provider, and the police officers with specific responsibility for liquor enforcement. The respondents who identified the boundaries depicted through the circle and the dashed line were mixed. Eight respondents also noted that events outside the LNEP have an impact on the number of assaults within it.

Figure 1b. Egress Routes. Commonly reported pedestrian egress routes are shown from the LNEP.

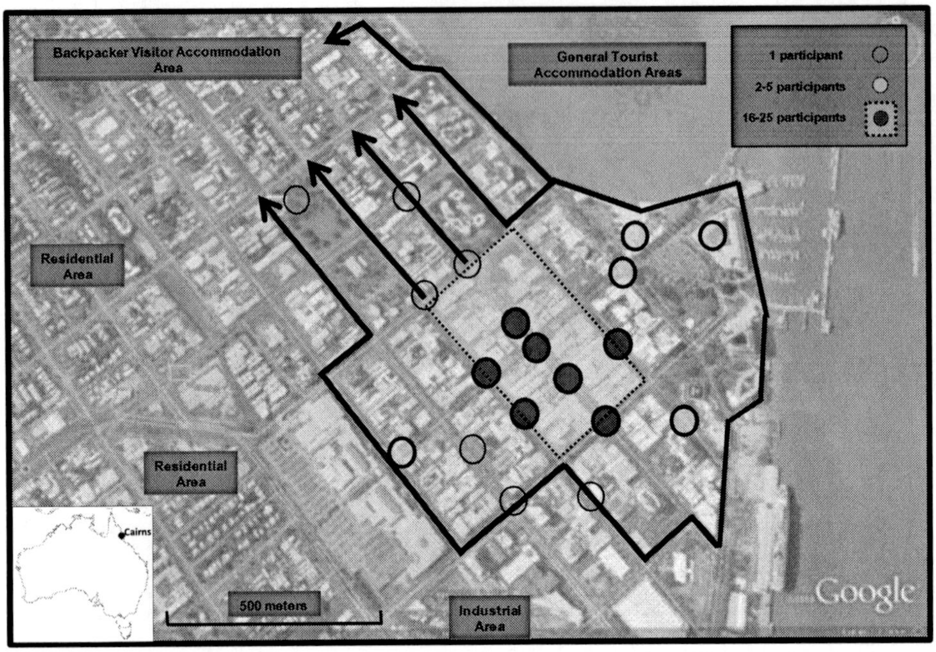

Figure 1c. Cairns – Late Night Entertainment Precinct (LNEP). Combination of delineated zones, pedestrian egress routes from the LNEP and identified hot spots. Twenty-one respondents regarded the central zone of the town as the main area of concern. This zone includes two venues, the taxi rank and the late-night food establishments. Most identified "hotspots" are at intersections. A number of respondents identified where the clientele from different styles of venues mixed as pedestrians and became regular locations for violence.

Co-ordinated Data Collection and Intervention Approaches

All the focus group interview respondents agreed that coordinated data collection and intervention approaches were feasible and desirable, if this placed no additional stress on current resources, and the identified agency-specific confidentiality requirements could be negotiated.

Interventions

Participant understandings of current intervention strategies are listed in Text Box 3. Liquor enforcement operations are prominent in participants' minds. Situational-environmental interventions comprise thirteen of the 24 existing interventions mentioned by respondents. The social marketing and education programs were broader and mentioned by comparatively few participants; five of the seven educational interventions identified by participants were broad population-level strategies. *Think the Drink*, a locally developed educational project that targeted senior school students, was identified as important. Apart from the Drug and Alcohol Brief Intervention Team (DABIT) initiative that was recognized as an important intervention by those who were aware of it, no respondent identified any of the individually focused psychological or counseling interventions.

Inter-agency communications forums were identified as important by a majority of participants. All four existing inter-agency forums are focused on the Cairns CBD and each serves a different stakeholder mix. There are significant overlaps. Among other existing interventions identified, six of seven regulatory and enforcement interventions are specifically situational and the seventh, "evaluation of location and patterns of violence," requires precise offense location data. Transport initiatives designed to quickly remove patrons from the LNEP, when they wished to depart, were also identified as important.

Further recommended interventions are listed in Text Box 3. Again, the regulatory and enforcement interventions are prominent with five of seven being venue and precinct environment-specific. Of the two that are not, one is a joint training initiative, which would be focused on operational processes within the LNEP, and/or it could be classified as enhanced communication processes. One calls for more severe sentences. Of the seven educational /awareness themed interventions that were suggested, five participants recommended enhancement of the existing programs. Two new interventions, community education on the role and scope of CCTV, and naming and shaming people presented to the ED, both have clear locational implications. Several interventions were suggested: two strategies would involve media; seven were specific situational-environmental interventions; and one recommendation was to remove patrons quickly from the LNEP at the end of their night. These suggestions were not accompanied by concrete procedures on how to implement them. The individual-level brief intervention work of the Drug and Alcohol Brief Intervention Team (DABIT) might focus on referral to those agencies that provide personal safety strategies and/or other counseling to prevent repeat victimization.

Text Box 3. Strategy Types in relation to existing practices and intervention to reduce alcohol-related violence in the Cairns LNEP (N=29 participants)

Strategy Type	Proportion (%) who reported awareness	Strategy Type	Proportion (%) who recommended enhancing and/or implementing the strategy
ENFORCEMENT		ENFORCEMENT	
Responsible Service of Alcohol regulations	45%	Restrict availability and enforce Responsible Service of Alcohol	59%
Liquor Enforcement and Proactive Policing officers	34%	Combined operations e.g. 'Amazon'	34%
Joint Operations and targeted Police	34%	Expand use of ID Scanners in clubs	31%
Council street-based security guards	14%	Target repeat offenders and ban from premises	24%
Last drinks venue recorded in assaults reported to Police	10%	Higher police visibility	24%
Police evaluation of patterns and locations of incidents	7%	Joint training Initiatives (venue and street-based security, Police)	17%

Text Box 3. (Continued)

Strategy Type	Proportion (%) who reported awareness	Strategy Type	Proportion (%) who recommended enhancing and/or implementing the strategy
Police Infringement Notice system available	3%	More severe sentences for offenders	7%
Education and community awareness-raising programs		Education and awareness-raising	
Responsible drinking generally encouraged	34%	Change attitudes to responsible drinking at population level	66%
'Think the Drink' program	24%	Enhance youth-focused interventions, e.g. 'Think the Drink' program	41%
Drug and Alcohol Brief Intervention Team (DABIT)	24%	Enhance brief interventions, e.g. role of DABIT	22%
'One Punch Can Kill' program - Queensland Police	10%	More community education on role and scope of CCTV	17%
Local newspaper	7%	"Naming and shaming" people presenting at Emergency Department	7%
'Don't Turn a Night Out into a Nightmare' national program 'Leggy not Legless' national program	3% 3%	Victim / offender narratives in the media Local newspaper initiated campaign (including narratives)	3% 3%
COMMUNICATION PROCESSES IN PLACE		COMMUNICATION and DATA SHARING i	
Between individual agencies	41%	Refine liquor accord to enforce more closely	52%
Cairns 'CBD Safety Summit' forum	38%	Enhance inter-agency co-ordination, communication, sharing information	34%
'Liquor Accord' and 'Cairns City Licensee Safety Association'	34%	Continue JCU Research Project	17%
Cairns Regional Council 'Community Safety Committee'	17%		
Environment-situational		Environment-situational	
Cairns Regional Council Closed Circuit TV surveillance	31%	Reduce venue density	24%
3 a.m. 'lockout' for premises trading until 5 a.m.	21%	Education and/or visible enforcement at late-night food vendors	17%
ID scanners for entry to licensed venues	17%	'Breathalysers' for self-testing - condition of entry to venues at 3am	14%
Additional lighting (and other CPTED principles)	3%	Enhanced use of CCTV	10%
		Crime prevention through environmental design to remove 'hot-spots'	10%
		In-venue educational resources	7%
		Provide snacks in venues	7%
Transport initiatives		Transport	
Secure taxi rank during peak times (one security guard and a Marshall)	21%	Getting people out of town quickly and safely: pedestrians, taxis, buses	38%
Late-night bus (since discontinued)	7%		

Focus group respondents stated that the methodology providing continuous feedback of the indicative results had been used to support funding applications and assisted with the tasking of operational resources, and it was viewed as an important step toward sustainability. There was a high degree of agreement supporting enhanced collaboration around data collection and sharing, provided that no stress would be placed on current resources (Text Boxes 2 and 3). There was recognition among all the interviewees that police statistics did not accurately reflect the actual number of assaults within the LNEP.

CONCLUSION

The process used to define and test the boundaries of the LNEP enhanced organizational understanding of the context in which ARAs and related injuries occur in the Cairns LNEP, and provided stakeholders within the network with new information and knowledge. Enhanced communication processes were recommended by a majority of stakeholders. The process of defining and testing the LNEP, and the qualitative analysis of the location of the assault incidents was reported by all participants as a significant step in embedding sustainable interventions. The independent role of researchers, signified by ethics approval and separate written agreements, was reported by respondents as important in establishing trust. These strong relationships were built on transparent information sharing that identified specific contextual complexities that were overcome early in the project. The role of researchers as technical advisors to local stakeholders has been recognized as a legitimate methodological function in evaluating the effectiveness of community action projects to reduce ARAs (Holmila et al, 2008). Lasting change in reducing alcohol-related harmful actions is most likely when those who are affected are part of the change process (Shepherd, 2003; Morgan & McAtamney, 2009; Graham & Homel, 2008; Alcohol Education and Rehabilitation Foundation, 2011; Stevenson & McClure, 2005).

In the view of the researchers this qualitative research process was an integral step to establishing a combined quantitative data collection framework. The community-action research framework used in Cairns provides the four conditions identified as necessary to build multi-sectorial partnerships for population-based health interventions (Fawcett et al, 2010). Participants reported that the information feedback loop connected or strengthened existing connections between multiple sectors. This contributed to shared responsibility for outcomes and the research itself became a "public" entity to reduce ARAs (Fawcett et al, 2010). The facilitation of collaboration and cooperation, and provision of information to stakeholders were identified as essential, reflecting previous research (Loxley et al, 2005; Hauritz et al, 1998; Law Justice and Safety Committee, 2010; Brennan et al, 2011; Fawcett et al, 2010; Shepherd, 2003; Morgan & McAtamney, 2009), and allowed stakeholders to make more informed judgments on resource allocation for effective interventions.

The development of a locally generated map provided new local knowledge, and in the view of the researchers this visual information contributed to a sense of shared responsibility for outcomes. The results of cognitive mapping highlighted unexpected findings related to the location of incidents and resultant interventions, for example, development of projects to facilitate patron egress from the precinct. The boundary of the Cairns LNEP as regulated through legislation was confirmed through this study. As there was a high degree of correlation among interview participants, where some of these participants contributed to the forums, this was not surprising. However, the research methodology refined the area of concern to describe four hot-spots of violence. The importance of the pedestrian egress routes was unexpected and significant. The majority of interventions identified or suggested through interviews were situational-environmental. With the exception of one individual-level intervention, one population-level educational campaign, and the enhancement of inter-agency links, all the existing and suggested interventions were focused on the defined LNEP. Importantly, every person who was interviewed highlighted generational and attitudinal issues as a necessary point of intervention. The importance of continued broad population level strategies was recognized. Additionally the *Think the Drink* program focuses on harm minimization education among senior students toward end of school student celebrations and this has clear situational-environmental implications in the sort of behavioral message delivered.

Recognition among all interviewees that police statistics did not accurately reflect the rate of assault actually occurring within the LNEP supports previous research that suggests ARA is under-reported in Australia (Graham & Homel, 2008). Recognition alone does not accurately inform public health or criminological strategies to reduce these assaults. The importance of a "safe brand" to tourism and the Cairns economy can be key drivers to willingness to effective collaboration among the stakeholder network.

Implications

Interventions to reduce alcohol-related assaults in the nighttime economy have been broadly categorized as educational and situational and the policy question in Australia as to whether universal or targeted strategies are most efficient and cost effective may still be current (Loxley et al, 2005). As the Queensland Government has recently defined LNEPs in every major city, it is worth noting the mixed evidence that has been published regarding the effectiveness of non-situational interventions to reduce ARA in LNEPs, based on diverse research from public health (Shepherd, 2003) and criminology (Graham & Homel, 2008). Two recent systematic reviews of effective interventions to reduce harm in and around licensed alcohol premises highlight the importance of defining the geographical scale of intervention, and variability in methodological rigor that is required for studying the effectiveness of these interventions (Jones et al, 2011). The views of Cairns stakeholders, however, clearly indicate the importance of community-level education as part of a systems approach to explore and offer solutions on the issue.

This present investigation reviewed in this chapter analyzed views of the key service delivery agencies in Cairns but not the persons involved in the violence or the consumers of leisure activities in the LNEP. Studying whether the LNEP patrons viewed the situational interventions or educational interventions as more important in reducing harm might reveal new knowledge. A recent report found that more than 60% of Australians aged 18-29 "drink to get drunk" (Alcohol Education and Rehabilitation Foundation, 2011). This culture of "determined drunkenness" when combined with the reason that LNEPs exist (Alcohol and Rehabilitation Foundation, 2011) suggest that it might be etiologically meaningful to view every assault that occurs in an LNEP as an ARA. Research testing of the motivational drivers as to why patrons are in the precinct might provide valuable insights into methodologies and intervention design. Additionally, analysis by police and/or the emergency departments of the trajectories of injury severity, and victimization or offending patterns of individuals repeatedly involved in assault incidents in LNEPs can uncover more intervention points. Such analysis requires precise locational information to identify whether an incident actually took place within the LNEP.

Problems with sustaining community-wide interventions are well documented in injury epidemiology and criminological literature (Loxley et al, 2005; Hauritz et al, 1998; Law Justice and Safety Committee, 2010; Brennan et al, 2011; Jones et al, 2011; Fawcett et al, 2010; Jones et al, 2011; Morgan & McAtamney, 2009; Graham & Homel, 2008). Lack of shared responsibilities and common goals are significant among these problems (Fawcett et al, 2010). The community-action qualitative research method described in this chapter demonstrates a process which began to overcome many of these issues. Independence, and the perception of it, is essential. Identifying boundaries of the LNEP and hot-spots within it, and testing these with stakeholders, was an important step in gaining agreement for coordinated quantitative data collection. In the view of the researchers this model is an essential plank in a scientifically defensible research design to evaluate the effectiveness of interventions to reduce ARAs in LNEPs. All stakeholders perceived the implications possible for focusing on situational crime reduction and harm minimization interventions. This process has policy implications for economic modeling in regards to cost effectiveness and cost-benefit analysis, refines the estimates of the burden on police, ambulance and emergency resources. Applying an epidemiological research method to the measurement of ARA-related injuries in Cairns has provided additional insights to traditional criminological methods. Formal application of an ecological study design to injury prevention (Stevenson & McClure, 2005) would refine these insights and offer suggestions for more targeted interventions. A specific area of research required in Queensland is an evaluation of the process and effectiveness of implementing the civil banning orders relating to 'Drink Safe Precincts'. The importance of the egress routes and timely exit from the precinct appears to have significant operational and policy implications. In Cairns, interventions to address this are currently being designed.

Whether research into alcohol-related assaults in LNEPs is conducted through a scientifically defensible criminological model or a public health framework for collaborative action, the processes of establishing the necessary stakeholder commitment for collaborative initiatives in these precincts requires more study. This chapter documents a process that was indispensable to the establishment of a coordinated framework for data collection and inter-agency sharing. Future research that replicates the process in the legislated 'Drink Safe Precincts' is recommended.

References

Alcohol Education and Rehabilitation Foundation, (2011). *Annual Alcohol Poll: Community Attitudes and Behaviours*, Deakin, Australian Capital Territory.

Basta, L. A., Richmond, T. S. & Wiebe, D. J. (2010). "Neighborhoods, daily activities, and measuring health risks experienced in urban environments," *Social Science and Med*icine, *71*(11), 1943-1950.

Bligh, A. (The Hon) & Lawlor P. (The Hon) (2010). *'Drink Safe Precincts' to offer local solutions to local problems*, Brisbane: Queensland Government, Premier and Minister for the Arts and Minister for Tourism and Fair Trading.

Braun, V. & Clarke, V. (2006). "Using thematic analysis in psychology," *Qualitative Research in Psychology*, *3*(2), 77-101.

Brennan, I., Moore, S. C., Byrne, E. & Murphy, S. (2011). "Interventions for disorder and severe intoxication in and around licensed premises, 1989–2009," *Addiction* (online).

Fawcett, S., Schultz, J., Watson-Thompson, J., Fox, M. & Bremby, R. (2010). "Building multisectorial partnerships for population health and health equity," *Prevention of Chronic Disease*, *7*(6) online (no pages).

Graham, K. & Homel, R. (2008). *Raising the Bar: Preventing Aggression in and around Bars, Pubs and Clubs*, Cullompton, United Kingdom Willan.

Hauritz, M., Homel, R., McIlwain, G., Burrows, T. & Townsley, M. (1998). *Reducing Violence in Licensed Venues: Community Safety Action Projects*, Canberra: Australian Institute of Criminology.

Holmila, M., Holder, H., Andréasson, S., Baklien, B. & Rossow, I. (2008). "Roles for researchers in community action projects to prevent alcohol and other drug problems: Methodological choices," *Drugs: Education, Prevention, and Policy*, *15*(4), 410-423.

Jones, L., Hughes, K., Atkinson, A. & Bellis, M. A. (2011). "Reducing harm in drinking environments: A systematic review of effective approaches," *Health Place*, *17*(2), 508-518.

Law Justice and Safety Committee, (2010). *Inquiry into Alcohol-related Violence: Final Report*, Brisbane: Queensland Legislative Assembly.

Loxley, W., Gray, D., Wilkinson, C., Chikritzhs, T., Midford, R. & Moore, D. (2005). "Alcohol policy and harm reduction in Australia," *Drug and Alcohol Re*view, *24*(6), 559-568.

Morgan, A. & McAtamney, A. (2009). "Key issues in alcohol-related violence," Research in Practice Number 4.

Pointing, S., Hayes-Jonkers, C., Stone, R., Brinn, D. & Clough, A. (2011). "Is it worth emergency departments recording information about alcohol-related assault occurring in inner-city, late-night entertainment precincts?" *Emergency Medicine in Australia*, *23*(1), 106-107.

Promotion, W. C. C. C. S., Institutet, K., Department of Public Health and Medicine, Department of Science, (2011). *Indicators for International Safe Communities*, [cited 25 March, 2011] > Available from: http://www.phs.ki.se/csp/who_safe_communities_indicators_en.htm.

Queensland, T. T. N. (2010). "Annual General Meeting Presentation," TTN Queensland Presentations to Industry.

Shepherd, J. (2003). "Violence as a public health problem: Combined approach is needed," *British Medical Journal*, *326*(7380) online (no pages).

Stevenson, M. & McClure, R. (2005). "Use of ecological study designs for injury prevention," *Injury Prevention*, *11*(1) online (no pages).

In: Assaults
Editor: Keith V. Bletzer
ISBN: 978-1-62808-051-3

Chapter 13

Firearm Deaths and Background Checks: Evidence on What Works & What Does Not

***Anantachai Panjamapirom*[1] *and Bisakha Sen*[2,*]**
[1]The Advisory Board Company, Birmingham, AL US
[2]Department of Healthcare Organization & Policy – School of Public Health
The University of Alabama at Birmingham, Birmingham, AL US

Abstract

There is much interest in how state policies might reduce firearm deaths. For example, a recent study found that using local agencies to perform background checks prior to a firearm purchase was associated with reductions in firearm homicide and suicide-deaths. We re-visit this issue, using sophisticated empirical model specifications that help reduce bias from confounders. We also explore the effects of comprehensiveness of other state policies related to gun background checks. State-level data for 1996-2005 are used. Data on state policies are from from the Survey of State Procedures Related to Firearm Sales, and data for firearm deaths are from the National Center for Injury Prevention and Control. Multivariate negative binomial models are used to estimate the relationship between agency levels and state policies for background checks, and firearm homicides and suicide-deaths, by race (all races, whites and blacks) and age (youth and adults). Models control for contemporaneous state characteristics, past firearm violence, past state-policy on background checks, and other proxy variables for unmeasured state-level heterogeneity.

We found little evidence that using local or state agencies as opposed to federal agencies impact firearm deaths. In fact, the use of state agencies as opposed to federal agencies except in certain instances is associated with higher firearm deaths. Firearm homicide-deaths were 11% and 37% higher respectively among Whites and Blacks in states using state agencies for background checks (reference group: federal agency). Firearm suicide-deaths among Whites and all adults were about 13% and 9% higher respectively in the states using state agencies. We found evidence that more comprehensive background checks at the state level are effective in reducing firearm deaths. We also found significant variation in results between suicide deaths and

[*] Corresponding author: Email: bsen@uab.edu.

homicide deaths, and between races and age-groups and states that have had background checks in place since before the Brady Act had fewer firearm deaths. The use of local or state agencies as opposed to FBI is not associated with lower firearm homicide-deaths or suicide deaths, whereas more comprehensive background checks regardless of agency before firearm purchase were associated with fewer firearm purchases.

Keywords: Homicide, suicide, firearms, gun, background-check, race, age-group

INTRODUCTION

Firearm violence remains a major issue in the USA. The year 2012 was a particularly horrific year in terms of mass shootings, including fatal assualts on movie-goers in Aurora, Colorado, worshippers at a Sikh temple in Wisconsin, which culminated in a fatal assault on several schoolchildren and teachers in Newtown, Connecticut. Firearms are also the most common method to commit suicide (Centers for Disease Control and Prevention, 2012; National Institutes of Health, 2012) and ownership of firearms in a household is associated with higher suicide risk (Miller et al, 2006). By some estimates the annual cost of firearm violence to the nation is as high as $100 billion (Cook & Ludwig, 2002), firearm violence takes away approximately 104 days from an average American life (Lemaire, 2005), and "willingness to pay" analyses suggests that U.S. society is willing to pay an average of $1.2 million for each prevented gun injury (Ludwig & Cook, 2001).

Gun control efforts, which prevent guns from falling into the "wrong hands," may be effective in reducing gun violence. Perhaps, the most significant federal effort towards gun control was the passage of the Brady Handgun Violence Prevention Act, signed into law on November 30, 1993, which mandated background checks and a waiting period on individuals who attempted to purchase firearms (Public Law No. 103-159). Prior to the Act only 18 states had an existing mechanism of background checks before a firearm purchase could take place (General Accounting Office, 1996). The permanent provisions of the legislation led the U.S. Attorney General to create the National Instant Criminal Background Check System [hereafter NICS], a computerized system that combines records provided by local, state and federal agencies, and helps determine eligibility of a prospective gun purchaser by a swift background check (Federal Bureau of Investigation [hereafter FBI], 2009). However, supply of records to the NICS is voluntary and pursuant to law in each state (Regional Justice Information Service, 2005). Substantial variability exists in State laws on different categories of prohibitory records that are included in the background checks, such as criminal history, restraining orders, mental illness, fugitive status and misdemeanors. Federally licensed firearm dealers are required to contact the appropriate state-designated agency for a background check on a prospective customer who is looking to purchase a firearm. Different states utilize different levels of agencies to perform these background checks. Some utilize the FBI, others utilize a single state agency, or local law enforcement agency such as amunicipal office or sheriff department (Regional Justice Information Service, 2006). State and local agencies have access to all the information available to the FBI through the NICS, the National Crime Information Center, and the Interstate Identification Index. In addition, state and local agencies can access additional information that is available exclusively to themselves.

Researchers have long been interested in links between policies on gun availability or gun restrictions and violent crime, though results have frequently been mixed. One early study using 1980 data from several U.S. cities, for example, found little association overall between gun restrictions and violent crime (Kleck & Patterson, 1993). Recent studies suggest more permissive state laws on concealed handgun carrying are linked to increased homicides (Ludwig, 1998; Rosengart et al, 2005), that the Brady Act reduced firearm suicides among older adults but did not have substantial impact on other firearm deaths (Ludwig & Cook, 2000), that child access prevention gun laws reduced youth suicide (Webster et al, 2004), and that minimum purchase age and possession age laws appeared to have little effect on firearm deaths (Webster et al, 2004; Rosengart et al, 2005). One study suggested that states where background checks are performed by state or local agencies have fewer suicides than states which depend on federal agencies (Sumner et al, 2008), though these results have been challenged by the findings of Sen and Panjamapirom (2011). This is a question of interest, since in recent years, including the period of this current study, there has been a trend in states moving from local or state agencies to perform these background checks to having them performed by the FBI. Finally, an association was found between the comprehensiveness of state background checks and gun homicides and suicides in states (Sen & Panjamapirom, 2012). In this paper, we synthesize the findings on the comprehensiveness of state background checks, the level of agency (federal, state, local) conducting the checks, and firearm homicide and suicide deaths in the state. Additionally, we explore the extent to which the results vary across whites and blacks, as well as youth and adults. As Figures 1 through 4 demonstrate, there is considerable difference in firearm homicide and suicide rates across races, as well as between youth, who should not legally possess a gun, and adults. Whites having higher age-adjusted suicide rates and blacks having higher age-adjusted homicide rates. Therefore, it is very likely that state policies on the background checks will have differential associations with firearm deaths across these different groups.

METHODS

In our analysis we use cross-sectional time-series data at the state level for the United States from 1996 to 2005. All the other data are described before their presentation.

Variables

Outcome Variables

The main outcome variables in this study are the total number of homicide-deaths and suicide-deaths caused by firearms, as well as the number of such deaths by race (white and black) and by age-group, which were retrieved from the Web-based Injury Statistics Query and Reporting System [hereafter WISQARS™], Centers for Disease Control and Prevention [hereafter CDC], 2008). Legal intervention homicide-deaths were excluded from the analyses, since these typically refer to law enforcement. WISQARS™ data are compiled from death certificate data from the National Vital Statistics System. WISQAR™ data are available by race for four races: White, Black, American Indian/Alaskan Native, and Asian/Pacific

Islander. Only the white and black races had a sufficient number of firearm deaths for statistical analyses with meaningful statistical power. For age-groups, analysis was done for adults (21 years and above) and youth who should not legally possess a gun (15-20 years). WISQAR™ data are free and publicly available, and their use has been deemed not covered by human subject research policies by the Institutional Review Board of the senior author's university.

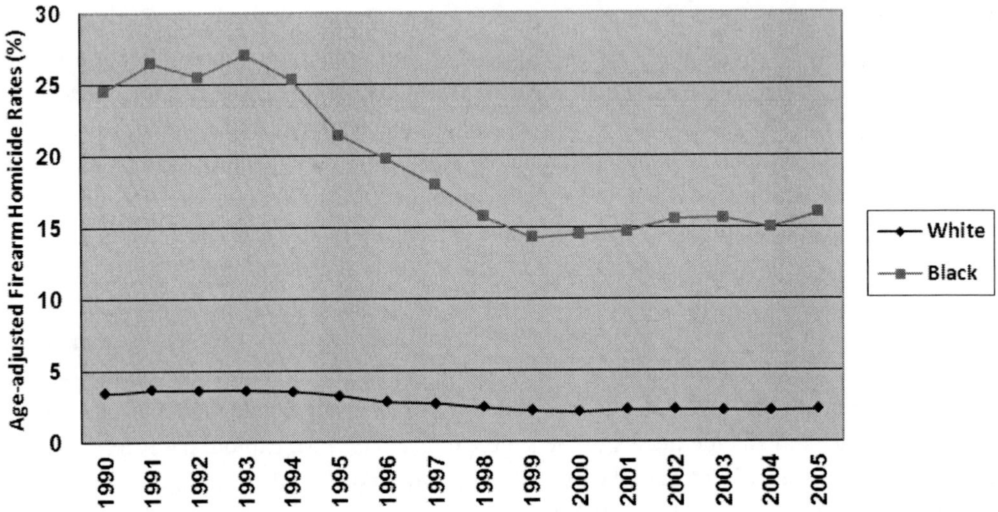

Figure 1. Age-Adjusted U.S. Firearm Homicide Rates by Race, based on the data from the Web-based Injury Statistics Query and Reporting System (WISQARS™).

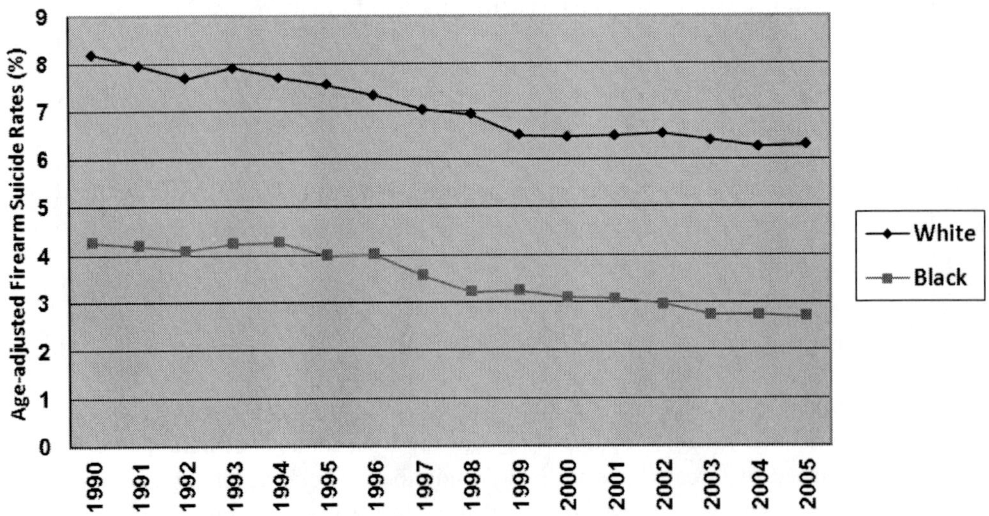

Figure 2. Age-Adjusted U.S. Firearm Suicide Rates by Race, based on data from the Web-based Injury Statistics Query and Reporting System (WISQARS™).

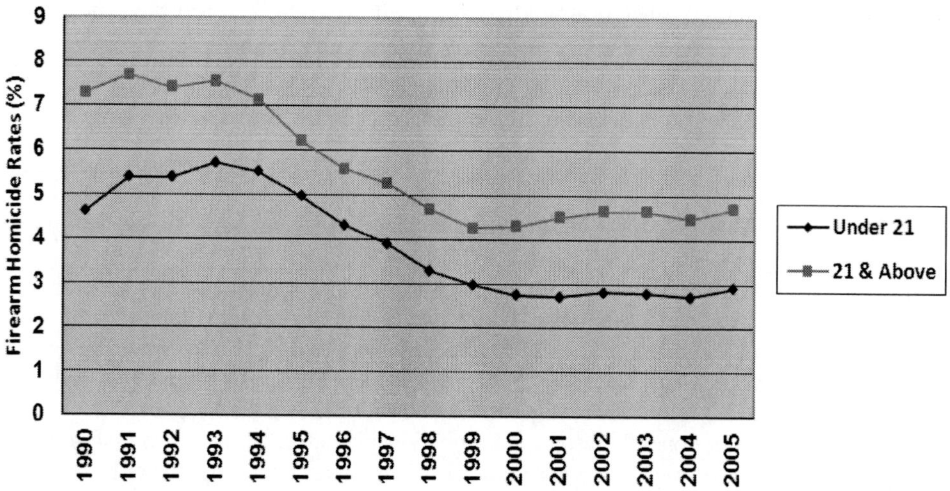

Figure 3. U.S. Firearm Homicide Rates by Age Groups (under 21 and 21 & above), based on data from the Web-based Injury Statistics Query and Reporting System (WISQARS™).

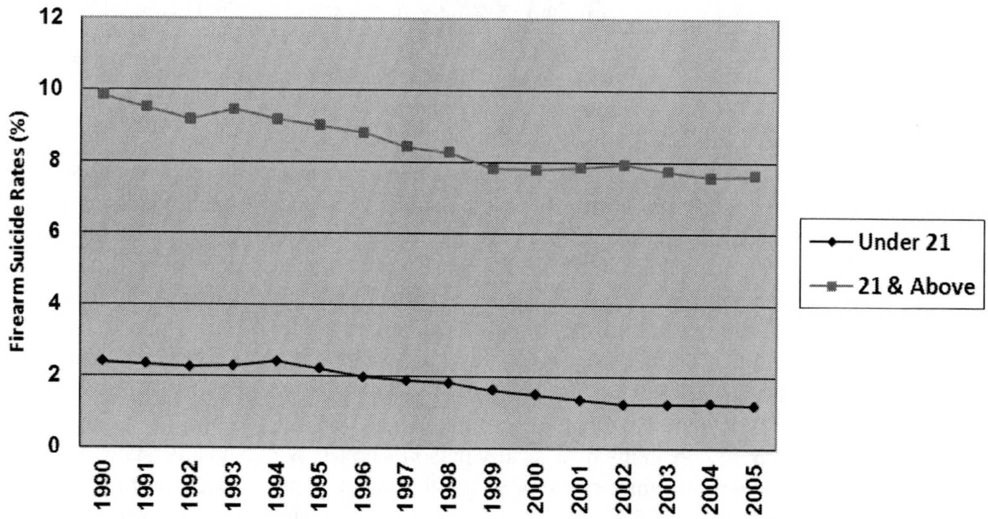

Figure 4. U.S. Firearm Suicide Rates by Age Groups (under 21 and 21 & above), based on data from the Web-based Injury Statistics Query and Reporting System (WISQARS™).

Main Policy Variables

The main independent variables of interest are the type of background information that the state uses to perform background checks on persons attempting to purchase a gun, and the level of agency the state uses to perform that check. Every state checks for criminal history, which is the "reference category." Additionally, some states check other information, such as restraining orders, mental illness, fugitive status and misdemeanor records. To prepare our analyses we retrieved data on type of background information from the Survey of State Procedures Related to Firearm Sales from the Bureau of Justice Statistics (Regional Justice Information Service, 1997, 1998, 2000, 2001, 2002, 2003, 2004, 2005, 2006).

The survey has been conducted annually from 1996 to 2005, and reported the following year, hence these are the years that we included in our study analysis. The survey was not conducted in 1998 (L. Gallaway, personal communication, July 11, 2008), and has not been available after 2005. Definitions of these prohibitory records are provided in Figure 5.

Type of Prohibitory Record	Definition[1]
Criminal history	All States maintain a central repository with criminal history records that include, at a minimum, felony arrests and dispositions. The first entry for a subject is normally an arrest record supported by fingerprints. Subsequent dispositions that may be recorded include dismissals of charges, guilty pleas, convictions, acquittals, admissions to and discharges from correctional facilities, and probation and parole events. Criminal history repositories also record modifications such as "expunging" or setting aside a conviction, pardon, or restoration of civil rights. Agencies that submit records to the repositories include police and sheriff departments, courts, prosecutors, jails, and prisons. State criminal record systems differ in regard to procedures, the extent of automation, and completeness and accessibility of their data. All states in our study checked criminal history records with the exception of Mississippi in 1996.
Restraining order	An order that restrains acts of domestic violence or other unlawful conduct is issued by a judge and usually entered by court or law enforcement personnel into a State system or NCIC or both.
Mental illness	Federal and State prohibitions encompass a variety of civil court orders, including a commitment to a mental hospital and a finding that a person is incompetent to manage his or her affairs. A prohibition may also be caused by a disposition in a criminal prosecution, such as a finding of incompetence to stand trial or a verdict of not guilty by reason of insanity. A criminal case disposition is usually reported by the trial court to the State's central records repository. Civil commitment records are often protected from disclosure by privacy laws.
Fugitives	The Federal Gun Control Act (GCA), at 18 U.S.C. 921 (a) (15), defines "fugitive from justice" as any person who has fled from any State to avoid prosecution for a crime or to avoid giving testimony in a criminal proceeding. Most States apply a similar definition and some limit the prohibition to persons who are wanted for certain types of offenses.
Misdemeanors	Types of misdemeanor-level offenses included in prohibitory statutes vary widely. Federal law and a few State codes only prohibit a misdemeanor offender who has been convicted of an act of domestic violence (generally, assault against a spouse, an intimate partner, or a child). Several other States deny a misdemeanor offender who has been convicted of any crime of violence or a firearm offense. Requirements for misdemeanor offenders to regain firearm rights after a conviction are generally less stringent than those for felons. A few States disqualify persons who have been arrested for or charged with certain misdemeanors.

[1] Survey of state procedures related to firearm sales, midyear 2004.

Figure 5. Definitions of Prohibitory Records.

We created an additive index of the number of background checks a state has in place. The higher the index score, the more comprehensive is the overall background check before a gun can be purchased. In addition, we use binary indicators of the level of agency that performs the check. The agency-level is coded as 'local' if it was a county police or sheriff department, 'state' if it was a centralized state department or division, and 'federal' if it was the FBI. Data for level of agency performing the check is obtained from the same sources described above.

Lagged Value of Outcome Variables

Stricter state background checks may be done in response to a prior history of gun violence. Alternatively, stricter state background checks might reflect a long history of support for gun control, even if the historic gun violence rates are low. Failure to account for this can produce biased estimates of the relationship between checking background information and firearm violence. We use an approach advocated by Woolridge (2006), where a value of the outcome variable from an earlier year is included in the regression equation to help reduce this type of estimation bias.

Other Control Variables

We control for various state-level variables that could potentially predict the prevalence of violent deaths in the state. Particularly important, we include a binary control for whether the state had a policy of doing background checks for gun purchases prior to passage of the Brady Act (Ludwig & Cook, 2000). Firearm violence is committed not just with guns acquired recently but also with guns purchased in the past. It is likely that states with background checks preceding the Brady Act would have fewer "guns in dangerous hands" already in circulation, since most the felons and other criminals would have been prevented for a longer period of time from legally purchasing guns. Thus, this variable might serve as an indicator of how many guns purchased with no background checks were already in circulation.

Other state-level controls include the state's annual per-capita-income measured in thousands of dollars, poverty-rate, unemployment-rate, divorce-rate, per-capita alcohol-consumption, police officers per 100,000 residents, and percentage of the state's population aged 16-and-over who were hunters. We include binary indicators for each year in our data to account for temporal shifts in factors that are relevant to the whole country, such as business cycles that impact the national economy. Finally, we include binary controls for the nine Census sub-regions to account for any unmeasured socio-cultural-demographic commonalities within each sub-region that potentially correlate to state gun laws and outcome variables for states in that particular sub-region.

The source of income data was the Regional Economic Information System, Bureau of Economic Analysis, U.S. Department of Commerce (Bureau of Economic Analysis, 2008). Poverty rates were retrieved from Housing and Household Economic Statistics Division, U.S. Census Bureau (Housing and Household Economic Statistics Division, 2008). Unemployment data were retrieved from the Local Area Unemployment Statistics Information and Analysis, U.S. Bureau of Labor Statistics (U.S. Bureau of Labor Statistics, 2008). The sources of divorce data included the Division of Vital Statistics, National Center for Health Statistics, CDC (National Center for Health Statistics, 2008). Per capita alcohol consumption data were retrieved from the National Institute on Alcohol Abuse and Alcoholism (National Institutes of

Health, 2008). Officers per 100,000 residents were from the Disaster Center (The Disaster Center, 2009). Percentage of population over 16 years who were hunters were obtained from the 2001 National Survey of Fishing, Hunting and Wildlife Associated Recreation (DeCicca et al, 2008).

Statistical Analyses

Firearm suicide and homicide deaths always take integer values and are not normally distributed. Certain state-year cells can have a value of '0' (zero) especially with analyses using demographic sub-groups. Therefore, we use negative binomial regression models to evaluate the relationship between the type of background checks and state suicide and homicide-deaths caused by firearm. In addition to all the control variables described in the previous section, we controlled for 'exposure' by including the state's population size for that sub-group, when analyzing by race or age-group, with its coefficient constrained to be '1'. The statistical software STATA version 11 was used. Statistical significance is reported at the levels of 0.05 and 0.10 with the latter deemed as "marginally significant."

DISCUSSION

Figure 6 provides descriptive statistics for firearm homicide and suicide deaths and rates for our pooled state-year observations, mean number of restrictions per state at three different points over our study period, and the sample means for all the other control variables.

Variable	Mean (N = 450)	Std. Dev.
Firearm homicide	59.08	127.66
Firearm suicide	85.43	196.93
Firearm homicide rate (per 100,000 population)	5.24	7.29
Firearm suicide rate (per 100,000 population)	4.50	4.83
Number of restrictions per state (all U.S.), 1996	2.40	
Number of restrictions per state (all U.S.), 2001	3.40	
Number of restrictions per state (all U.S.), 2005	4.30	
Real income (inflation-adjusted)	16,162.60	2,431.67
Poverty rate (%)	11.85	3.22
Unemployment rate	4.73	1.13
Number of officers (per 100,000 residents)	227.81	51.01
Divorce rate	4.21	1.10
Per capita alcohol consumption (N=1,400)	2.25	0.46
1990 Firearm homicide rate (per 100,000 population / all states)	7.12	9.91
1990 Firearm suicide rate (per 100,000 population / all states)	5.56	6.94
Number of states having background check law before 1994 Brady Act	18.0	--
Percent of state population over 16 years who are hunters (2001 data)	8.68	5.41

Figure 6. Descriptive statistics from Pooled Cross-Sectional Time-Series State Level Data.

	Full Sample		White		Black		Youth		Adults	
Variables	Firearm Homicide	Firearm Suicide	Firearm Homicide	Firearm Suicide	Firearm Homicide	Firearm Suicide	Firearm Homicide	Firearm Suicide	Firearm Homicide	Firearm Suicide
Index of background check laws	0.93*** (0.000)	0.98** (0.009)	0.97* (0.077)	1.00 (0.673)	0.93** (0.005)	0.94** (0.002)	0.94*** (0.001)	0.96** (0.011)	0.93*** (0.000)	0.98** (0.025)
State level agency	1.10* (0.078)	1.03 (0.136)	1.11** (0.040)	1.13*** (0.000)	1.37*** (0.000)	1.09 (0.233)	1.17** (0.015)	1.01 (0.886)	1.09* (0.073)	1.09*** (0.001)
Local level agency	0.99 (0.920)	0.89*** (0.000)	0.94 (0.244)	0.85*** (0.000)	1.19** (0.032)	1.00 (0.986)	1.00 (0.934)	0.85** (0.014)	1.00 (0.982)	0.85*** (0.000)
Pre-Brady background check policy	0.87*** (0.001)	0.87*** (0.000)	0.81*** (0.000)	0.85*** (0.000)	0.81** (0.003)	0.67*** (0.000)	0.88** (0.041)	0.83*** (0.000)	0.88*** (0.001)	0.85*** (0.000)

Data used is cross-sectional time-series data at the state level for the U.S. from 1996 to 2005, with year 1998 omitted due to lack of information on state laws. N=450. Numbers shown in the tables are Incident Rate Ratios or IRR, with p-values in parenthesis. * $p < .10$; ** $p < .05$. *** $p < .001$

All models include the state population, with its coefficient constrained to be 1. Robust standard errors are calculated. All models control for state income, poverty, unemployment rate, per capita police officers, state divorce rates, per capita alcohol use, the suicide or homicide rates in 1990, percent of population who are hunters, year and Census sub-region fixed effects. The nine sub-regions are: *East North Central* (OH, IN, IL, MI, WI), *East South Central* (KY, TN, AL, MS), *Middle Atlantic* (NY, NJ, PA), *Mountain* (MT, ID, WY, CO, NM, AZ, UT, NV), *New England* (ME, NH, VT, MA, RI, CT), *Pacific* (WA, OR, CA, AK, HI), *South Atlantic* (DE, MD, DC, VA, WV, NC, SC, GA, FL), *West North Central* (MN, IA, MO, ND, SD, NE, KS) and *West South Central* (AR, LA, OK, TX).

§ - the reference category is basically a criminal background check.

Figure 7. Adjusted IRR from Negative Binomial Models for Firearm Homicide and Suicide, and All Homicide and Suicide.

Figure 7 provides results from the negative binomial models. For economy of space, we only present the *incidence rate ratio* (IRR) and p-values pertaining to the index of comprehensiveness of background checks, the level of agency performing the check, and whether the state had pre-Brady background check policies. All models include the other control variables. Results for these variables for the full sample are virtually identical to those reported in a recent analysis that we conducted (Sen & Panjamapirom, 2012). Results for control variables by race and age-group can be made available to interested readers upon request.

Results from using the index show that additional background checks are associated with fewer firearm homicides (IRR: 0.93, $p<0.05$) and suicide deaths (IRR: 0.98, $p<0.05$) among the overall population. Analyses by race show that for whites, the association with reduced firearm homicide deaths is marginally significant (IRR: 0.97, $p<0.10$), and the association with firearm suicide deaths is not significant. For blacks, there is a strong association between comprehensiveness of background check index and fewer homicide deaths (IRR=0.93, $p<0.05$) and suicide deaths (IRR=0.94, $p<0.05$). Associations between more background checks and fewer firearm deaths were found in case of youth homicide deaths (IRR=0.94, $p<0.001$), youth suicide deaths (IRR=0.96, $p<0.05$), adult homicide deaths (IRR=0.93, $p<0.001$) and adult suicide deaths (IRR=0.98, $p<0.05$).

There is little evidence that having a state agency perform background checks as compared to federal agencies is associated with fewer firearm homicide or suicide deaths. In fact, for the overall sample, there is a weak but positive association between state agencies doing background checks and the number of homicide deaths (IRR=1.10, $p<0.10$). However, there does appear to be an association between local agencies doing such checks and reduced suicide deaths in the overall population (IRR=0.89, $p<0.001$), particularly among whites (IRR=0.85, $p<0.001$). In contrast, for blacks, state or local agencies performing the checks as opposed to federal appears to be associated with more firearm homicide deaths (IRR=1.37, $p<0.001$, and IRR=1.19, $p<0.001$ respectively). State agencies doing background checks also appear to be associated with more homicide deaths among youth (IRR=1.17, $p<0.05$), while local agency checks are associated with fewer suicide deaths among youth (IRR=0.85, $p<0.001$).

Having background checks in the pre-Brady period is strongly associated with reductions in both firearm homicide (IRR=0.87, $p<0.001$) and suicide deaths (IRR=0.87, $p<0.001$) in the overall population. Similar, highly significant associations are found between the pre-Brady background checks and fewer firearm deaths for both races, and youth and adults.

CONCLUSION

The topic of gun control remains in dispute among U.S. policy-makers, though it is generally accepted that it is best to keep guns out of the hands of those whose main inclination is to use them to inflict harm upon themselves or others. The question remains about what methods might be best to attain that end.

This current study explored relationships among comprehensiveness of background checks, the type of agency performing the checks, and firearm homicide and suicide deaths in the state. We used data from 1996-2005 which is primarily dictated by the years of availability of the annual Survey of State Procedures Related to Firearm Sales. We conducted our analysis using an index of the number of background checks that a state requires, binary indicators for whether state or local level agencies perform the check, and control for state characteristics including whether the state performed background checks prior to the Brady Act. On balance, our evidence suggests that having more comprehensive background checks is associated with decline in firearm deaths. The associations appear stronger for blacks than whites.

The associations are also strong for youth firearm deaths, suggesting that more comprehensive background checks can prevent the 'illicit' gun purchases that are more likely to end up in the hands of underage youth. States with background checks prior to the Brady Law have fewer homicide and suicide deaths, and the results are strongly significant for all sub-groups. This suggests that the longer background that checks have been in place, the fewer guns there are in circulation which might have been purchased with no background checks. Of course, it is possible that having background checks prior to the Brady Act suggests that these are the states which, in general, do not have a strong 'pro-gun' culture, and ultimately it is this difference in culture that actually is reflected in having fewer firearm deaths.

Unlike Sumner and colleagues (2008), we do not find evidence that states using local agencies have substantially lower firearm deaths. Indeed, we find that firearm homicides among blacks are higher when state or local agencies perform the checks. However, we did find some evidence that local agencies performing background checks are associated with fewer firearm suicide deaths among non-blacks, and among youth. In contrast, having state agencies rather than the FBI performing the checks appears to be associated with an increase in homicide deaths, including among youth. In summary, our findings suggest that the fact that seven states moved from state agencies to FBI over the course of this study period (Sen & Panjamapirom, 2011), while Minnesota and other states are about to follow suit, is not a major concern in terms of increased gun homicide. If anything, it indicates that background checking procedures need to be comprehensive to be effective.

Thus, the findings of this study tentatively suggest that, by and large, the more comprehensive background checks at the state level prior to firearm purchase can reduce firearm deaths.

Findings suggest that it is not important that the background checks be done by state or local agencies rather than the FBI in order to be more effective. Notably, these results are not sufficient to definitively establish causality, since there are certain underlying confounders that this study cannot account for. For example, this study does not control for factors like cross-border smuggling of guns, the ease of illegal acquisition of firearms in black markets (Atwell, 1999; Kopel, 2000), existence of unaccountable transfers of firearms between gun dealers and traffickers (Fallis, 2010), popularity of gun shows where there typically is a lack of background checks for gun purchases, or how a state regulates gun transactions in the secondary market (Open Society Institute, 2000). It is anticipated that this study will lead to further research that incorporates those factors.

REFERENCES

Atwell, C. (1999). "Brady Act in Alaska," *Alaska Justice Forum*, *16*, 1-8.

Bureau of Economic Analysis, U.S. Department of Commerce, (2008). "Regional economic information system: State per capita income," http://www.bea.gov/regional/reis /default.cfm?selTable=CA1-3&section=2, accessed on August 18, 2008.

Centers for Disease Control and Prevention, (2008). "Injury prevention & control: Data & statistics (WISQARS™)," http://www.cdc.gov/injury/wisqars/index.html, accessed on April 8, 2009.

Centers for Disease Control and Prevention, (2012). "Suicide: Facts at a glance – 2012," http://www.cdc.gov/ncipc/dvp/suicide/suicide_data_sheet.pdf, accessed on December 14, 2012.

Cook, P. J. & Ludwig, J. (2002). *Gun Violence: The Real Costs*. Oxford University Press, USA.

DeCicca, P., Kenkel, D., Mathios, A., Shin, Y. J. & Lim, J. Y. (2008). "Youth smoking, cigarette prices, and anti-smoking sentiment," *Health Economics*, *17*, 733-749.

Fallis, D. S. (2010). "Virginia gun dealers: Small number supply most guns tied to crimes, Washington Post," http://www.washingtonpost.com/wp-dyn/content/article/2010/10/24 /AR2010102402221.html, accessed on February 22, 2011.

Federal Bureau of Investigation (FBI), (2009). "NICS: The National Instant Criminal Background Check System," http://www.fbi.gov/about-us/cjis/nics/nics, accessed on June 10, 2010.

General Accounting Office, (1996). "Gun Control: Implementation of the Brady Handfirearm violence Prevention Act, in GAO/GGD-96-22 report," US Government Printing Office, Washington, DC.

Housing and Household Economic Statistics Division, U.S. Census Bureau, (2008). "*Poverty Status by State and Ten Large Metropolitan Areas*," http://www.census.gov/hhes/www/ cpstables/macro/031997/pov/25_000.htm, accessed on August 8, 2008.

Kleck, G. & Patterson, E. B. (1993). "The impact of gun control and gun ownership levels on violence rates," *Journal of Quantitative Criminology*, *9*, 249-287.

Lemaire, J. (2005). "The cost of firearm deaths in the United States: reduced life expectancies and increased insurance costs," *Journal of Risk and Insurance*, *72*, 359-374.

Ludwig, J. (1998). "Concealed gun-carrying laws and violent crime — evidence from state panel data," *International Review of Law and Economics*, *18*, 239–254.

Ludwig, J. & Cook, P. J. (2000). "Homicide and suicide rates associated with implementation of the Brady Handgun Violence Prevention Act," *Journal of the American Medical Association*, *284*, 585-591.

Ludwig, J. & Cook, P. J. (2001). "The Benefits of Reducing Gun Violence: Evidence from Contingent-Valuation Survey Data," *Journal of Risk and Uncertainty*, *22*, 207-26.

Miller, M., Azrael, D., Hepburn, L., Hemenway, D. & Lippmann, S. J. (2006). "The association between changes in household firearm ownership and rates of suicide in the United States, 1981-2002," *Injury Prevention*, *12*,178-182.

National Center for Health Statistics, (2008). "Divorce rates by state. Center for Disease Control and Prevention," http://www.cdc.gov/nchs/fastats/divorce.htm and http://www. cdc.gov/nchs/products/pubs/pubd/nvsr/nvsr.htm, accessed on September 17, 2008.

National Institutes of Health, (2008). "National Institute on Alcohol Abuse and Alcoholism, Per capita ethanol consumption for States, census regions, and the United States, 1970–2007," http://www.niaaa.nih.gov/Resources/DatabaseResources/QuickFacts/Alcoholsales/Pages/consum03.aspx, accessed on April 8, 2008.

National Institutes of Health, (2012). "National Institute of Mental Health, Suicide in the U.S.: Statistics and prevention," http://www.nimh.nih.gov/health/publications/suicide-in-the-us-statistics-and-prevention/index.shtml, accessed on December 14, 2012.

Open Society Institute, (2000). "Gun control in the United States: A comparative survey of state firearm laws," http://www.soros.org/sites/default/files/GunReport_Chart1_0.pdf, accessed on June 12, 2012.

Regional Justice Information Service, (1997). "Survey of state procedures related to firearm sales, 1996 (NCJ 165705)," http://bjs.ojp.usdoj.gov/index.cfm?ty=pbdetail&iid=1063, accessed on July 15, 2008.

Regional Justice Information Service, (1998). "Survey of state procedures related to firearm sales, 1997 (NCJ 198830)," http://bjs.ojp.usdoj.gov/index.cfm?ty=pbdetail&iid=932, accessed on July 15, 2008.

Regional Justice Information Service, (2000). "Survey of state procedures related to firearm sales, 1999 (NCJ 179022)," http://bjs.ojp.usdoj.gov/index.cfm?ty=pbdetail&iid=931, accessed on July 15, 2008.

Regional Justice Information Service, (2001). "Survey of state procedures related to firearm sales, 2000 (NCJ 186766)," http://bjs.ojp.usdoj.gov/index.cfm?ty=pbdetail&iid=924, accessed on July 15, 2008.

Regional Justice Information Service, (2002). "Survey of state procedures related to firearm sales, 2001 (NCJ 192065)," http://bjs.ojp.usdoj.gov/index.cfm?ty=pbdetail&iid=923, accessed on July 15, 2008.

Regional Justice Information Service, (2003). "Survey of state procedures related to firearm sales, 2002 (NCJ 198830)," http://bjs.ojp.usdoj.gov/index.cfm?ty=pbdetail&iid=922, accessed on July 15, 2008.

Regional Justice Information Service, (2004). "Survey of state procedures related to firearm sales, 2003 (NCJ 203701)," http://bjs.ojp.usdoj.gov/index.cfm?ty=pbdetail&iid=920, accessed on July 15, 2008.

Regional Justice Information Service, (2005). "Survey of state procedures related to firearm sales, 2004 (NCJ 209288)," http://bjs.ojp.usdoj.gov/index.cfm?ty=pbdetail&iid=911, accessed on July 15, 2008.

Regional Justice Information Service, (2006). "Survey of state procedures related to firearm sales, 2005 (NCJ 214645)," http://bjs.ojp.usdoj.gov/index.cfm?ty=pbdetail&iid=907, accessed on July 15, 2008.

Rosengart, M., Cummings, P., Nathens, A., Heagerty, P., Maier, R. & Rivar, F. (2005). "An evaluation of state firearm regulations and homicide and suicide death rates," *Injury Prevention*, *11*, 77–83.

Sen, B. & Panjamapirom, A. (2011). "Types of background information checks prior to gun purchase and violent deaths," *Southern Economic Association 81st Annual Conference*, Washington, D.C.

Sen, B. & Panjamapirom, A. (2012), "State background checks for gun purchase and firearm deaths: An exploratory study," *Preventive Medicine*, *55*, 346–350.

Sumner, S. A., Layde, P. M. & Guse, C. E. (2008). "Firearm death rates and association with level of firearm purchase background check," *American Journal of Preventive Medicine*, *35*, 1-6.

The Disaster Center, (2009). "United States: Uniform crime report 1960 – 2009," http://www.disastercenter.com/crime/uscrime.htm, accessed on October 9, 2009.

U.S. Bureau of Labor Statistics, (2008). "Local area unemployment statistics information and analysis," http://www.bls.gov/lau/data.htm, accessed on August 18, 2008.

Webster, D. W., Vernick, J. S., Zeoli, A. M. & Manganello, J. A. (2004). "Association between youth-focused firearm laws and youth suicides," *Journal of the American Medical Association*, *292*, 594-601.

INDEX

A

B

D

E

G

H

I

J

K

L

M

N

O

P

S

W

Y